Andrew Stanway, MB, MRCP, worked on the Professorial Medical Unit of a London teaching hospital until 10 years ago. He now lectures, broadcasts, writes and makes films on medical topics, both for the medical profession and for the general public.

He has written many books including the *Boots Book of First Aid; Alternative Medicine – A Guide to Natural Therapies; Why Us?* – a guide for the childless; *Taking the Rough with the Smooth* and *A Dictionary of Operations*. The *Pears Encyclopaedia of Child Health* and *Breast is Best* were written jointly with his wife, Penny. They live in Surrey with their three children.

MIND (National Association for Mental Health) is a mental health charity with two main aims: to improve public awareness of the needs of mentally ill and mentally handicapped people and their families, and to work for better services, both on their behalf and on behalf of the staff who provide them.

Depressives Anonym··········support, voluntary organ··········sion and their families.

D0892346

Overcoming Depression

Dr Andrew Stanway

Hamlyn Paperbacks

OVERCOMING DEPRESSION
ISBN 0 600 20332 8

First published in Great Britain 1981
by Hamlyn Paperbacks
Copyright © 1981 by Dr Andrew Stanway
Reprinted 1983

Hamlyn Paperbacks are published by
The Hamlyn Publishing Group Ltd,
Astronaut House,
Feltham,
Middlesex, England

Printed and bound in Great Britain by
Cox & Wyman Ltd, Reading

To Ben, our stillborn son,
through whom I came to understand depression

ACKNOWLEDGEMENTS

I should like to thank the following who helped me with this book: The Director, the Librarian, the Information Dept and the staff of MIND (National Association for Mental Health), and especially Tessa Jowell. Keith Middleton, Honorary Chairman of Depressives Anonymous. Neville Symmington of the Tavistock Clinic. The Librarian and staff of the Royal Society of Medicine who supplied me with all the key literature on depression for the last ten years. All the patients on whose experiences I have drawn so freely.

I would especially like to thank Dr H Steven Greer, consultant psychiatrist to King's College Hospital, London, and senior lecturer in Psychological Medicine, University of London, whose help, encouragement and comments on the final typescript were so valuable.

CONTENTS

FOREWORD

Depression is an inevitable part of the human condition. It is a normal emotional response to certain distressing events such as the loss of a loved person. The essence of depression is captured in Shakespeare's poignant words:

> But day doth daily draw my sorrows longer
> And night doth nightly make grief's
> strength seem stronger

In some cases, depression becomes more severe and lasts much longer than seems appropriate to the individual's circumstances; such a person is no longer merely depressed, he or she is developing a depressive illness. The distinction is not always clear-cut, but individuals who suffer from depressive illness are usually miserable, tearful and unable to concentrate; they lose interest in the world around them, have no energy or appetite, sleep poorly, complain of various physical symptoms and become immersed in feelings of hopelessness which may, on occasion, be so intense as to lead to suicide.

Although depressive illness is common and its effect on individuals and their families is often striking, public knowledge in this area remains meagre. To take one example, it is still, unfortunately, common practice for people with depressive illness to be told to snap out of it. Well meant though it may be, such advice is foolish and dangerous. Not only is it impossible to carry out, but it may well make matters worse by reinforcing the very feelings of guilt and worthlessness which form part of the picture of this illness. A more informed public attitude towards depressive illness is clearly highly desirable and may, indeed, help to save lives.

Where, then, can the ordinary person obtain information on this important subject? There are numerous textbooks and learned papers in scientific journals, but these are often written in technical language, sufficiently obscure to put off any but the most persistent reader. Dr Stanway has surveyed much of the scientific literature, noted salient facts and insights contained therein, and presented them here in colloquial English.

In this book, the reader will find accurate and useful information about many pertinent questions, for example: how one can recognize depressive illness; what is known – and not known – about its causes; which warning signs indicate a serious risk of suicide; what kinds of treatment are available and how effective they are. In addition, Dr Stanway indicates ways in which the relatives of depressed patients can help. The author is reassuring without offering false optimism and provides simple explanations without ignoring the complexity of the underlying issues. To face the possibility of depressive illness in oneself or in close relatives and friends is never easy. Yet a knowledge of the facts can dispel unnecessary fears and increase understanding. With these laudable aims in view, Dr Stanway has written a book for people with inquiring minds.

H Steven Greer
Senior Lecturer in Psychological Medicine
University of London

PREFACE

We all get depressed from time to time – it's a normal part of life. A death in the family, a business setback, a disagreement with someone close to us, marital disharmony, the end of an enjoyable holiday and a host of other things can leave us feeling low or 'blue'.

For the vast majority of us such emotional setbacks come and go. Sometimes we're happy and sometimes we're sad and we accept such variations in mood as a part of the pattern of life.

Occasionally, however, the low or 'blue' feelings linger on long after the original provoking agent has disappeared and we realize that our 'normal' reaction has become something else . . . a depression adversely affecting our lives.

This is what this book is all about – depression serious enough to alter people's lives.

The impact of depression on a family can be devastating. Familial, sexual, social and economic disaster can follow closely in the wake of depression if it isn't recognized and treated effectively. For many thousands of families, depression causes untold misery, much of which could be prevented.

Unfortunately, too many families either don't know how to recognize depression or find it hard to come to terms with the fact that someone close to them isn't in control of his or her life and seems to be going to pieces. There is still a deep-seated fear of insanity and a reluctance to involve outside help before things get really serious, just in case the loved one is 'taken away and locked up'. On top of all this, many relatives and friends feel helpless when someone close to them becomes depressed. After all, if someone close who cares can't help – who can?

Thank goodness mental disease is rapidly becoming more accepted by the public. This has mainly come about as a result

10

of the greater publicity that mental diseases have enjoyed in recent years. At last mental illness is coming out of the cupboard. People are always amazed at how common mental disorders are (they fill more hospital beds in the UK than any other group of diseases) and are greatly relieved to learn that their relative isn't quite the freak they feared.

Of all mental illnesses, depression is by far the most widespread and has been called 'the common cold of psychiatry'. Unlike the common cold though, it regularly kills people and that's why it is so important to recognize it and get help as soon as possible. This book tells you how.

Depression is a disabling condition, yet with modern therapy some sufferers can be quickly cured and returned to a normal life. Far too many people – including doctors – think of depression as a rag-bag of emotional and physical complaints that are a nuisance, yet not serious. To the sufferers and their families the impact of depression is real enough – it's just as real to them as an obvious physical illness; yet all too often depressives and their complaints are not taken seriously. This has come about partly because the public and medical professionals alike use the word 'depression' too glibly. Unhappiness has become equated with real depression in the minds of many people and the result is that they tend to react similarly to people suffering from both conditions. We shall see that this is not only unfair, but can also be frankly dangerous.

This book tries to answer most of the questions that people have put to me about depression over the years. It is aimed at depressed people who are still not too seriously affected by their condition and at all of those who have to live or work with a depressive. Because most seriously depressed people will, by definition, be incapable of going out and buying a book, let alone reading it, most of this book is written for those who have to cope with the problem in others.

In many places it has not been possible to be as dogmatic as most people would like, simply because there are so many grey areas in our understanding of depression. A lot is known though, and it's time that the veil of secrecy and misconceptions was lifted. In order to be able to do this, I have searched through world medical literature so as to be able to give hard, factual information whenever possible. Depression is a subject on which too many people have said and written too many woolly half-truths and promoted a lot of homespun philosophies. Throughout the book I have tried to avoid this, though at times I'm sure I will have failed, like others before me.

It's unfortunately true that many doctors treat depression very badly and that many health care professionals are still ill at ease with mental disorders unless they are used to dealing with them. All this makes it difficult for relatives and even for depressed people themselves to get all the information they really need. I hope that this book supplies it.

Dr Andrew Stanway
October 1980

CHAPTER 1
Depression under the microscope

What is depression?

Depression is a highly complex condition which can be defined in many ways. To the average man in the street it usually means a low feeling or 'the blues'; but to a psychiatrist it can also mean something very much more serious – an illness that can lead to suicide.

I think it's fair to say that 'depression' is one of the most over-used and misused words in the English language and it's because of this that the real nature of the condition is so badly understood by the public. 'She's just had a row with her daughter and she's terribly depressed', is the sort of remark we hear almost every day. 'Depression' has become interchange-able in everyday speech with 'unhappiness'.

This is all very well and really would not matter over-much if the two emotional states were *in fact* the same – but they're not. By no means all those who are unhappy are depressed; but almost all depressed people are unhappy.

So before we go any further let's agree what depression is medically accepted to be. As you can imagine, there have been scores of different definitions, even among the experts. But the one that seems most acceptable to me is that coined by the US National Association for Mental Health: 'Depression is an emotional state of dejection and sadness, ranging from mild discouragement and downheartedness to feelings of utter hopelessness and despair.'

Depression then is a continuum from sadness and unhappi-ness at one end to a mental disorder serious enough to require emergency hospitalization at the other. It is because it's such a wide spectrum disorder that it is difficult to understand and classify – indeed, the medical literature contains thousands of

13

learned papers that dispute almost every facet of the condition. Some experts doubt whether the vast majority of what is generally called depression should be so labelled at all, and argue that the word should be reserved to describe only seriously 'medically' ill people. Such an approach would disqualify about three-quarters of the so-called 'depressed' at a stroke and relabel them simply as 'unhappy'.

Is depression new?

Without a doubt the answer to this must be 'no', but one could be forgiven for thinking that it was. The public's awareness of a disease is to a great extent the result of the medical profession's current interest in it. The medical profession is known for its fads and fashions, which, it has been unkindly said, differ only from those in the clothes trade in their cycle length! Clothes fashions change every year but medical fashions come and go in about twenty-five to thirty year cycles.

Until about twenty-five years ago there was very little active research going on into depression: schizophrenia, the anxiety states and the neuroses were the main areas of interest. Over the last quarter of a century the medical profession has really gone to town on depression and there are now thousands of medical papers on the subject. This has come about partly because of a general change in attitude within psychiatry, which has taken it out of the realms of anecdotal case studies and firmly into the laboratory and the world of computer-assisted clinical trials. Psychiatry has grown up in technological terms over the last twenty years and depression has been the first subject to be put under the technological spotlight. We are also hearing more about depression because society is becoming more open and because the man in the street is more willing than he used to be to admit to mental and emotional illness and to seek ways of relieving them.

Ironically, although depression is, and probably always has been, the commonest of all emotional disorders, we find relatively few descriptions of it in very early medical writings. These authors described hysteria with its dramatic signs and schizophrenia with its own peculiar 'poetry' but depression is relatively poorly documented, partly because it tends to produce 'non-symptoms' – passivity, inactivity, resignation and despair.

The history of depression in the western world is the history of *melancholia*, described in the fourth century BC by Hippocrates, the so-called father of medicine. Hippocrates, although he thought depression was caused by an accumulation of black bile, was the first to describe the brain as the seat of all emotions, as this quotation from his writings shows:

> Men ought to know that from the brain only, arise our pleasures, joys, laughter and jests, as well as our sorrows, pains, griefs and tears.

The Old Testament too has many references to depression and Job was a classical depressive. In the first book of Samuel we find:

> And it came to pass, when the evil spirit from God was upon Saul, that David took an harp, and played with his hand: so Saul was refreshed, and was well, and the evil spirit departed from him (1 Sam. 16:23).

This early 'music therapy' obviously did the trick and was repeated many times. Music and the singing of epic tales by a bard date from Homeric times. The bard was what we would call an entertainer/therapist today. Here are a few comforting words from a century after Homer:

> . . . for though a man choose sorrow and grief in his newly troubled soul, and lives in dread because his heart is distressed, yet when a singer . . . chants the glorious deeds of men of old and the blessed gods who inhabit Olympus, at once he forgets his heaviness and remembers not his sorrows at all.

The next major milestone in the historical understanding of depression was instigated by a seventeenth century vicar at Christ Church, Oxford, named Robert Burton. In 1691 he wrote an enormous book entitled *The Anatomy of Melancholy*

15

which brought him considerable fame. He publicized his own depression in the book, which he wrote as a result of his insights into and perceptions of his own suffering. 'Other men get their knowledge from books', he wrote, 'I get mine from melancholizing'. He was way ahead of his time when he recognized that hostile feelings were at the root of much depression. He talked about the internal struggles and emotional ambivalence of the condition and postulated that depression was caused by 'an inherited predisposition, a lack of affection in childhood and sexual frustration'. Even judged by our so-called 'enlightened' modern standards of knowledge, he was very near the mark. His recommendation that the sufferer 'seek a trusting friend' to whom he can confess his grief must surely be one of the earliest references to what we call psychotherapy.

Greek medicine from Hippocrates to Galen was a systematic and physiological business. At this time, the word *melancholia* meant that there was an excess of black bile or gall, and it was widely held that this produced the bitterness and anger seen in depression. Galen described depressed people as being 'black-bilish'.

Psychological and social factors weren't ignored though and Soranus, for example, wrote in the second century about drinking, drugs, sex, grief, anxiety and strain due to study, business and social ambition. He rejected the black bile theory and said that depression was caused by black rage.

Galenical medical thought was unchallenged until the sixteenth century, when men such as Vesalius and Copernicus began to question previously held beliefs – often at great personal danger. In the late sixteenth century Felix Plater, a Swiss professor of anatomy, began to visit the dungeons where the mentally ill were kept. He was probably the first person since Hippocrates to stress that the brain was the seat of the problem in depression and went on to write very detailed descriptions of depression that weren't matched for three hundred years. His textbook of medicine written in 1602 was the first to include psychiatry.

The father of our modern understanding of depression is Emil Kraepelin. His concept of depression as a physical disease dominated nineteenth-century psychiatry, and in 1899 he amalgamated this with the thoughts of many others and created the concept of manic-depressive illness in the sixth edition of his textbook. This was counterbalanced by the publication, early this century, of Freud's *The Interpretation of Dreams* which put the emphasis back on to the psychological causes of depression.

Since Freud, numerous theoretical 'models' of depression have been postulated and are being added to each year. There are currently five dominant schools of thought; not all of them psychological in their approach. To those of a psychological bent, depression represents the internalizing of the hostility arising as a result of ambivalent feelings towards a loved person (or a reaction to separation from a person or object that's important to us). To the behaviourist, depression is a set of maladaptive behavioural responses that is further reinforced by the sick role. The sociologist sees depression as the outcome of a social structure that deprives individuals of certain roles. To the existentialist, depression is the result of the individual discovering that the world has lost meaning and purpose and lastly, to the biological psychiatrist, depression is the behavioural output of a genetically vulnerable nervous system depleted of certain essential chemicals.

Readers could be forgiven for feeling that, for all the wonders of modern science, we are even more confused than the ancients were – and they'd be right. Every new door that opens on our understanding of depression reveals another room with many more doors and it'll be a very long time before we have the keys to most of them.

However, this doesn't mean that we don't already know quite a lot, because we certainly do, and we know enough to be able to help a large number of those who suffer from depression.

How common is it?

We have seen how difficult it is adequately to define depression, so it's understandable that no one can say how common it is. It has been calculated that between eight and fifteen million Americans are being treated for depression at any one time, and there is no reason to assume that the proportion of the population which is depressed there is

17

substantially different in other western countries. It is generally accepted that for every depressed person being treated in hospital there are about ten others suffering from depression outside. This raises an important question for the whole of our understanding of depression – that of the 'population' being studied. The vast majority of studies on depression have been done on hospitalized patients; yet, as we have seen, they probably represent a very atypical tip of the iceberg of depressive illness in society – if only because people in hospital behave differently from those living in the community. General practitioners and family doctors the world over see the majority of people with depression and, of course, very substantial numbers of people never seek any kind of treatment at all.

What is certain is that few families in the land will go through life without one of their members suffering from depression. This makes it a very common problem indeed. In certain sections of the population, depression is exceptionally common. A survey carried out in 1980 of over 10,000 young women found that eight out of ten of them were suffering from, or had suffered from, depression (defined as 'feeling more than a bit blue'). As many as one in seven were thought to be suffering from true, clinical depression and as many again had suffered from various depressive symptoms but may not have been actually depressed in 'medical' terms. Age didn't seem to be a factor in this survey, but it was found that girls with better jobs (managerial etc) were less likely to be depressed than others. Better educated girls seemed to suffer less too. For almost half of the girls, relationships with the opposite sex were the cause of their depression.

Research shows that depression in other specific groups of people is also surprisingly common, as we shall see in chapter four in which we look at depression at special times of life. It also results in the hospital admission of more people than any other mental disorder, but this is discussed in more detail in chapter eight.

Depression around the world

It has been calculated that each year about 100 million people in the world develop clinically recognizable depression which could benefit from qualified help, and there is every likelihood that this figure will rise. I say this for several reasons. First, life expectancy is increasing in most countries and, as a result, the numbers of those at a higher risk of developing depression (the aged) are also increasing. Second, as the world becomes more complex and stressful, rapid rates of social change will produce more situations in which people will become depressed. At a time when growing numbers of individuals all over the world are being uprooted and their families fragmented, and with the consequent spread of social isolation, it is unlikely that psychiatric disorders such as depression will do anything but increase. This is one of many prices people pay for becoming westernized. Third, there is a marked increase in certain physical diseases which have been shown to produce depression in about twenty per cent of cases. These diseases include long-term cardiovascular disease, rheumatic diseases, cancer, certain endocrine disorders and diseases of the blood vessels in the brain. Fourth, certain drugs, known to produce depression (see page 70), are being consumed in ever-increasing quantities and new drugs, as yet undiscovered, may well add to this pool of depression still further.

In addition to all of these reasons, there is a growing readiness to diagnose depression, partly because of the reduced fear of mental diseases, the reduced social stigma connected with them and the very real belief (which is often erroneous) that modern drug treatment has all the answers. It's also interesting to note that as the Third World becomes westernized, more and more people are verbalizing their problems in terms of depression, whereas previously they would have received other diagnoses. As standards of living rise in these countries, more medical services become available and the diagnosis of depression is made with increasing frequency.

Even allowing for the different ways in which depressive episodes are measured and recorded, there are still considerable differences in the levels of depressive illness around the world. Sub-Saharan Africa, for example, has always been said to have very low levels of depression and, when it does occur, it is thought to be milder among Africans than among whites. The most recent studies are, however, finding that depressive disorders among black Africans are commoner than was previously thought.

It's interesting that depression manifests itself in very different ways around the world. As long ago as 1921, it was found that depression in Java was characterized by excitement and confusion and that ideas of sin and suicide were absent. Depressed Africans in Kenya, when studied in 1958, showed no signs of guilt or poor self-esteem. The Chinese seem to have more hypochrondriacal depression than we in the West and never complain of symptoms related to guilt and sin.

In a study of people in southern India in 1966 anxiety, agitation, bodily complaints and suicidal tendencies were found to be the most common depressive symptoms. Feelings of sin, guilt and self-reproach were very uncommon. Endogenous depression in the western world is characterized, as we shall see, by feelings of guilt, loss of self-interest, poor self-esteem, a sense of hopelessness and helplessness, slowness of thinking and some bodily symptoms.

In the West Indies, more than three-quarters of depressed people go to their doctors with bodily complaints (as opposed to about twenty to forty per cent of Western people).

Just why people complain of very different symptoms in depression isn't known, but we are beginning to realize that even among the white populations of the West, the ways in which they describe their depression to the outside world varies considerably. We shall see on page 40 that between twenty and forty per cent of all depressed people seen by general practitioners in the West complain primarily of bodily symptoms and *not* emotional or psychological ones. Unfortunately, most depressed people who complain of physical symptoms end up 'doing the rounds' of specialist after specialist, until someone realizes that the real problem has been depression all the time. This is happening even more often among other racial groups resident in the West, because they have different ways of expressing emotional and psychological turmoil and don't manifest their depression in a way that is easily recognized by white, middle class doctors. In psychiatric illness, symptoms which are assigned the status of an illness by the group to which the patient belongs become those that are subconsciously chosen as the most appropriate ones to complain of.

Relatively unsophisticated cultures (in Western terms) tend not to describe psychological symptoms and Indian patients, for example, tend to use bodily symptoms to express mental disease. Even when depressed Indian people complain of guilt feelings, for example, they are not describing the same feelings as a European would. To Indians, guilt is an impersonal matter. Present suffering is attributed to possible bad deeds in a previous life, and need not be a consequence of current actions. Individualized guilt is seen less often, and then only in well-educated people. Also, the average Indian views a life role more as part of a social system than as belonging to a unique individual. In the face of failure, lowered self-esteem results from feelings such as 'what will others say?' rather than from what he or she sees as personal shortcomings (real or imagined). Westerners, on the other hand, assume a greater degree of individual responsibility and independent role-playing, and these are more likely to foster a sense of guilt resulting from one's own failures. The strong Christian concept of original sin also probably contributes to much of the sense of guilt so widely experienced in the West.

So, as we have seen, the way that different individuals from various cultural backgrounds 'complain' of their depression varies considerably. This is often forgotten, especially in the UK and the US where there are many people of non-white origin whose cultural reactions to disease, and especially psychiatric disease, are very different from those of whites.

Who gets depressed?

The short answer is 'anybody'. Depression is no respecter of persons. One of the first reactions people have when learning that a friend or relative is depressed is, 'Oh he couldn't possibly be, he's too intelligent' (religious, sensible, nice, happy, normal).

Anyone can feel blue and therefore anyone can become depressed.

Having said this though, there are certain people, or groups of people, who are more likely to get depressed and we shall be considering them in more detail in chapters two and four.

It is said that twice as many women as men suffer from

21

depression, though even this is open to debate. It is now generally accepted that women and men probably have the same amount of depressive illness, but that in men much depression is 'masked' (see page 39) and masquerades as physical illness, alcoholism and antisocial behaviour. If all those men who behave antisocially, all the male alcoholics and all the 'classically' depressed men are added together then the sex statistics even up. This is not to say, however, that all or even most antisocial behaviour can be explained (or excused) as a symptom of depression.

Many researchers have wondered whether women do in fact have more stressful lives and whether this makes them more prone to overt depression. Quite a lot of 'life events' research has linked the onset of depression to negatively charged life events, especially those involving loss, but there are no consistent differences between the sexes on life event scales. Nor, it seems, do women weigh stressful events more heavily than do men. Nor do women in western cultures feel freer to express their changes of mood and emotion. Perhaps the way that men and women complain of depression is related to the way each group thinks it should express psychological symptoms. Women generally use more health services than do men, attend doctors and out-patient clinics more and consume more mind-altering (psychotropic) drugs than do men. Women also seek help for minor illnesses more than men do. Why?

One possible explanation is that women are going through a very difficult and confusing time, with the coming of the women's movement. Various researchers have found that the rates for several varieties of mental illness are higher in married women than in single, divorced and widowed women. Marriage, it seems, protects men from depression but has a detrimental effect on women. The most vulnerable time for women to get depressed is from puberty to the age of forty-five. After fifty-five the incidence for the sexes evens out.

During the decade of the '40s there was more mental illness among men than among women, but since 1964 men have never been ahead in the statistics. The long-term trend since 1940 has been for women to suffer from more overt depression than men and as each decade passes the gap is getting wider. The traditional female role is being questioned and this is causing much confusion among women of all social classes. Both housewives and working wives experience more depression than do working men; suggesting that for women, work outside the home is not protective. It is possible that men are protected because they have two sources of satisfaction – job and family – while women have only one. This doesn't, however, explain the working wives' greater likelihood of becoming depressed.

Some researchers feel that women get depressed more because they suffer from learned helplessness (see page 64), a situation in which nothing the person does has any effect on the rewards obtained. As more women enter the labour force they are, it is argued, opening themselves up to more negative reactions, during which they learn that nothing they do greatly improves their lot. Most women work in male-dominated settings and it has been found that men usually ignore a woman's attempts to influence the group in which she works. In one study, women who persisted in trying to influence their group were labelled as 'difficult' and were often isolated as a result. Traditionally female fields are less prestigious than male ones and, in general, women don't have to achieve as much as men to come up to people's expectations of them. If a woman tries to advance beyond society's expectations of her, rewards will be withdrawn from her in other ways. Men view such assertive, achieving women as less desirable co-workers and this, along with other things, makes their work less valued than men's. So, it could be argued, women over the last twenty-five years have become programmed by society to expect to achieve, but when it comes to the crunch they are poorly rewarded (either financially or in esteem). They learn that they are essentially helpless and cannot win either way and so become depressed.

The sad thing is that many health professionals may well be labelling some women as depressed simply because they have difficulty conforming to society's changing stereotype of womanhood. Health professionals, known for their love of pigeon-holing people who seek help, may be diagnosing role confusion-induced unhappiness as depression. This could make more women appear to be depressed than is in fact the case.

Of course there may be other causes for the greater numbers of female depressives, and hormonal ones are usually cited. Several studies have found that a larger proportion of depressed women are admitted to hospital in the twelve days of the month around ovulation, premenstrually and during menstruation, than in the rest of the menstrual cycle. This fact, and the finding that women's suicide attempts were also clustered around these times, led many to suggest that a hormonal change might be at the root of female depression as opposed to that in men. In spite of these seemingly convincing findings, there is little evidence linking the increased levels of depression in women to hormones alone.

Other 'at risk' groups are discussed fully in chapter two. The following list outlines the main groups of people more likely than average to suffer from depression.

Women, especially if they have several young children under the age of fourteen

Those who have a close relative who is, or has been, depressed or who has committed suicide

Those with an alcohol or drug problem

Those who have just been bereaved

Women who have just had a baby

People taking certain drugs that cause depression

Those suffering from certain physical diseases that cause depression

Those sensitive to certain foods

Those who have had certain infections

Those who have certain glandular (endocrine) disorders

Those who have had a surgical operation

Those who have lost a part of their body

Those with a long-term, debilitating illness

The mentally and physically fatigued

Those who have suffered a significant loss in life (real or imagined)

Those whose lifestyle has been changed (widowed, divorced, retirement, displacement, loneliness)

And those with a history of depression (especially manic depression)

What are the different types of depression?

The medical world has been arguing over the classification of depression for decades and the discussion will no doubt continue for a few more yet. The problem is that, with an ill-defined condition such as depression, it is very difficult to group those suffering from it into useful categories that help the patient.

Basically, medical opinion is split into those who think depression is an illness which can vary in form and intensity, depending on the circumstances and personality of the individual, and those who think that there are at least two clear-cut and different kinds of depression. Depending upon how one interprets the medical literature, one can accept either or even both points of view. To the depressed person though, results are what matter . . . so I have grouped the types of depression according to the way they are treated, rather than according to notional academic concepts.

To cut a very long story short, I find it useful to think of depressive illness as falling into five main types.

The first is 'true depression' or endogenous (coming from within) depression. The second is 'reactive depression' – so called because it occurs as a reaction to life's stresses and strains. The third type is a genetically-inherited one in which attacks of depression alternate with periods of elation and overactive (manic) behaviour. The fourth contains some of the small numbers of truly mentally ill people who have depression as a part of some other psychiatric illness and the last group consists of the so-called 'masked' depressions. In this last group, sufferers complain mainly or entirely of physical symptoms that do not suggest depression unless the person hearing the complaints is aware of what they are *really* saying. Treatment of the depression will often result in the disappearance of the physical symptoms.

It's impossible to be dogmatic about the proportion of depressives that fall into each of these groups, but suffice it to say that groups three and four are rare and that group two is by far the commonest. What most doctors and the public refer to when talking about depression is reactive depression. It probably accounts for eight out of ten of all depressions. Group five depressives are mostly seen by general practitioners, but a few eventually get through to psychiatrists when all their bodily symptoms have defeated their family doctor, physicians and surgeons.

Why, you might ask, bother to group depressives at all? Quite simply, it all comes down to treatment. Endogenous depression responds well to anti-depressant drugs and electro-convulsive therapy (ECT), while reactive depression does not. Manic-depression is treatable with lithium carbonate (see page 153) but the drug has little or no effect on the other three groups, and depression as part of a serious mental illness needs diagnosing because the more serious underlying condition may have been missed.

Having said this, depression in any one individual can often be difficult to label, though it can be very helpful to do so when trying to select the right treatment. Some depressed people fall 'neatly' into one category or another; but many have features of reactive and endogenous depression combined.

All depressions can be mild, moderate or severe. All but mild depressions need medical help. Not only can the severity of the condition vary, but so too can the duration. *Acute* depressions come and go in about a week, and often disappear without any treatment. *Recurrent* depressions are characterized by repeated acute episodes with normal periods in between, and *chronic* depression lasts for months or even years.

Let's look now at the four main types of depression, bearing in mind all the time that there can be a considerable overlap between the groups and that few individuals fall into one category as typically as I am describing.

Endogenous depression

Endogenous literally means 'coming from within'. Such depressions are by definition the ones that arrive from within the sufferer and seem to have no triggering factor from outside. No sooner have we said this than it becomes very apparent just how unsatisfactory such a label can be. How can we say with any certainty whether or not there has been a provoking factor which the depressed person has forgotten, overlooked, or even actively withheld from the doctor? Clinical experience shows that the majority of endogenous depressions do not in fact occur 'out of the blue', but that there usually is an underlying causative factor, if only it can be found. The danger of the 'coming from within' label is that the sufferer and the doctor alike may overlook or choose to ignore external causes that could be remedied and so make a recurrence of the depression less likely.

But perhaps the biggest potential drawback to thinking of depression as coming from within (i.e. that it is caused by a 'plumbing' fault) is that it tends to suggest that a person's mind and body are separate entities. This opinion is becoming increasingly difficult to hold to as the overlap between mind and body is found to be far greater than we in the West ever thought. By thinking of endogenous depression as some kind of plumbing fault we do ourselves a disservice, because there is almost certainly a psychological (reactive) element to most endogenous depressions.

Endogenous depression occurs at any time of life but is especially common around the menopause; as a part of manic-depressive illness; in the elderly; after childbirth; on taking certain drugs; after some infections; with some glandular (endocrine) disorders; after severe injuries and operations; with some diseases and as a result of chronic fatigue (mental or physical). All of these are discussed in depth in chapter two.

The features of endogenous depression, when typical, are those of 'classical' depression or melancholy. They include:

Sadness
Feeling worse in the morning and getting better as the day goes on
Sleep problems, particularly waking in the early hours of the morning
A general slowness of thought
Reduced appetite
A loss of interest in life
Diminished sexual interest
Self-neglect
A loss of self-confidence
A sense of guilt and unworthiness
A preoccupation with body functions or bodily symptoms
An inability to concentrate
An inability to make decisions

27

A poor memory
Agitation and anxiety
Irritability
An increased tendency to cry
A fear of being left alone
Unnatural fears about death
A sense of hopelessness and helplessness
Extreme bodily weakness and tiredness
Delusions
Suicidal thoughts

No one depressive will necessarily experience all of this list, but it is not uncommon for someone with moderate or severe depression to suffer from most of them at some time during his or her illness. We shall see how to deal with each of these symptoms in chapter three.

Endogenously depressed people tend to have these symptoms more severely than do the reactively depressed and tend to experience more bodily symptoms (as opposed to psychological ones) than do reactive depressives. By and large, endogenous depression occurs later in life and responds well to anti-depressant drugs and electroconvulsive therapy. It is said that the endogenously depressed feel worst in the morning and get better as the day goes on, but that this doesn't apply to the reactively depressed. The endogenously depressed are said to go off their food, while reactives often eat more; the endogenous group awake early in the morning and the reactives have difficulty falling off to sleep yet wake at the normal time after a fitful night's sleep. Such differences are often of theoretical rather than practical value, but can be helpful to a doctor in deciding which type of depression he's dealing with and so which treatment to use.

Reactive depression

This is the commonest form of depressive illness but it tends to be rather less severe than does endogenous depression. Some people with a reactive depression can have many of the symptoms listed above. True reactive depression can be difficult to differentiate from the depressive *reaction* (sadness and so on) that people experience as a natural, normal part of life and often it is impossible to do so. After all, sometimes it is simply a matter of degree. If life's stresses get on top of you it's not unnatural to lose some sleep, not feel much like eating, become irritable with those around you and so on. But however many of these things you experience, you're still in charge of your life and your emotions. When control slips away from you and the symptoms begin to rule *you*, then you know you've crossed the line from a depressive *reaction* to a depressive *illness*.

Reactive depressions tend to occur in those who are more neurotic than average and, because of this, some doctors call them 'neurotic' depressions. Because reactive depressions are by far the most common, let's see what neuroses are and how they predispose a person to reactive depression.

Human beings are highly complex creatures emotionally. From the moment we are born we crave love and attention, probably more than other creatures because we are dependent upon our mothers for so long. Because we need not only food, for which we are totally reliant on our mothers for many months, but love as well, we realize in our earliest days that our mother's ability to withhold these things from us can make us anxious and fearful. This is our first conflict in life – a conflict which is probably increasingly common and even more apparent as today's woman becomes less 'cow-like' towards her babies, is parted from them more, breast-feeds them less and spends less time in physical contact with them. All these things increase the baby's sense of dependence and vulnerability and in turn mould his adult personality. Mothers who have treated one child in the 'modern' way and another in the traditional 'animal' way tell of the completely different personalities of the children as they grow up and their very different ways of responding to life's stresses. I believe that the treatment of this, the commonest form of depression, starts in the cradle with a secure, very close, loving mother-baby relationship.

For most of us though, the fear of what our supplier of love and food can withhold from us produces hate, and we then feel guilty because we sense that we shouldn't feel so strongly about our provider. This ambivalence is the source of the child's first major conflict and sets the pattern for the rest of life.

'Normal' people come through the emotional upheavals of infancy and childhood relatively unscathed, secure in their view of themselves and able to function effectively in the outside world. They can also get pleasure out of life.

But being normal isn't easy in our western society because it very often presents us with conflicting demands. For example, we are expected to be nice to other people yet the whole of our culture emphasizes competition and striving, often at the expense of someone else. Such competition is seen not only in business, but at home between husband and wife, brother and sister, father and son and so on.

When such conflicts mount up in us we display neurotic symptoms. These include anger, fear, resentment, suspicion and apathy. Such feelings are normal, of course, but when they're present in inappropriate situations or in inappropriate doses we say the reaction is neurotic. Neurotic reactions don't alter a person's life: they're part of it and often a healthy part. The normal person isn't *always* anxious, resentful, angry or whatever, nor so afraid as to become timid or apathetic. Most of the time such a person isn't at either end of the scale of neurotic symptoms, but somewhere in the middle.

Neurotic people, however, often don't know how to react or behave. They are their own worst enemies, often deeply unhappy and don't know what to do for the best. The obsessive-compulsive person is one of the best examples of a neurotic, and is a good one to look at because sufferers from this condition can all too often become depressed.

Obsessive-compulsive people are excessively rigid perfectionists who feel there is only one way to do anything and that they have to do it that way all the time. They are incapable of changing their ideas and minds, plan their lives carefully and are punctual to a fault, intolerant of those who don't behave as they do and are plagued by the sloppiness of others. Such people live by the letter, not the spirit, of the law.

'Now', you may say. 'I'm a bit like that myself, but am I an obsessive-compulsive neurotic?' Well, to find out if you are, ask yourself honestly if you can dismiss your obsessive thoughts and willingly and easily stop a compulsive act and go on to the next thing you are going to do. If you *can*, then you're not neurotically obsessive.

The trouble with neurotically obsessive people is that their behaviour uses vast amounts of nervous and physical energy. The endless straightening of books on the coffee-table, the emptying of an ashtray before the cigarette butt is cold, the obsession with personal cleanliness, neat handwriting and a host of other things simply wears them out. They feel they can't let up from their vigilance in their endless quest for perfection and over the years wear themselves down. Then, if a crisis occurs, their emotional and psychological bank balance is so low that they easily go 'into the red' and become depressed.

Today's world calls for an almost infinite ability to change and this leaves the obsessive-compulsive especially vulnerable to depression, sometimes right from childhood. Unfortunately, because of deeply felt emotions in infancy and childhood that they dared not express (for fear of losing loved ones or the approval of society) the mental hurt lies there festering for years. Slowly they find a way of coping with the emotional pain and adopt various emotional 'escapes', many of which involve controlling their environment. Alas, the emotional escapes provide only short-term benefit and as time goes by the neurotic becomes tyrannized by new sources of pain – neurotic symptoms. A neurosis starts off by being a way out, but sadly the way out is often merely a cul-de-sac which provides no long-term answers.

Because neuroses are learned patterns of behaviour they can be unlearned; although it's easier for young people to do than it is for older people. Much of the treatment of reactive depression involves the use of techniques that help people to come to terms with their neuroses and personality problems and so take less out of themselves.

Reactive depression arises as a result of a definite and perceivable stress or stimulus, of which loss (real or imagined) is the commonest. The loss can be of a loved one, a concept or idea, a job or many other things. We shall look at this in more detail in chapter two. Such depression, unlike endogenous depression, is often (some experts say, always) accompanied by anxiety.

The relationship between anxiety and depression is a vexed question because anxiety neurosis (a condition in which the sufferer is crippled by inappropriate anxiety) and depression

31

are often seen in the same person at the same time. Anxiety is an acute or chronic response to a threat (real or imagined) to an individual. It is not in itself abnormal and is frequently useful. Problems can arise though when anxiety is too intense and when it occurs inappropriately.

We all need some anxiety in our lives. For example, when we sit an examination or put on a performance of some kind, anxiety makes us more alert, helps us put on the best show we can and generally stimulates all our senses. Excessive anxiety, though, would mean a poor performance because our minds would flit from idea to idea, our hands would be too restless to write, our legs too restless to stand and we'd frequently be rushing to the lavatory to pass water. Somewhere between the two extremes of 'not caring' and being overanxious is the best place to be, so that we can function effectively in any given situation.

Because anxiety manifests itself in many different ways, it can be mistaken for other things. The main psychological symptom of anxiety is fear and it's an unpleasant state to be in. The emotional feelings of anxiety and fear are accompanied by an overactivity of the sympathetic nervous system, which in turn produces a fast pulse, palpitation, nausea, numbness, tingling in the hands and feet, sweating, a desire to pass water and even to open the bowels.

Such a state of excessive arousal need not be seen as totally negative though, and in a sense anxiety is the price we have to pay for being vigilant – on our guard against the stresses of the outside world. It is highly unlikely that we are born anxious, but rather that we learn to be anxious. Some situations are more dangerous or anxiety-producing than others and most of us learn to be anxious when we don't get what we want in our earliest days of infancy.

Most anxiety then is protective, alerting us to very real dangers; but the anxiety neuroses seen so commonly with depression are destructive rather than helpful to the sufferer. No one knows why, but women seem to show anxiety symptoms more obviously than men, who tend to convert them into physical disorders such as peptic ulcers and high blood pressure.

Anxiety and depression are closely linked, especially in

reactive depressions, but they are by no means one and the same thing. Depression refers to the past and a feeling of hopelessness. Anxiety refers to the future with a feeling of helplessness. A person can't be anxious about what has already happened – he is afraid of what will happen. A man who fears he may have got a girl pregnant is not anxious about what has happened, but is apprehensive that her pregnancy will become a fact and worried about how it will influence their lives. In these circumstances depression could develop as a result of the guilt feelings about the experience. Depression could also come on once he learns that she is pregnant.

Depression is a passive emotion whereas anxiety is an active one. The prototype of anxiety is fear and that of depression, grief.

Frustration is something else again. This arises as a result of perceiving a need to do something or a desire to have something; while at the same time realizing one can't do it or have it. Frustration can produce a sense of helplessness but rarely produces depression.

So, in general terms, it's the destructive sort of anxiety that produces problems and can lead on to or be a part of depression. This sort of anxiety arises because we all have within us a collection of feelings and emotions, a large number of which contradict each other. Many of our emotions ought to be expressed somehow, but we overrule them because to express them at a particular time or place would be inappropriate. If some of these impulses are so strong that the personality can't cope with bottling them up, anxiety is the result. For example, people who get mad at their bosses are likely to be fired so they repress their feelings, however strong they are. There are two aspects of the anxiety that follows. First they fear that if they are unable to control their feelings they may well not be able to control other feelings and that this could be dangerous. Second, they are anxious because of the possible outcome if they *were* to lose their temper with their bosses.

Anxiety is such a common feature of depression that many experts feel that the two conditions are both part of an anxiety-depression continuum, in which some people are more anxious and others more depressed. If we expect to suffer, we are anxious and if we have no hope of relief, we despair. Therefore

33

anxiety and depression are closely related and interlocked forms of emotional response in both normal and ill people. Most people affected by anxiety neuroses also experience depressive episodes, but severe and persistent depression is more common among the depressed. Similarly, research has shown that although anxiety and periods of strain are common in the depressed, anxiety neurotics experience these feelings more often. One large study of a group of anxious and depressed patients found that both, although labelled differently by psychiatrists, had a considerable degree of symptom overlap. While panic attacks, attacks of unconsciousness, severe agoraphobic symptoms, depersonalization and distortions of reality were largely confined to the anxiety group, symptoms of generalized anxiety, 'dizzy' attacks and mild agoraphobic symptoms were common among the depressed patients.

This same study found that neurotic illness in parents and personality disorders in both parents and siblings were much more common in the anxiety group. Anxious patients also reported parental disharmony and poor relationships with parents more often than did the depressed ones. The anxiety group described themselves as poor mixers and as being easily hurt by trivial remarks and criticisms and thought that they suffered easily from the stresses of everyday life. The anxiety group admitted to more frequent depressive swings and were more concerned with their health than were the depressives.

Overall in the study, the depressed patients were found to be more stable, mature and independent than their non-depressed counterparts. But, having drawn all these differences, the researchers felt bound to conclude that although it is possible to distinguish two groups of symptoms, those that are substantially 'anxious' and those that are substantially 'depressed', 'the hypothesis that there are two separate patient groups corresponding to those symptoms was not confirmed'.

So, as we have seen, anxiety and depression often go hand in hand. Which predominates varies according to the particular person, personality and many other factors. In some circumstances the overt manifestations of one end of the anxiety/depression spectrum may be overwhelmed by the other, only to reappear when healing begins to take place. This is often seen when anxiety 'breaks through' as people recover from their depression.

When anxiety and depression are both of equal intensity, the condition is called *agitated depression*, and where anxiety is low yet depression marked, the term *retarded depression* is used. Again, these classifications are helpful in choosing the best treatment because retarded depression improves dramatically with electroconvulsive therapy (ECT).

This then is the picture of reactive depression. But, as we have seen, there is often a considerable overlap between it and endogenous depression. There are some basic differences which are worth mentioning. Endogenously depressed people feel sad and empty within themselves, overwhelmed with their own guilt and unworthiness. Reactive depressives have the same feelings, but sense that something outside has 'done it to them' and link their feelings to their loss or other life events. Because of this, reactive depressives usually retain their self-esteem, whereas endogenous sufferers are convinced that they are fundamentally hopeless and worthless. The families of the two types also react differently to the sufferer. Endogenously depressed people make everyone irritated and impatient. The family can't help it. They simply can't see a cause for the depression and so can't understand why their relative should be behaving in this way. It is under these circumstances that the typical 'Pull yourself together', 'Just snap out of it', remarks are made so thoughtlessly, yet not with any intent to hurt. Endogenously depressed people are no more capable of 'snapping out of it' than someone who has pneumonia, and any expectation that they should do so only serves to deepen their depression because it confirms that the person making the remarks doesn't know what the sufferer is going through.

With reactive depression the person's friends and relatives tend, if anything, to rally round because they can readily see the loss, grief or whatever and usually try to help all they can. However, if neurotic symptoms predominate, the family, whilst feeling sympathetic, still gets very annoyed because after a while they can't take any more of the depressed person's behaviour.

Reactive depression is by far the commonest type and probably accounts for eight out of ten of all depressions.

Manic-depression

This is a form of endogenous depression but is so characteristic that it deserves a category of its own. It is also the only type of depression that is definitely known to be inherited and is one that can be treated effectively and even prevented.

Manic-depression is a condition which is characterized by episodes of depression and mania. Mania is a very active, over-excited state in which the sufferer feels 'high'. The alternating moods of 'high' (mania) and 'low' (depression) occur in cycles of between six months and five years. It's an uncommon cause of depression but it is still very important. It has been calculated that the average general practitioner in the UK will have about twenty manic-depressives on his list of 2,000 patients and that many of these will one day have a nervous breakdown of some kind as a result. The reason why these people have to be diagnosed and treated is that they form a very high percentage of known depressives who eventually kill themselves. We have seen already that manic depression can often be very successfully treated, so by recognizing it lives can be saved.

Unfortunately, not all manic-depressives go to their doctors complaining of depression. Many show up with family or social problems such as shoplifting, traffic offences, marital breakdowns, heavy drinking or failure at important tasks in life. If these crises were handled in the normal way and the underlying diagnosis missed, the patient would lose out and might commit suicide.

Although the name suggests that the sufferer should have equal numbers of episodes of depression and mania this is not usually the case. Most manic-depressives only have attacks of depression. Relatively few people have true mania and when it occurs it is usually seen either before or after a depression.

The saddest thing about manic-depression is that those affected by it are often very talented and able people. Many of the world's great artists and creative people have been manic-depressives, whose bouts of creativity have often coincided with their overexcited phases. Handel, Rossini and Schumann were people with the condition. A significant number of modern entertainers and public figures, for example, are either manic-depressives or have a mood-swing personality that is one step away from true manic-depression.

This type of personality is called cyclothymic (see page 43).

The manic-depressive personality is in many ways an attractive one to an outsider but not to the sufferer and the family. When manic-depressives are on a high they spend freely, often looking for new ways of getting rid of their money, going on a spending spree just for the sheer joy of spending. At times they'll almost get out of touch with reality. They sleep little but wake up ready to go all over again. In the most severe stages of mania they hardly sleep at all, often for days on end. They eat poorly (because they're so busy) and are brimming over with madcap plans and schemes, many of which seem very plausible.

Hypomania is the stage just short of this. Sufferers are still very much in touch with reality, in fact more in touch than those around them. They tend to develop a sixth sense about gambling and think they can control the many thousands of variables involved. They are very competent and jump into any situation, are greedy for knowledge, very perceptive, over-aggressive and overactive. Because they feel invincible they can gamble, quite effectively if they are not on too much of a 'high', and in business hypomanics often do very well. Such a person is always first in the office in the morning and last out in the evening. They have more energy than anyone else and love to build empires. Alas, they overextend themselves only to fall precipitously. Successful hypomanics surround themselves with good lieutenants who take advantage of their enormous energy and ability when they're 'up', but water down the more mad-brain ideas and keep them and the business going when they're 'down'.

Almost every hypomanic or manic will eventually crash and, when they do, they spend a lot of time brooding on real or imagined losses and problems. Some such people become deluded into believing that they have lost everything, that they have no money, that nobody likes them and that they are worthless. Then true depression may set in.

The most dramatic feature of these depressions is that they contrast so severely with the person's normal life and personality. They lose their ability to get pleasure out of anything, can't work properly, worry about their health, wake early in the morning and exhibit all the other signs of an endogenous depression. This first bout of depression may well be treated with anti-depressants or even ECT if it is serious enough, and within a few weeks or months the person is usually better. Unfortunately, as we have seen, in the case of manic-depressives this is unlikely to be the last episode of depression, though many years may go by before the next one.

No one knows what causes manic-depression. It's certainly inherited (like colour blindness) and those who have had a manic-depressive relative form a substantial percentage of all depressives. One survey found that one-third of all manic-depressives had had a relative in a mental hospital. In one form of the condition the gene is carried by the X chromosome. Consequently a woman will carry the gene and not have the illness yet will pass it on to half of her sons. This has some practical implications because in such affected families it becomes possible to predict with a fair degree of probability which individuals are likely to be manic-depressives and which are not.

But having said all this, just because you or someone you know is subject to 'highs' and 'lows' doesn't mean that he or she is more likely to suffer from manic-depression. Some people naturally function quite normally and effectively at what you would call a 'low' level, whereas others are amazing doers and are active all the time. Neither of these personality types is in any danger of becoming manic-depressive – they simply represent both ends of the scale of normality.

However, any substantial mood change, towards either depression or mania, should be reported to a doctor because once it is serious enough to alter people's lives, and especially if they seem to have lost touch with reality, they need help and need it quickly.

Lithium carbonate is now the drug of choice in the treatment of manic-depression and is highly effective both in controlling the acute phase of the disease and in preventing a recurrence of depressions. For more details of drug therapy, see page 153.

Depression associated with psychotic mental illness

Some mental illnesses are so severe that they make the sufferers lose hold on reality, retreat completely into themselves and live in a world entirely of their own making. People suffering from such diseases are labelled *psychotic* and are what the average layman would call 'mad'. Psychotics used to form the bulk of the long-term patients within mental hospitals, but today many can live near-normal lives in the community because of modern drug therapy.

The commonest of all the psychoses is schizophrenia, which affects about one per cent of the population. This is no place to talk about schizophrenia at any length, but there is one type of the disease that includes depression, and because of this the more serious underlying psychosis can be diagnosed.

Often, the story starts with a young person who spends a lot of time moping around the house, showing no interest in anything and wanting to be alone a lot of the time. Slowly the other signs of schizophrenia begin to manifest themselves. Familiar things and people appear strange to the sufferers; they may have hallucinations; they may be deluded into believing that people are against them; they may sleep all day and stay up all night; they may use strange words in a language all of their own; and slowly retreat into a private world.

At this stage depression sets in and it becomes increasingly difficult to distinguish the real from the unreal. Slowly the schizophrenia and the depression become intertwined and both need medical treatment. In the US, schizophrenic depressions account for the largest proportion of suicides in men and women between the ages of fifteen and twenty-four. Once the depression is treated, the schizophrenia can be tackled, often with very good results.

Masked depression

So far I have described types of depression which are readily recognized by doctors and patients alike; but there are many millions of people in the western world alone who are severely depressed yet are not recognized as such. This comes about because, although depression is more widely recognized than ever before, many people present their depression to the medical profession in a disguised form. Not uncommonly in such cases, a suicidal act is the first outward sign that depression is the underlying condition.

Obviously, if someone complains of the classic emotional and psychological symptoms of depression, everyone will know what is wrong. But for some unknown reason (although many psychiatrists have elegant theories) some depressed people complain of almost no psychological symptoms, merely of somatic (bodily) ones. As many as forty per cent of all depressed people go to their doctors complaining of bodily symptoms alone and as a result end up doing the rounds of increasingly frustrated specialists. Gradually, they become more and more convinced that they have a terrible, undiagnosable illness that everyone is missing. Often, so many body systems are involved that the patients think their whole body must be going bad. Ironically, this very fear is the key to the diagnosis of an underlying depression, because it is extremely rare for a person to have symptoms from many organ systems at once, and it is even more rare for them to continue for months or years without coming to a head in some physical way.

In such depressed people, the results of the tests they have (and they have them in abundance) are always negative, or if there is any abnormality it is insufficient to account for the severity of the symptoms they suffer. Anyway, the pattern of the symptoms follows no known physiological or anatomical pathways and they don't respond to the non-specific medicines that so often help others. Quite soon these patients become labelled as hypochondriacs by their family, their friends and ultimately their doctors and, after causing a great deal of agony to everyone, eventually get referred for a psychiatric opinion as a desperate last ditch stand. By this stage, quite understandably, patients are resentful at what people think of them; sick of trailing around 'experts' who can find nothing wrong; worn down by their symptoms; upset that people think (or even say) that they're imagining them; and worried lest being referred to a psychiatrist means that they really are 'mad'.

There have been many studies of bodily symptoms for which no bodily cause could be found and which get 'miraculously' better when the person's depression is treated. Some of the symptoms most complained of are:

Headache
Weakness and shakiness

Dizziness
Palpitation
Blurred vision
Loss of control with a tendency to drop things
Burning pains in the limbs
Difficulty with breathing ('can't draw a good breath')
Constipation or diarrhoea
Abdominal pains
Nausea
Unusual facial pains
A sense of food 'sticking' at the top of the stomach
Pains, aches or cramps in the legs and back
Excessive sweating
Itching

In one study of patients complaining of symptoms for which no cause could be found, ten per cent were found to be severely depressed and half of them had been ill for more than ten years. Many had already had numerous investigations and even (unnecessary) operations.

The real diagnosis becomes apparent when the doctor seeks other evidence of depression. Such symptoms are invariably present but are never volunteered by the patient. Unfortunately, some doctors discard such findings (even if they are present early on), considering them to be the *result of* the as yet undiagnosed underlying condition instead of the *cause* of it. True hypochondriasis is usually life-long, but a preoccupation with bodily symptoms which comes on out of the blue is nearly always of depressive origin. Such a preoccupation, together with early morning waking, is almost diagnostic of depression. Feelings of guilt, self-recrimination, desperation and worthlessness are usually there if they are asked for. As a final clincher, these depressives are almost always far more disabled socially and physically than their symptoms or clinical findings on physical examination suggest. They become very limited socially, often staying close to or at home for weeks or months on end; yet they are remarkably fit when compared to patients with a similar disability who aren't depressed.

The early recognition of this kind of depression can save the

41

sufferer and the family a lot of heartache, money, inconvenience or even unpleasant investigations and unnecessary operations. It can even prevent suicide. Depression with so-called hypochondriacal symptoms has a particularly poor outlook if left untreated and makes the sufferer a very high suicide risk.

But depression in adults isn't just disguised as physical illness – it can be disguised as a personality disorder too. Shoplifting, especially in women over the age of forty, is not an uncommon way for depression to show itself. These women are usually of perfectly good character and the charge of shoplifting comes as a shock to all who know them. Usually, the stolen article is of little value and the women could easily have afforded to pay for it. They admit guilt readily and give a self-incriminating story to the police. Fortunately, the courts now deal very sensitively with such women who are obviously not criminals.

Serious drinking and gambling or hard drug taking occurring for the first time in middle age can be a pointer to an underlying depressive illness. (For more details see page 74.)

Depression commonly presents itself in 'masked' or atypical ways in children, adolescents and in the elderly but these are considered separately in chapter four.

Is there such a thing as a depressive personality?

Whenever someone we know becomes depressed we try to look for things that could explain why it all happened. If several people we know, especially in the family, are, or have been, depressed we often start to wonder if there's a particular type of personality that's more likely to become depressed. If there were any barn door links between certain personality types and the likelihood of getting depressed, perhaps we could do something either to change susceptible people's personalities or to react swiftly in situations likely to make them depressed and so prevent trouble.

The whole subject has been much debated in the medical profession and it is only recently that there has been any kind of agreement.

Certainly it's fair to say that nothing is as simple as a 'depressive personality', but there are common personality types which seem to be linked to specific types of depressions. For example, it is now fairly widely agreed that of those who first become endogenously depressed in middle age, the pre-depressive personality is often found to be obsessional. Such people are inhibited with a tendency to be quiet, unobtrusive, serious, worry a lot, intolerant, sensitive, extremely honest, frugal, stubborn, of unbending moral code, lacking humour, over-conscientious and given to self-punishment. Often their interests are narrow, their habits stereotyped, their behaviour predictable, and their real pleasures and friends in life few. This doesn't mean to say that anyone with this sort of personality will become depressed, but that of all those becoming depressed for the first time in middle age this sort of personality tends to prevail.

When it comes to reactive depression, most experts agree that the majority of sufferers have been more neurotic (before the onset of the depression) than other people. Endogenously depressed people tend to have been more stable, more submissive and to have had more mature personalities before their depression. Contrast this with the person destined to become reactively depressed who is basically pessimistic, easily lonely, obviously dissatisfied, generally unhappy and feels guilty and inadequate. It isn't a long step from this kind of personality to a frank reactive depression, given the right trigger factors.

Overall, it's probably fair to say that the type of depression people suffer from is to some extent pre-determined by their pre-illness personality. Hysterical people (those who are emotionally insecure, are dramatic attention seekers and enjoy manipulating people) tend to suffer from hysterical signs and symptoms when depressed; obsessionals will have obsessional depressions and so on.

Manic-depression has been most widely studied in this context and it is generally agreed that the underlying personality type is one which is called cyclothymic. This term means that the person consistently displays mood-swings of a range and intensity that are beyond what most of us would consider normal. Such people have frank, open personalities, and are either bright, talkative, optimistic, aggressive people who make light of everyday affairs or alternatively take a

43

gloomy outlook and make mountains out of molehills. Many of these character traits are often combined, making the person emotionally unstable and difficult to live with.

Psychiatrists of all schools have had a field day characterizing the personalities of depressed people generally and many have come up with plausible ideas. Some describe the depressive as a 'love addict' in a perpetual state of greediness; some characterize depressives as people of insatiable demands; some see depressive personalities as manipulative, using their depressive symptoms to manoeuvre people and life to suit them; and yet others talk of the depressive's extreme emotional dependency.

In general, depression-prone people are exceptionally dependent upon the outside world to supply them with boosts to their self-esteem. Their frustration tolerance is low and they employ various subconscious techniques to maintain their ambivalent relationships in life. A tendency towards envy, fear of competition, underselling of the self and a lack of interest in or ability to deal with interpersonal relationships are also commonly seen.

Psychoanalysts talk of many depressives being 'oral' – by which they mean that they exhibit behaviour which is centered around the mouth and digestive system. They argue that such a fixation comes about as a result of poor mother-baby relationships early on in life, but we shall see more about this in chapter two.

So, in summary there seem to be some predisposing personality types that are more likely to become depressed than others, but there are no definite cause-and-effect links, except perhaps for manic-depressive illness.

Personality *will* undoubtedly colour the way in which depression manifests itself. It may also render people more or less susceptible to certain stresses, especially the loss of significant individuals and objects or of their self-esteem. Personality greatly affects the way people seek (or don't seek) treatment; react to psychological therapies; their willingness to take drugs; and their response to all of these – even to electroconvulsive therapy (ECT). Their underlying personality so colours their disease 'face' that it can substantially alter the way doctors, nurses, other health professionals and even family, react to and handle the depression. Personality, especially in people under middle age, can be modified, often quite considerably if the person is sufficiently motivated and is led by a good therapist. In some cases, modifying one's personality or one's reactions to it can be very helpful in treating the overall depression. Depressed people are often trapped within their own personality but can release themselves, given the right help and guidance. Many features of our personalities are learned and can, often with some difficulty, it's true, be unlearned. Too many people simply throw up their hands and say, 'I'm just obsessional, there's nothing I can do about it'. It's often not easy, but there is usually something that *can* be done.

Alcoholism, drug addiction and depression

It is widely held that women are about twice as likely to suffer from depression as are men, and we have examined one theory as to why this should be the case on page 22. However, it is becoming increasingly clear that alcoholism and drug addiction are often male equivalents of depression and that men (who currently greatly outnumber women with these conditions) sometimes express their depression by resorting to alcohol or drugs.

Alcohol has a long history of being used as a mental painkiller. It is certainly the oldest of tranquillizers and is readily and socially available. Many men turn to the bottle instead of to the doctor, as women do. Unfortunately, alcohol not only gives only short-term relief from their mental and emotional agony, but it also depresses brain activity chemically. So, cruel though it may seem, it actually adds to the problem of depression.

The second problem with a depressive's taking to alcohol for relief is that it answers nothing and can even mask the underlying problems that caused the depression. It's all too easy for a family to get wrapped up in Dad's drinking and for everyone to focus on it when underneath there is a depression getting deeper by the month, which no one diagnoses. Of course depression isn't the only reason people become alcoholics: there are lots of other causes but depression is a major, often treatable and potentially lethal cause.

There are parallels with drug addiction too, especially in

the young. Several surveys have found that experimenting with drugs starts during a period of depression in adolescence – a depression which has all too often been completely overlooked by family and doctors alike. Just as alcohol can produce temporary oblivion, so too can hard or even soft drugs; but this slippery slope is even more dangerous and each year growing numbers of young people, especially in the US, die from hard drug addiction.

People with a tendency to depression, or those in the early stages, often feel tempted to take mind-altering drugs. This is very dangerous and should never be done. If ever you feel you might be getting depressed, don't take the odd anti-depressant or sleeping tablet without first telling your doctor. There are many treatable causes of depression and you may have one of them. Simply masking the symptoms with self-medication is pointless and could be dangerous. *Never ever take anybody else's anti-depressants anyway*.

Does depression run in families?

When the cause of a disease isn't known, many of us wonder whether it might be inherited and mental illness very often provokes this response. The science of genetics is a fairly recent one, yet we now know quite a lot about inherited susceptibilities to various illnesses. Some conditions are inherited in well-proven and predictable ways and others are inherited in the form of rather indefinable susceptibilities. In the former conditions, no matter what your environment or the way you behave, you can do little to influence whether or not you'll suffer from the condition. In the second group, however, it is likely that the environment plays a final deciding role in whether or not you end up with the disease in a clinically recognizable form. It follows from this that people with certain susceptibilities can, by manipulating their environment, prevent the onset of a condition which might easily have been a problem in another environment. In this way, for example, the exclusive breast feeding of infants by mothers whose families have a clear family history of allergies can substantially protect them from developing allergies.

So it is with depression. It is likely that many of us inherit a tendency to depression that can be either nurtured or prevented from developing, according to our upbringing. In the majority of such people it is thought that the right environment, especially in the first few formative years of life, can more than compensate for any such underlying depressive trends.

There are, however, some very clearly inherited types of depressions, as the latest research is beginning to show.

The finding that families with mania had a larger than expected number of members with mood and emotional disorders in two consecutive generations suggested that manic-depressive illness might be inherited. This has been found to be the case, with at least one sub-group of the condition being inherited on the X chromosome – just like colour blindness. A woman who is a carrier for this type of manic depressive illness will, therefore, pass it on to half of her boys who could suffer from the disease itself.

Other research has found that those suffering from ordinary, endogenous depression can be divided into two groups according to inherited characteristics. *Pure depressive disease*, as one expert has called it, occurs when the patient is a middle-aged man with a strong family history of depression in first-degree relatives of both sexes and *depressive spectrum disease* occurs when the patient is a young woman with depression in female, and alcoholism and social problems in male, first-degree relatives.

Other studies of the families of depressed patients have shown that the risk of close relatives developing a similar illness is greater when the index case (the patient being studied) becomes depressed in early life. This has led to the theory that there are several different sorts of depression and that the genetically based ones appear earlier in life and the situational or environmental ones occur later.

Clearly, whether or not people will suffer from depression depends on many factors: their genetic make-up; the way in which their threshold for depression is modified by their upbringing; their vulnerability to emotional and other stresses; and their personality.

So, as with so much in the study of depression, the answer isn't simple. It is clear now that some forms of depression are inherited but, apart from the X-linked inheritance of certain

47

types of manic-depression, it is thought that all the others can be modified by upbringing to such an extent that depression need never occur because of an inherited 'weakness'.

The outcome of depression

Being able to predict the outcome (prognosis) of a condition is a very difficult part of medicine. Most people, when they fall ill with something, are naturally only too keen to know when it might end. Some conditions and diseases run well-defined courses and the end can be predicted with certainty. Depression, however, isn't like this and even in the best medical circles it can often be a guess as to how long a particular bout of depression will last.

Mild bouts of the blues, such as those coming on after a marital problem, business loss, or other setbacks, usually subside as the life event that provoked the situation resolves itself. In such circumstances a mild reactive depression will frequently last only a few days anyway and a few good nights' sleep, an improvement in a relationship or a short holiday will see most people right again in no time.

When it comes to more serious depression, studies have shown that over forty per cent of patients experience no more than one episode, even when follow up is continued for as long as forty years. Other studies show that a single episode of depression does nothing to impair the brain or intellectual functioning. This is encouraging to many who think that they'll in some way be changed mentally for ever. The American Psychiatric Association has crystallized the current thinking on this very reassuringly: 'In general, the assumption of normal activities by countless thousands of people who have been successfully treated for depression is compelling evidence that the existence of an episode of depression in a person's medical history should be considered in the same manner as a wide range of other successfully treated illnesses.'

So in between episodes of depression the vast majority of depressives are completely healthy and lead normal lives. But, as we have seen, over half of those who have one depressive episode will have another. Having had depression confers no immunity to further attacks, especially if someone has a personality, or lives in an environment, which is conducive to depression. This is especially true of reactive depression.

It's paradoxical that modern treatments have made it more difficult to be able to predict disease outcome in depression and indeed some other diseases. Before we started 'interfering' with drugs and ECT, the course of a depressive illness was clear. Such studies found that, left completely alone, the average depression lasted for about eighteen months, at which time it disappeared spontaneously. Unfortunately, many people never get this far down the natural recovery route because they kill themselves as a result of their depression. Today, things are very different. Drugs are often given so early (and often inappropriately as we will see on page 158) that the depression can't even properly be classified and classification is one of the helpful things in predicting outcome. Often, by the time a specialist sees the depressed person, the illness has been so modified by drug treatment that he has no hope of knowing how far into the disease the person is and so cannot predict an outcome or duration.

The age of the patient, the family history and a personal history of previous depression can all be helpful to the doctor in making some prediction as to the outcome. Younger people are more flexible than older patients and fare better in reactive depressions. Older people, however, often respond better to drugs and ECT because they are usually suffering from endogenous depression. A strong family history of depression could mean that the person has inherited a tendency to become depressed and since most of such depressions are endogenous in type, there is a better chance that they'll respond to therapy. However, it could mean that because of social and emotional vulnerability, they'll be subject to even more similar episodes unless something can be done to break the cycle.

Certain features in a given person do seem to be helpful in predicting the outcome of depression in particular circumstances. The presence of physical disease and disabling conditions usually means that the depression will do rather badly. However, one study of elderly people living in the community found that their physical diseases and their psychiatric disorders pursued independent courses. A deterioration in the physical illness was sometimes associated with a lessening of the depression.

In general, the longer a person has been depressed, the poorer the outlook for a complete recovery or a depression-free future – but even this generalization is constantly being proved wrong.

Of the illness features, loss of weight and early waking are related to a good outcome. Panic attacks and other signs of anxiety setting in are not a good sign. People with hypochondriacal symptoms also tend to do rather worse than other depressives.

So if your doctor tells you how long he thinks your depression will last, remember that at best he can only give an informed guess and that because there are so many variables it might not be a very accurate one. Truly depressed people don't think about outcome – they're too wrapped up in their illness to do that, but their relatives certainly will wonder just how long it can all last. As we have seen, there really is no magic answer to this, but what can be said is that the family and friends of depressed people can greatly influence their speed of recovery and even whether or not they'll suffer from another episode. If each of us were to use a depressive episode in our family as a trigger to examine what might have brought it on, to re-examine our interpersonal and family relationships and to take stock of our lifestyles, then we might not only prevent future depressions in our ill relative but also even safeguard our own futures a little. After all, depression doesn't just happen to other people – the same cluster of circumstances that produced a depression in one member of the family could well do so in another if no avoiding action is taken.

Is depression all bad?

Depression is Nature's way of enabling us to endure loss, sorrow, bereavement and a host of other negative situations in life and, although depression is mentally and emotionally painful, it's almost certainly part of Nature's survival kit. After all, if you're slowed down and miserable, you won't have the energy to commit suicide (see page 209).

Depression can, however, have more practical day-to-day pay-offs than this and, although I'm not saying that most people would go as far as the character in a Nestroy play who says, 'If I could not annoy other people with my melancholia, I wouldn't enjoy it at all', there *are* advantages to being depressed. We learn right from childhood that when we lose something or do badly at an examination, our parents console us and we like it. They reassure us and boost our self-esteem. By doing this they counter the sense of loss and help prevent depression from setting in.

In later life many adults resort to the same tactics. When they feel emotionally depressed or insecure they use depression to elicit love and concern from those around them. Many of the most experienced people working with depressives tell of the extraordinarily manipulative form that the disease can take in people. This manipulative behaviour is often subconscious; but sometimes it is perfectly conscious. Remember that all but the most severely depressed are perfectly 'with-it' mentally and know exactly what they're doing.

Depression starts off by affecting only the sufferers, but as the condition progresses they may find they actually get satisfaction out of the situation. At the very least, they become the centre of attention, especially if they have to go into hospital. As one man told me: 'Now she [his wife] can't ignore me, I really must be ill or they wouldn't have taken me into hospital'. A diagnosis of depression can also take the pressure off the sufferers, pressure they'd sooner be without. In this way they escape the real problems of life and throw them firmly at the feet of those around them. This may, of course, be what their depression is all about anyway. In their new 'invalid' role, they couldn't possibly (in their eyes) be expected to cope with everyday life and all its obligations. So depression can be an escape, albeit that most depressed people don't consciously contrive it to be so.

The feelings of worthlessness and inferiority that most depressives experience are also sometimes used to their advantage. By constantly demonstrating their misery to those around them they (often implicitly) make others feel guilty. This may lead to emotional blackmail – often of their nearest and dearest. If someone keeps telling you that he's unloved it almost forces you to say the opposite if you care for him at all. This often provokes tremendous internal conflicts with the friend or relative, because such reassurances are usually made

51

at a time when one feels decidedly unloving towards the depressed person. In this way, any real symptoms associated with depression (and we have seen how these are modified by the person's underlying personality type) can be effectively 'beefed up' by depressives to further manipulate people and situations over which they would otherwise have little control. In a few depressions, the gains are so substantial that they actually get in the way of treating the depression.

What doctors can do

Although some types of depression can respond dramatically to modern therapy, the majority of those with depression are not easy to treat and are probably mistreated. One US expert has claimed that of the eight to fifteen million depressives in his country only about 1.5 million are being treated properly for their condition. There is no comparable estimate for the UK, but it is unlikely that the figures would be substantially different.

In this section we'll look at the commonest problem areas in depression and see what doctors generally have to offer. A more detailed discussion of the various specific treatments for depression can be found in chapters five, six and seven.

Bereavement is a common cause of reactive depression and a natural response to the loss we experience when someone dies. The death of anyone diminishes us all, since it reminds us that we too will die, perhaps sooner than we'd like to admit. In the early days doctors usually offer some sort of sedative to calm the bereaved. A nighttime dose may enable the person to sleep. The commonest drugs used in this sort of situation are Valium (or a similar drug) as a tranquillizer and Mogadon as a sleeping tablet. Neither drug should be needed for more than a few weeks at most and many bereaved find that if they need to take anything at all then a few days' worth of tablets are often enough. This is especially the case with night sedation which can, even in the absence of true drug dependence, produce a 'hypnotic habit', as doctors call it. Such a person becomes psychologically used to needing sleeping tablets and can't sleep without them.

When the immediate bereavement pains are over these drugs should be discontinued because there is evidence that they inhibit the natural process of mourning. Some surveys have shown that those who don't take any drugs for such bereavement crises do better than those who do. There is a positive value in crying, for example, and I have found that a few sleepless nights do no harm either in such circumstances. Weeping, feeling sorry for oneself, the sympathy of others, the wretched feelings of guilt, anger, resentment, self-reproach and so on, are all a normal part of mourning and must be given expression. If you dampen them down with drugs they'll come out in other ways at another time, perhaps later as a true depression.

Normal grief has two stages. Early on, the person withdraws from any forward-looking activities and concentrates on and is preoccupied with the past. The dead person dominates the thoughts. Slowly, the current world begins to reassert itself and the dead person becomes a memory. To be fair, some people may never be the same again after a bereavement and some of these are likely to become depressed. If you feel you aren't coming out of a bereavement in a normal way, do talk to your doctor.

Mourning and grief in our society are very repressed and it's often difficult to talk about the dead person. Talking is understandably of therapeutic value in such circumstances and many find comfort in their doctor, vicar or even a friend who isn't involved with the family. Ideally, of course, the family and close friends should help the grieving person, but all too often this help (which can also be of value to those giving it) is bypassed in favour of drugs. There is certainly no place for anti-depressant drugs in the depression following bereavement unless it becomes very longstanding and serious – which it rarely does. Prolonged grief reactions do respond dramatically to anti-depressants.

Mild and moderate depressive episodes are common and most people turn to their general practitioners in these circumstances, if indeed they do anything at all. When faced with the problem the majority of general practitioners will respond by prescribing a drug. One study of five urban UK practices found that medication was the prime treatment offered for all depressions and that it was often prescribed or taken in inadequate dosage. In this study, half of all the depressed patients could not carry out their normal work because of their depression yet only a quarter of the patients were prescribed anti-depressant drugs in the full dose, and half were given too low a dose. Eight per cent were given tranquillizers and only three per cent were given psychotherapy. It is hardly surprising that few of the patients thought that there was a therapeutic value in the doctor-patient relationship! A stress factor was present in eighty-one per cent of the patients, but no doctor in this study attempted to do anything at all to modify or influence the precipitating factors. No social agencies took part in the treatment of any of the patients.

The study reflects the findings of many others which show that unless you're lucky, you are not going to be very well treated for your depression by your general practitioner. This is unfortunate and could even be serious, because many of those going to their doctors are not suffering from trivial depression, as this study showed. Even people who usually like and are helped by their doctors feel that the doctor-patient relationship isn't much help in depression and this state of affairs is being made worse as patients return to see different doctors in a group practice. Perhaps the saddest finding of this survey was that the longer a person remained ill, the less likely he was to receive effective treatment.

It is widely held by general practitioners that they have a considerable advantage over consultant psychiatrists in that they know the family and social setting in which every case of depression arises. Unfortunately, even if family doctors do indeed have this knowledge they seem to use it to little advantage in most cases of depression; though some of the better family doctors will make time on their calls or clear a gap in their appointment system in order to devote half an hour to a depressed person. The majority cannot or will not make such efforts and rely on drug therapy to tide the person over until nature cures the condition or the placebo effects of the drug begin to work. Anti-depressant drugs, if they're going to be used, must be prescribed in full doses and taken properly by the patient. If you are prescribed the drugs, don't forget that in the early days you might be drowsy and so shouldn't drive or operate machinery. All the side-effects of these drugs are described on pages 149-56.

It's probably fair to say that severe depressives are better treated in general practice than are mild to moderate ones, but even then, many severely depressed people are undiagnosed, as we saw on page 39. If patients respond to anti-depressants they'll be kept on them for about three months and then an attempt should be made to stop them. If there is no response after three to four weeks on a full dose and the depression continues to be serious then new treatment will be needed. A change of drug may do the trick, but sometimes electroconvulsive therapy (see page 178) will be thought necessary.

Moderate to severe depressions are seriously crippling both to the sufferers and to those around them and certainly need careful medical treatment – if only because these patients often kill themselves. Seriously depressed people may have to be taken into hospital. In general, the appearance of delusions, severe guilt and a loss of touch with reality, with or without suicidal impulses, will make hospital the safest place at this stage of the disease. Social circumstances, too, play a major part in deciding whether a particular depressed person should go into hospital.

Such severely depressed people will usually be given drugs and/or ECT. If the depressive is very agitated a tranquillizer may be used (see page 144) and a sleeping tablet may be given at night.

Anxiety often goes hand in hand with depression, as we have already seen and if this occurs, mono-amine oxidase inhibitors (see page 152) can often be highly effective. Most experts think it inadvisable to take separate anti-depressant and anti-anxiety drugs.

Recurrent depression is a very difficult treatment problem and frequent recurrences can be very distressing for both patient and family, even if they are not very severe. Most doctors treat recurrent depression (without manic swings of mood in between) with long-term courses of tricyclic anti-depressants or lithium carbonate (see pages 147 and 153 respectively). Some people are kept on such drugs for years. Just how desirable this is is not known. Manic-depressives certainly benefit from long-term treatment with lithium, but there is disagreement among doctors as to how long to continue tricyclic anti-depressants for recurrent depression. What is

55

certain is that if you are given anti-depressant drugs you really do have to take them in full dosage and regularly. If the side-effects are too unpleasant, tell your doctor rather than simply stopping the drug or reducing the dose. He may be able to find you one that suits you better.

Not uncommonly, depressive illness persists despite all attempts at treatment and this can become very frustrating for all concerned. It is unlikely that a doctor will call a condition *resistant depression* unless it has not responded to treatment within six months. Any adequate treatment trials, especially if more than one drug is involved, could easily take this time. Most experts agree that before patients are labelled as 'resistant' to treatment they should have received a full course of tricyclic anti-depressants, a course of mono-amine oxidase inhibitors and at least one course of ECT. If, after all this, they are still depressed, then they'll have to be completely re-evaluated to look for other causes of the condition. Some people don't seem to want to get better and no amount of medical treatment can *will* a person to be happy. Such people may need psychological therapy or may have an underlying physical disease that has been undiagnosed. Those who are resistant to all other forms of therapy can occasionally be helped by brain surgery, although such operations are very rarely done (see page 189).

To be fair to doctors, depression can be a very difficult condition to manage. Some people's threshold of unhappiness and inability to cope is so low that almost any setback in life sends them running for tablets. Others walk around severely depressed for years, completely undiagnosed and then kill themselves. Either way doctors feel inadequate and indeed they are. They cannot make the world a happy place and can do little to help the general public come to terms with their distress. Too many people today see the medical and caring professions as their refuge in any storm. Suffering isn't popular any more. People are increasingly unwilling to 'grin and bear it' and the stiff upper lip of the British is in need of new starch. Against this background the public demands miracle cures for depression and unhappiness and then grumbles when all the medical profession can offer is a little time and lots of drugs.

What most depressives need is what most doctors cannot give – time, a loving family and good interpersonal relationships. We are wrong to expect that the medical and caring professions could or should help us out of every twist and turn of life but, alas, for many people there is no alternative. It is against this backdrop that many of us will become depressed and get better or not as the case may be. And we'll do all of this in spite of the medical profession rather than because of it.

Things depressed people say

Here are a few of the things that depressed people have said either during or after their depression. The range of experiences in depression is, of course, as varied as the people experiencing them but I hope these selected comments, all from people seeking aid, will help both the depressed readers and the relatives of the depressed to see that they are not alone.

> My depressive experience has been predominantly one of inadequacy, indecision, a fear of intellectual impairment and a loss of memory and concentration. I have a feeling of complete hopelessness, uselessness and desperation at myself – longing to no longer exist – and an inability to move my mind from myself on to other things.

> I feel as though a black raven has settled itself on to my brain with outstretched wings – letting no thought in or out – crushing all emotion but allowing through a little light . . . Just enough to see the next dreaded day appear.

> Let me say straightaway I have not lost, nor do I have any doubts about, my faith – it is simply that I doubt my own ability to preach the word of God. To experience depression in such a painful manner is doubly distressing as I recognize that I am expected and wish to give solace and comfort to so many sorrowing bereaved families. Communication is difficult, if not impossible. Despite my faith I feel alone. (A clergyman)

> I'm too depressed to talk to other people – terribly

isolated in the middle of the night when Mummy is asleep and the radio just plays music and no one talks.

I can't stand the inadequacy – the not wanting to cope rather than an inability to cope. I try not to think about problems. I kid myself that if I don't think, they will go away. I feel so terribly alone even though I have a mother who cares a great deal and I reproach myself for this feeling . . . feel guilty that I am so selfish. I only think about myself.

After being under psychiatric treatment for five years I am now on MAOI treatment but still endure bouts of terrible suffering and my life is nigh on unendurable. I have just about reached the end of my tether. *Can you help me*? I have tried so hard to help myself – I have taken my medication without fail – nothing helps.

The thing that troubles me particularly is the *isolation*. I have no family or friends, no real home and I am utterly alone – loneliness that has obsessed and pursued me since a very early age. I am an only child. My only relief is to travel constantly. I'm always on the move from one hotel to another. I can speak several languages but I go for days without saying a word excepting 'good morning' to the girl at reception or to order a meal in restaurants.

So often you hide your feelings – the depth of them – the hopelessness, loneliness, exhaustion etc, because you know that people cannot understand – that you must be the abnormal one to be feeling these things that no one else would understand.

The isolation is a terrible thing – knowing you are alone inside your head with the frightening thoughts. It's horribly frightening that you can be so close to someone yet no one else ever really knows exactly what it is like to be someone else – to experience their situation, emotions and thoughts . . .

I find it awful to be with other people – to be sitting there with them, yet in my mind I'm miles away. Their laughter seems so utterly foreign and trivial when I am feeling drastic and terrible. I'm afraid I think, 'How can you ignore it and go on as if what you are doing is so important?'

A frown instead of a smile can ruin my day. I lack faith in my own abilities, I'm eager to attempt unwanted tasks but really expect to fail. My frustration can lead to my making brusque statements which are upsetting to others but I'm immediately apologetic.

I find writing very difficult but I've tried phoning Depressives Anonymous most days. My trouble is that I'm constantly apologetic, constantly reproaching myself.

I feel that God has taken the phone off the hook. I know he's still there but we don't talk any more. I haven't lost my faith but it's absolutely no use to me at the moment.

I thought I'd phone my boyfriend in a fit of depression and to my amazement his wife answered the phone. After talking it all over with a friend I realized that I'd completely lost track of time. It had been fifteen months since I last went out with him yet I'd thought it was recently.

I have lots of physical complaints. Dry mouth and lips, a stiff neck, weakness in my legs and so on. I hate the out-patient set-up at the hospital – they don't know how to handle my trivial complaints. Now to cap it all my wife has left me to go home to her mother. She tried to strangle our fourteen year old son.

I often put on a cheerful, happy expression because I feel my family, general practitioner and psychiatrist want me to.

I was getting terribly run down because we were so hard up. We couldn't afford our mortgage payments and this made me terribly stressed. My husband was put on to short time working. Imagine my surprise when I went with my husband to see my boss (a woman) who told me she'd been depressed too. She was surprised by my approach and was very reassuring about my job. I was then able to go to the building society manager and he was very understanding too.

I have a wonderful and secure marriage but I feel very inadequate and insecure. Everyone seems normal except me and this makes me feel so isolated. I feel I want lots of reassurance and encouragement all the time!

I'm so depressed that I can't even get any pleasure out of my grandchildren.

I'm a professor of psychology so it's doubly difficult for me because I have a foot in both camps. When I'm depressed, even though I know all about it I still need support and real understanding.

I'm in my thirties and married to a wonderful husband – in fact I think he's over-understanding. I'm agoraphobic and also keep on washing and cleaning everything. I first got depressed at sixteen after a bereavement and I get these periods of frustration when I'm terribly violent verbally. The trouble is that these can be brutal to my husband and even to myself.

Self-recrimination – out of all proportion to events or situations, occurring on the way down or on the way up. It endlessly goes round and round in my head till I would do almost anything to escape from myself even for a few moments. It's dangerous – but I feel everyone would understand if I took my life. It would be a relief for them and not upsetting.

Ever since I was admitted under Section I've been terribly anxious and hate being labelled as mentally ill.

CHAPTER 2
The causes of depression

It's a part of human nature to want to know why things happen – and in a baffling condition such as depression, which can so alter people's lives, the search for a cause is especially understandable. It is only through a knowledge of the cause of a disease that modern medicine can hope to find cures, so it will come as no surprise to learn that thousands of doctors and other researchers the world over have devoted much of their lives to the search for provable causes of depression and ways of overcoming them. As a result we now know that many cases of depression are curable, simply by removing the cause, and that certain others are preventable in the first place. This is important because too many doctors and their patients believe that depression occurs out of the blue and cannot be influenced. True, many of the causes outlined in this chapter can't be readily avoided – but this is not to say that we need to be fatalistic about depression.

Depression can be seen as the final common pathway that emerges from the maze of a person's life. It comes about as a result of a combination of many factors, one of which often appears to be dominant, but may in fact not be. There are five main factors that go into the melting pot in any case of depression.

1. *Genetic vulnerability* This has been shown to be of possible importance in manic-depressives and in people who suffer from recurrent episodes of depression. For more details of depression in the family, see page 46.
2. *Developmental events*, for example the loss of an important person early on in life which then renders the person more vulnerable to psychological pain later in life.

3. *Psychosocial events* in adult life that so stress the person that he can't cope and becomes depressed.
4. *Physical and psychological stresses* such as operations, serious illnesses, drugs and childbirth that produce depression in people who otherwise wouldn't necessarily have become depressed.
5. *Personality traits* that predetermine the way any given person reacts to a situation.

There are hundreds of different causes of depression but very few automatically bring about depression in everyone who is exposed to them. Depression is the outcome when the 'cause' piece of the jigsaw puzzle fits perfectly into the rest of the picture painted by the five things listed above. Many of us go through life and never experience depression because the depression 'cause' pieces don't fit into our life's jigsaw to complete the final picture. We may come near to it when the cause piece is a big and powerful one (such as a death in the family), but if the rest of the jigsaw doesn't fit, we don't get depressed. A substantial proportion of the population has a life jigsaw that is permanently near completion for depression and all they need at any one time is the final 'depression cause' piece to throw them into true depression. Unfortunately, the way society is developing, increasing numbers of people seem to be in this situation.

Let's look now at some of the proven causes of depression. They are not listed in any particular order; certainly not in order of importance.

Psychological causes of depression

Given that depression is to a large extent a psychological disease, it makes sense to look first at the possible psychological causes for it. Unfortunately, many of the psychological causes are still greatly debated both within and outside the medical profession. In fact, the psychological causes of depression probably remain one of the most controversial areas of the whole subject. Freud and his followers saw depression as the inward turning of an aggressive feeling that for some reason isn't directed at the appropriate person or situation. They also maintain that the loss of a loved person or situation can produce depression. Unfortunately, the anger part of this theory is difficult to prove, and experiments aimed at getting depressed people to express their anger towards outside objects haven't been useful in treating their depression. There is no doubt that a loss of some kind is at the heart of many cases of depression but this theory isn't an all-embracing one.

Other psychoanalysts have focussed on the helplessness side of depression. Bibring, a leading researcher in this field, maintains that depression overcomes people when they recognize a goal but also become aware that they are helpless to attain it. According to this theory, depression occurs when one can't live up to one's expectations of oneself and others. Hostility and anger are not often seen and, when they are, they are used only against people or situations which prevent the attainment of desired goals.

Beck, the distinguished behaviourist, maintains that it's disordered thinking that makes us depressed. Because some of us have learned that we don't get pleasant feedback from a lot of things in our lives, we build this assumption into our thinking and gradually come to expect very little from life. According to this viewpoint, hopelessness and helplessness are at the heart of depression. Individuals find that the world presents them with insuperable obstacles and respond by feeling hopeless and helpless, eventually slipping into a state in which they believe that they cannot and never could control their lives.

This theory is interesting because it breaks away from psychoanalytic principles and stresses the importance of disordered thinking. It correlates well with thoughts expressed by the severely depressed and suicidal and gives a useful starting point for psychotherapeutic treatment. If people can be taught how to 'unlearn' this negative view of their ability to influence their destiny, then they will get a lot more out of life and will not be depressed.

Seligman and his colleagues extended this theory one stage further. They were experimenting with a learning theory that involved the administration of unavoidable electric shocks to dogs. The behaviour that they accidentally discovered may have some bearing on our understanding of human depression.

What they found was that during the inescapable electric shock phase of the experiment (the dogs were not allowed to take any action that would prevent further shocks) the dogs became used to the shocks but did not like them. In the second part of the experiment the dogs were unharnessed and the shocks readministered. This time, rather than jumping out of the box (which they could easily have done), the dogs sat there and took more shocks. They seemed to give up and passively accept the unpleasant stimuli. Seligman thought that there were important parallels between this work and human depression and used the term 'learned helplessness' to describe both conditions.

It certainly makes sense to suggest that when we are confronted with negative stimuli in life we should try to get away from them or avoid them. However, if it's your boss, your son, your wife or the only home you can afford, to quote a few simple examples, you may not be able to get away in any real sense. You learn to live with the dilemma and, as other similar situations build up, you soon begin to realize that there's very little point trying to avoid life's stresses and knocks – so you give up. It can be demonstrated that a state of learned helplessness affects other areas of people's lives as well as those in which they learned to be helpless in the first place.

Seligman's theory is certainly an elegant explanation of the way in which depression paralyses people with helplessness, passivity and an inability to assert themselves. But this relatively recent theory has come in for a lot of criticism from others in the psychiatric and psychological world, not least because the experiments involved cruelty to dogs which many people, including most psychiatrists, find unacceptable. Moreover, such extremely stressful conditions are never encountered by the vast majority of humans with depression.

Another psychological cause of depression is really one that maintains it once it's there. Many researchers have found that a proportion of depressives get such rewards from the 'sick role' that this prolongs what would otherwise be a short episode of depression. We saw on page 50 that depression is by no means always bad for the sufferers and is in fact often the only way they know of manipulating their environment to make it bearable for them.

Separation and depression

There's a lot of research available on the subject of separation and depression and it has all shown that the breaking of close bonds (usually parental) early in life has a lingering traumatic effect both on the growing and on the fully grown animal. A great deal of work has been done both on primates and on children separated from their mothers, all of which demonstrates that the young whose maternal bonds are broken react in a depressed way. More recent work has found that adults who become depressed for the first time in adulthood are more likely to have lost a parent (usually a mother) early in life than adults who don't become depressed. It's rather upsetting to find that this depressive reaction can occur not only if the loss of an important relationship was real, but also if it was imagined or even fairly trivial. Thus a child whose father has gone away from home for a long period on business or to war is seen by the young child as having deserted him, and this builds into the child's subconscious mind the concept that someone who loves him dearly can hurt him in this way. I suspect that mothers who leave their babies and very young children to go out to work for long periods may also have a negative effect on susceptible children, but there is no concrete proof of this as yet.

The loss of a loved one or a valued situation in life was first highlighted as a potent cause of depression by Freud in his *Mourning and Melancholia*, probably one of the most influential pieces of writing on depression ever. He stressed the link between separation in adult life and depression, and bereavement and separations in childhood and adult depressions. Although it has often been difficult to prove that separation causes depression, recent research has definitely proven that 'exit' events in life (usually involving loss, separation, bereavement etc) are the most common stressful events that cause depression. (See also pages 90-94 for more details of this.)

Apart from the subject of death, and even this is open to debate, there is evidence to suggest that the situation might not be as simple as I have just suggested. It could be, for example, that potentially depressive people behave in such a way that others around them become alienated and, as a result, bring about situations which are viewed by the 'depressives' as loss situations. This is particularly true of interpersonal relationship problems which are at the root of a substantial number of depressions. Potentially depressive individuals act in a way which makes relationships falter and eventually impossible for the other person. They then leave, or the relationship breaks down in other ways, and the depression-prone person perceives a loss and becomes depressed.

Some authorities suggest that the loss of a father between the ages of ten and fourteen years is the most critical loss for predisposing one to adult depression and that a similar loss between the ages of birth and four years can produce delinquent behaviour. Generally though, the loss of a mother in childhood seems to cause more depression both in childhood and later in life than does the loss of a father.

But a loss severe enough to produce depression need not be as dramatic as the death of a parent. It can be a loss of esteem, a job, the loss of a goal or ideal and all kinds of other far less tangible concepts. Some people even become depressed by the *fear* of a serious loss.

Biochemical causes of depression

For years scientists have been searching for an abnormality of body chemistry that could explain depression. Evidence in animals suggests that anything (physical or psychological) that interferes with the workings of a particular part of the brain called the *diencephalon* renders the animal unable to respond to pleasant things in its environment. Because depressives have exactly this as their major problem, scientists naturally started looking for chemicals in the brain that might be altered in depression. They clearly hoped that one day a specific abnormality of brain chemistry would be found and that it would be amenable to treatment with drugs. This goal has not yet been achieved.

There's a lot of research in animals that shows that two chemical groups called amines (catechol amines and indole amines) significantly affect the functioning of the 'reward' and 'punishment' centres of the brain. Drugs such as the amphetamines are known to increase drive, motivation and activity when injected into 'reward' areas of the brain and anti-depressant drugs are known to boost this reaction. Stimulation along these 'reward' pathways in the brain, whether from artificially instilled drugs or from psychologically received stimuli, has the same effect. It produces pleasure in the animal. Any disturbance in the levels of these amines, induced either artificially or psychologically, results in the animal's inability to respond to pleasurable stimuli.

The research has not been easy and there are still many conflicting schools of thought, but what is encouraging is that of all the amines looked at (and there are many in each of the two groups mentioned above), lowered *serotonin* looks like being important in both depression and mania and an elevation of catecholamines seems important in the switch from depression to mania. The role of catecholamines in depression itself is still a subject of considerable controversy. The idea that a specific chemical event in the brain produces a particular type of behaviour is, however, an intellectual leap of gigantic proportions and is not accepted by most experts. The human brain just isn't that simple. As one expert has put it, 'One can be certain that all reductionist attempts to explain "mind" in terms of brain chemistry (only), or reinforcement schedules (only), or computer logic (only), or any combination of these, will fail. The facts of conscious experiences are irreducible and must enter in their own right as basic irreducible elements into any comprehensive account of the mind.'

This doesn't mean that twenty years of studying brain chemistry has all been wasted, but rather that we should now see chemical changes as the *result* of genetic and environmental stimuli and not the *cause*.

Animal work throws some interesting light on this. Two researchers, for instance, swam rats to exhaustion and found that their brain serotonin levels were increased by ten per cent and their catecholamine levels were raised by twenty per cent. Other animal work has backed this up in various ways. Group-reared mice and those reared in isolation have also been found to produce different levels of these brain chemicals when subjected to the same stimulus as adults. The separation of infant rhesus monkeys from their mothers causes a marked increase in the enzymes involved in producing these brain amines and this must alter the way we think about the causes of depression. Many elegant theories have suggested that a primary disorder of brain amines is the cause of depression. I maintain that such changes are real and measurable; but that they are secondary to a variety of stimuli. Thus they are the result of depression and not the cause of it.

So in summary, various stimuli produce biochemical changes within the brain in a way which we don't yet understand. These chemical changes affect the pleasure (reward) and punishment centres so as to alter the person's mood adversely. This alteration of mood is what we call depression. Anti-depressant drugs have been found to alter the levels of these amines in the brain, but they are simply treating the symptoms just as an aspirin treats a headache. In both examples, drug intervention is justifiable – but we should not delude ourselves that we're curing anything. A cure will only come about by reducing the stimuli that produced the amines in the first place.

Social causes of depression

Doctors have substantially 'taken over' depression because it is generally thought by society to be a 'disease'. Sociologists, however, argue that depression very often isn't a somatic disease at all but a sociological 'illness'. At least a quarter of working class women with young children living in London suffer from a condition which, if they went to a psychiatric clinic, would be labelled as depression. Women with similar aged children living on the crofts of the Outer Hebrides are, on the other hand, practically free of depression no matter what their social class.

Clearly the sociological view of depression doesn't ignore genetic susceptibility and the possibility that people will get depressed as a result of many of the causes outlined below; but it does stick uncomfortably in the throat of the medical model of depression which demands that people be categorized and placed in biochemical or other pigeon-holes.

Certain social factors appear to make people (and especially women) more vulnerable to depression. Social class, for example, seems to be important. Working class women are especially at risk, even when they are living in the same environment as other classes. Women with no close confiding relationships (boyfriend, spouse or similar) also fare badly when life gets tough, as do women with three or more children under fourteen at home, those without any employment and those who lost their mothers before the age of eleven.

All these are social vulnerability factors, which may actually *cause* depression in some cases, but certainly do put a woman at greater risk when the going gets tough.

The low rate of depression in the Outer Hebrides is probably explained by the fact that their culture and society protects their women, and as a result increases their sense of self-esteem.

So it can be seen that social disadvantage, whether it is being unemployed, poor, divorced, living in tower blocks of flats or one of a host of other variables, can predispose to depression in a way which complies with the psychological theories outlined above. People in such states come to think of themselves as losers in life's battle and then when a stressful factor hits them, they cannot cope and become depressed.

To summarize, then, what the sociologists say is that some people – and there are millions of them – are born into or find themselves in a situation which predisposes them to depression in a way that would not affect others. If one isn't careful, this type of argument can easily become a political one because one can all too easily equate the 'downtrodden' working classes with depression-producing lifestyles.

Although there may be some merit in this argument, since it is certainly stressful to be poor, homeless, unemployed or a single parent, it should be remembered that many middle class people with none of these problems nevertheless also suffer from depression.

Depression is not, however, a social disease, even though social factors can play an enormous part in producing it. Unfortunately, as doctors find every day of their lives, it's often impossible to change social circumstances quickly enough to be able to help any one particular patient. All the social problems go on whatever the medical profession does. They are called upon to pick up the pieces when social breakdown occurs. Doctors can't create jobs at the local factory, nor rehouse those in need; they can't force people to marry more suitable partners (even if they were able to tell who would be suitable); and they can't run people's lives to make things easy for them.

Social factors may well be the cause of a person's smoking, but knowing this is of little use to surgeons battling to save the person's life as they remove the lung cancer.

Doctors should certainly take social situations into account when dealing with depression but, to be realistic, many of these factors are beyond their control. Unfortunately, there is little doubt that society is developing in a way which is likely to produce more depression. There are no answers to this dilemma short of a complete re-think of western culture – which is unlikely to happen in the foreseeable future.

Drugs that cause depression

The relationship between the taking of a drug and the onset of depression can, of course, be a coincidence, but certain drugs are known to produce depression as a direct result of their chemical actions in the body. These drugs don't, however, produce depression in all who take them – those with a history of depression and those with a genetic sensitivity to the particular drug are most at risk.

Over 200 drugs have been claimed to cause depression in certain people, but only a few do so with any frequency. Some drugs (e.g. reserpine) cause depression as a side-effect of their therapeutic use, whilst others (e.g. fenfluramine) cause depression only if they are withdrawn too rapidly.

As there are so many drugs that *can* cause depression and since so many people are taking drugs at any one time, it's always worth thinking of a drug cause of depression, because stopping the drug could be the answer to the depression. But if you think a drug might be causing your depression, don't just stop taking it: this could be dangerous. See your doctor at the first opportunity and discuss the matter first.

Alcohol

Of all the drugs that can produce depression, alcohol must be the most widely used. The depression occurs as the heavy drinkers' blood alcohol level is falling. Those who drink heavily run a greater risk of suicide than the rest of the

70

population, partly because an underlying depression probably led them to drink in the first place and also because the alcohol itself causes further depression.

Sedative and anti-anxiety drugs

Barbiturates, non-barbiturate sedatives, sleeping tablets and tranquillizers all have an additive effect with alcohol. They also seem to increase the risk of depression and suicide in those who depend on them. It can be argued, of course, that normal, healthy people don't use this group of drugs anyway so people who do take them are already an 'at risk' population.

Painkillers and anti-rheumatic drugs

Ordinary aspirin-like painkillers don't seem to cause depression. Many people who consume large quantities of compound powders containing aspirin, phenacetin and caffeine complain of depression, but it is not known whether it's the caffeine or the painkillers in this mixture that causes the depression.

People who are dependent upon narcotic analgesics (the powerful painkillers such as morphine) often complain of depression as their drugs are withdrawn. The pethidine-type drug, diphenoxylate, also causes depression.

Over the last two decades a group of anti-rheumatic painkilling drugs has been introduced with great success in the treatment of joint and muscle pains. This group includes phenylbutazone, indomethacin, ibuprofen and many others. These three drugs are said to cause depression in some people. However, the underlying arthritis for which the drugs are being taken is also known to cause depression (see page 77), so just how much of the depression can be attributed to the drugs alone is difficult to say.

Stimulants

Amphetamines produce depression as they are withdrawn. Fenfluramine (an appetite suppressant and stimulant drug used in the management of obesity) also causes depression if it is withdrawn too rapidly. Some experts think that these groups of appetite suppressant drugs shouldn't be given to anyone who is depressed.

Drugs used in mental illness

Phenothiazines are used not only in the treatment of schizophrenia but also by some doctors in the treatment of anxiety and depression. Mild to serious depression can occur with any of this group of drugs and is just as likely to occur if the drug is taken as a depot (injection) preparation or by mouth.

Blood pressure drugs

Several drugs used in the treatment of high blood pressure produce symptoms like those of depression. Methyldopa, reserpine, guanethidine and bethanidine can all cause depressive symptoms. Unfortunately, both high blood pressure itself and anti-hypertensive drugs such as these produce symptoms that are so like depression that it's very difficult to know which is responsible for the depression. It is generally accepted that a person with a history of depression should not receive reserpine in particular and some experts are cautious when using other blood pressure treatments too.

Some patients being treated with beta-blocking agents such as propranolol and oxprenolol for their high blood pressure or angina report depressive symptoms and the beta-blocking drug clonidine, used in treating hot flushes of the menopause, can also do so.

Steroid drugs

There is confusion as to whether or not these compounds produce depression. Naturally-occurring increases in steroids in the body (such as occur with the disease known as Cushing's syndrome) seem to produce depression, but steroid tablets or injections appear to make some people elated and euphoric.

Oral contraceptives (the Pill)

It has been estimated that over two million women in Britain alone are taking oral contraceptives, so any psychological side-effects would certainly be of considerable interest. There has long been a controversy as to the psychological side-effects of the Pill and over forty learned papers have 'proven' that depression can occur in women on this form of contraception. Many other studies, however, have not been able to confirm these findings and the balance of opinion (often based on double blind trials in which women on inactive placebo tablets also become depressed) today is that the Pill does not cause depression. Several studies have remarked on the astonishing frequency of depressive symptoms in both the Pill and non-Pill women they studied. Some researchers have noted that in women on the Pill, any sign of depression is immediately attributed to the medication, whereas all too often there are very obvious precipitating factors that are nothing to do with the Pill. The Pill has probably been used as a scapegoat not only by Pill-takers but by Pill-prescribers, who put down any signs of depression to the Pill and don't even bother to look for other causes.

There seems to be a consensus of opinion that women with a past history of depression are more likely to become depressed on the Pill and so should be carefully observed while they are taking it.

Sulphonamides (a group of anti-bacterial drugs)

The older sulphonamides were well known to cause depression and nalidixic acid, a related drug (widely used in the treatment of urinary infections), can cause psychological disturbances, including depression.

Other drugs

Anti-parkinsonian drugs are well known to cause depression as do some anti-cancer drugs.

Metronidazole (used for trichomonas infection of the vagina) and griseofulvin (an anti-ringworm drug) can also cause depression.

Certain anti-tuberculosis drugs also cause depression.

Digitalis and digoxin are also responsible for many psychological disturbances, including depression.

Insulin and oral anti-diabetic tablets can produce depression via their blood sugar-lowering effects and anti-thyroid drugs can do so as a result of the low thyroid activity they cause. Even the anti-depressant lithium carbonate, which is used in the treatment of manic-depression (see page 153), *can* produce depression in normal (non-depressed) people. Tryptophan, a drug little used in the treatment of depression, actually *increases* depression when taken in high doses.

Alcoholism, drug abuse and depression

We saw on page 45 that depression is often the underlying cause for people becoming addicted to alcohol and hard drugs but, sadly, the reverse also happens. Many of those who start off taking alcohol or 'drugs' in a healthy mental state end up becoming depressed as a result. Depression occurs frequently among alcoholics, especially among female ones. The depressive picture (which develops a lot later in males than females) is very similar in the two sexes; but male alcoholics tend to have a higher level of depression among first-degree relatives than do female alcoholics. So 'normal' is depression among alcoholics that in one study the researchers remarked that if an alcoholic patient shows little overt depression the staff tend to wonder what is wrong and are sceptical as to the patient having sufficient insight for successful treatment.

Some researchers now feel that alcoholism is intrinsically a depressive disorder and that those destined to become alcoholics in later life have always had a poor ability to enjoy life and their own successes. For too long depression has been seen as a relatively unimportant side-effect of the alcoholic personality and of alcohol itself.

The treatment of alcoholism is often extremely difficult. An important part of the treatment is a clear understanding of the vicious circle of depressive personality – excessive drinking – alcoholism – depression. To break this circle, the alcoholic must be helped not only to stop drinking, but to come to terms with his depressive personality.

Hard drug addicts suffer from many emotional problems and one of the main ones is depression. Hard drug users are more depressed on average than soft drug users. Rather as with alcoholism, many drug users have a life-long history of frustration, poor expectations and little pleasure from life. Treatment aimed at curing the actual addiction and introducing more pleasurable experiences into the user's life are beginning to yield good results. Just as with alcohol, the drugs themselves can actually produce depression, which then adds to the underlying depression that led to the addiction in the first place.

Infections that cause depression

Depression can be brought about not only by infections of the brain and nervous system, but also by generalized body infections. Meningitis and encephalitis (in which the brain is affected directly) can produce delirium and coma in the acute phase. Once this phase of the illness is over, depression often sets in and can last for several months.

Generalized infections, particularly viral infections such as influenza, hepatitis and infectious mononucleosis (glandular fever), can produce depressions that last for months. In fact, depression is often the most unpleasant part of these diseases, simply because it goes on for so long.

No one knows why such depressions occur but they always get better and respond well to simple anti-depressant therapies.

Depression after surgical operations

No one knows why, but a substantial number of those who undergo a major surgical operation feel low afterwards and some actually get depressed. Many people feel weak for months after an operation and no explanation has yet been found for this either.

Operations that have involved body disfigurement or the removal of a part of the body (an amputation of a leg or a breast for example) are more likely to result in depression post-operatively. Very often this depression comes about because the person's sexuality and attractiveness to the opposite sex are reduced (at least in his or her own eyes), but in other cases the person's whole life is altered and such a major change is reason enough to explain the depression. Someone who is left partly or totally invalided as a result of an operation will clearly be at greater risk of developing depression and needs counselling before and after the operation to minimize the problems.

Although many operations can undoubtedly cause post-operative depressions, there are few that have been so well researched with depression in mind as have hysterectomies. Hysterectomy (the removal of the womb) is the second commonest operation in women. By the age of seventy-five, nearly one in five women will have undergone the operation –

nearly one in three hundred of the female population over the age of twenty has her uterus out in any year. The operation is also being carried out in increasingly younger women.

All this raises many questions, but the one we're concerned with here is the depression that follows a hysterectomy. It has been found that women who have had hysterectomies are four times as likely to become depressed within three years of the operation as are women who have not had the operation. In one survey, six per cent of the operated women had to be admitted to mental hospital within three years of the operation. It might have been expected that women who had had no children at the time of the operation might be more likely to become depressed – but this isn't so. Younger women who have a hysterectomy *are* more likely to be subsequently admitted to a mental hospital when compared with older women who've had the operation.

Overall, about seventy per cent of hysterectomy patients have post-operative depression and an almost equal number have hot flushes, tiredness and urinary symptoms. Obviously this level of depression is much higher than for other operations but, to be fair, few have been so carefully scrutinized with post-operative depression in mind, so the incidence may well be higher than we think for other less emotionally charged operations. Perhaps if the extent of the depression suffered by people after the loss of certain body parts were better understood, surgeons would be even more cautious about removing them in the first place. There is ample evidence, for example, that far too many women have their uterus removed unnecessarily. This is undesirable for many reasons, not the least of which is the mental illness it creates.

Depression with serious physical disease

People who are suffering from all but the mildest of physical diseases are likely to become depressed and many with longstanding illnesses do so. In one US survey of 150 medical (as opposed to surgical) in-patients, nearly a quarter were found on objective testing to be depressed one week after admission to the ward. Most of the depressions were mild, but they were almost all unrecognized by the attending medical and nursing staff. Nearly two-thirds of the severely ill were depressed in this survey, as opposed to one in five of those with minor ailments. Depression was commoner in patients confined to bed, those in pain and those with diminished alertness. Depression was also found to occur more commonly in those in whom there was a poor outlook. In general, the depressions tended to be mild.

Although most in-patient physical illness seems to produce fairly mild and totally understandable depression, other surveys have found that there is a high correlation between suicide and physical illness. One worker found that seventy per cent of those who committed suicide had one or more active illnesses, fifty-one per cent of which were considered to have contributed to the suicide. Rheumatoid arthritis, peptic ulcer and high blood pressure were found to have the most powerful 'suicidal' effects. This fits with doctors' experiences (and those of relatives) that physical illness is a key factor in suicide.

It is not uncommon for individuals with such physical illnesses to be unable to share their feelings of hopelessness and dependency with others, especially if their interpersonal and marital relationships are not very strong. Gradually, they become isolated within themselves, fearing the outcome of their condition and move on to the slippery slope to depression. This is especially true of chronic disease which is known to be 'irreversible'. Many chronically ill people adapt to their illness perfectly well, but others see so many losses ahead of them (in social, psychological, economic and physical terms) that they can't cope with the future as they see it. Once depression develops in such people, they are weaker and more tired than would be expected, spend a lot of time in bed and may start to produce new pains. Depression often becomes a way of life and is soon inextricably mixed with the chronic physical disease. This can make the depression difficult to treat. Careful and persistent treatment can be of help and anti-depressant drugs can work wonders in such cases.

Contrary to what one might think, longstanding pain *per se* does not necessarily produce depression. One major survey found that of those attending a pain clinic for uncontrollable pain, the majority were either only mildly depressed or not depressed at all. The high level of depression found in those with rheumatoid arthritis (probably about a third of whom are

77

clinically depressed) can probably be explained by the adverse effects of the deformities and the fear of being crippled by the condition, rather than by the pain itself.

Nearly one in three men in the West will die of coronary arterial disease, mostly in the form of a heart attack (myocardial infarction). If a study carried out in a psychiatric hospital in Jerusalem is anything to go by, it looks as if depression may well predispose men to having a coronary. The research team scrutinized the medical and psychiatric histories of all those patients who had a myocardial infarction whilst admitted as in-patients in the hospital over an eight year period. In this time thirty-four depressives had infarctions, whereas there were only five other heart attacks among all the other patients in the whole hospital over this period. The time relationship between the depression and the heart attack varied enormously, and another study of post-coronary patients found that they had had short periodic depressions more frequently in their pre-infarct past than had matched control patients. So all of this raises the possibility that depression may well have to be regarded as a risk factor in heart attacks, along with all the other known factors.

Once someone has had a heart attack there is an increased risk of his suffering from a depression and some patients are particularly at risk. Those who are depressed after a coronary report more stressful events in the year before the attack; but this may simply be a reflection of their pessimistic and depressed view of life generally.

It has been suggested that the overactive post-coronary patient needs restraint during his convalescence and that the depressed one needs encouragement. Giving the wrong treatment to the wrong group could be fatal, it is argued, so the diagnosis of depression in the post-heart attack patient seems to be more than just a luxury. The Toronto Rehabilitation Centre team, for example, is highly successful at getting severely depressed people back to full employment after a heart attack; whereas many others have found they have a long-term problem with post-heart attack patients developing a 'cardiac neurosis'. It is somewhat ironic to save a man from death so that he can become a mental cripple, a burden on his family and a misery to himself. The correct handling of post-heart attack depression can often prevent this.

Depression and cancer

Guy (1759) was of the opinion that depressed women were more prone to breast cancer and in so saying was echoing the earlier belief of Galen who thought melancholic women suffered from more cancer than did other women. Speculation has raged on the subject of cancer-prone personalities for years now, and many experts have even suggested that cancer is a psychosomatic disease. There is as yet no final verdict on this matter and there probably won't be for some time; but there is no doubt that the various personality types fare differently once the cancer has been diagnosed.

Several surveys have found that people who are depressed stand a greater than average risk of dying prematurely than do others of the same age. A six year follow up of psychiatric patients who had suffered from mood disorders, including depression, found that they had a higher than expected level of malignant disease.

The link between cancer and depression has not yet been proved – if indeed there is a link. It has been suggested that the depression preceding some cases of cancer could be caused by a tiny seed of the cancer in the brain. It is well known that brain tumours themselves can cause depression, so perhaps a tiny tumour, carried from the distant mother tumour, could be causing the depression. At least that's how the story goes.

There may also be other connections in rather the same way that some people with cancer get muscle and nerve troubles, even when the cancer does not directly involve either tissue directly. Many tumours produce hormone imbalances. Perhaps it is these that induce the depression. Hormone changes in breast cancer, for example, can produce high levels of calcium in the blood and naturally-occurring tumours of the parathyroid glands (which control calcium in the body) are often accompanied by depression. Carcinoma of the pancreas is very commonly associated with depression – a depression which always comes on before the cancer itself is diagnosed. No one knows how all these things are linked.

It is possible that in older patients, especially as the immune system of the body begins to age, cells that would have hitherto

79

been recognized as cancerous and destroyed are allowed to grow. Several studies have related a previous stress to the development of a cancer. Perhaps the person's immune system (known to be affected by stress) is temporarily 'stunned' and lets cancer cells 'take root' when they normally wouldn't. One researcher has found that there is a depression of immunological mechanisms following bereavement, for example.

Perhaps cancer and depression are genetically linked. Certainly, it has been found that there is a higher than expected incidence of cancer in the mothers of those who are depressed. In one survey of suicides caused by depressive illness, there was a higher than expected rate of cancers found at postmortem and only half had been diagnosed during the suicide's lifetime.

A lot more research is needed in order to be able to make any links between cancer and depression.

Glandular trouble as a cause of depression

Most of us have known someone with 'glandular trouble' or have had such an illness ourselves. In these conditions, one or more of the hormone-producing (endocrine) glands of the body go wrong and produce either too much or too little of their normal hormones. Either extreme of hormone production can cause depression.

Thyroid disease is a fairly common glandular cause of depression. Those with a low thyroid state are often depressed and those whose thyroid glands are overactive are often both agitated and depressed. Cushing's syndrome is the overactive disease condition of the adrenal glands and Addison's disease the underactive state. Both can produce depression as part of their clinical picture. Disorders of the pituitary gland can cause depression too.

Curing the underlying glandular condition usually cures the depression.

Food allergies and intolerance causing depression

There is an increasing body of knowledge on food allergies and their common manifestations. One of these is depression. It has now been proven fairly conclusively that certain foods, especially cows' milk, eggs, wheat flour and its products

80

(including bread) and cereals can cause bouts of depression and headaches in susceptible people. The link between certain foods and migraine headaches is now well established and some experts are linking the Pill with food allergy migraines.

The idea that an allergy or intolerance to specific foods can cause illness is not new. It was first mentioned by Hippocrates and was revived in the 1920s and '30s by the Californian physician Dr Albert Rowe. Both Hippocrates, Rowe and present day allergists cure many food allergies by eliminating the suspected food from the affected person's diet. Re-introduction of the food in question into the diet produces symptoms of depression if it is in fact causing the condition.

Most family doctors and many specialist physicians are not very well informed on the subject of food allergy and many even doubt its existence. There is now, however, no question that food allergies exist and that they cause all kinds of psychological syndromes.

A lot more research is needed before we can establish a link between depression and food allergies in many people, but the signs are very hopeful that in some people simply removing a food from the diet will produce dramatic results. This is difficult to achieve in many cases because wheat flour, for example, is present in so many made-up foods that it is virtually impossible to eliminate from the diet unless you know the exact contents of commercial foods. It certainly makes sense to avoid foods that you suspect of producing depression, but in order to achieve anything more sophisticated than this you'll need to get a good book about food allergies to see which foods contain the substances you think you might be allergic to. Many doctors won't know the answers to the questions you're likely to ask and many psychiatrists won't even recognize food allergy as a possible cause of depression, so you may not get a very sympathetic hearing on this subject.

Babies and children as a cause of depression

One of the most depressed groups of people in the West are mothers of young children, since it has been shown that babies and young children in our society are a potent source of stress and depression. Several surveys have found that mothers of young children living in Central London and other cities are very likely to become depressed, and one such study found that fifty-two per cent of the depressed mothers they looked at had had moderate or severe emotional problems in the previous twelve months. High rise tower block living and many other socially disadvantageous factors have been implicated in this high depression rate, but I think we need to go back to birth to see the real roots of the problem.

'Post-natal depression' is a term commonly used to describe the uniquely female experience of weepiness on the one hand and full blown depression on the other, experienced soon after having a baby. If the condition is mild it is usually called the 'baby blues'.

About half of all recently-delivered mothers experience some form of 'baby blues', but this usually lasts only a day or two. Some studies have found that transitory, mild depressive feelings and a tendency to be easily upset are present in up to eighty per cent of women in the week or so following birth. These emotions may or may not be accompanied by a feeling of anxiety around the time of taking the baby home from the hospital. This is especially true of first babies, which understandably produce more anxiety in their mothers.

Post-natal depression itself is a term used to describe a depression that, whilst unpleasant for the woman, is usually not serious enough to prevent her from functioning fairly normally. It is not helpful to debate whether it is a reactive or endogenous depression because whatever the cause (and no one knows for sure what the cause is) the woman will have to be treated in the best way for her particular case and not according to some ready-made rules.

The symptoms are much like those in any other depression but with certain additional features. A woman with post-natal depression cries at the slightest provocation and often for no reason at all; feels she can't cope with her baby; is critical or even openly aggressive towards her husband; feels guilty about not loving the baby enough; loses her appetite; goes off sex; can't sleep (even when the baby lets her); has nightmares; may be afraid to leave the house (agoraphobia); and may have anxious 'panic' attacks. Very few women suffer from this whole list, but even a few of these troublesome symptoms can temporarily wreck a woman's life and make her feel very wretched.

Depression of this severity starts at any time from two to three weeks after the birth to six months later. About one in ten women are said to suffer from this more serious kind of post-natal depression, but the figures may be even higher. Women who have such a depression are unlikely to have had a previous psychiatric illness. One key study found that post-natally depressed women had few pregnancy symptoms, were anxious during the first three months of pregnancy and elated in the last six months, and were keen to breast feed.

Puerperal psychosis is not nearly as common as post-natal depression, occurring as it does in only 1 in 500 newly-delivered mothers. This is a serious mental disorder occurring after birth, which can be so severe that emergency admission to hospital has to be arranged. Although there are several types of the condition, about two-thirds of the affected women manifest their illness as depression. A very small proportion of such women become so ill that they have thoughts of killing their baby and themselves and a few actually go so far as to do so.

The law officially recognizes the fact that some women become severely emotionally disturbed after the birth of a child. The Infanticide Act of 1938 states that a woman can't be found guilty of murder if she kills her own child within twelve months of the birth provided 'the balance of her mind was disturbed by reason of her not having fully recovered from the effect of giving birth'. There is a one in five chance that a woman who has suffered from this kind of serious mental reaction post-natally in one pregnancy will do so in a subsequent pregnancy.

All but this last very serious kind of post-natal depression are very common, as was found in one UK survey carried out in 1979. This careful study of sixty-six women having their first babies found that eighty-four per cent experienced post-natal blues; seventy-seven per cent were anxious; thirty-three per cent had a depressed mood; and twenty-four per cent had depressive symptoms. The authors suggest that feeling depressed after giving birth to a baby should therefore be seen as normal and that *not* feeling depressed is abnormal.

Just why so many women should feel depressed after having a baby isn't known, but there are three main schools of thought: the hormonal, the psychoanalytic, and the psychosocial. According to the first, some kind of hormone imbalance is responsible for the depression. Progesterone is a hormone manufactured by the placenta. Levels of this hormone rise during pregnancy and fall rapidly after delivery. Superficially, this seems an adequate explanation of the depression most women experience: after all, there is a measurable fall of this potent hormone. Unfortunately, things aren't this simple because whilst such an explanation could (and probably does in my view) explain the blues that occur three or four days after birth, it is very difficult to see how it could explain the post-natal depression that comes on weeks or months later when the hormone state is back to normal. Secondly, almost no research has been done to equate hormone levels with women's mental states. Third, these very same hormones are held responsible for the depression of pregnancy (in which progesterone levels are high, not low).

The psychoanalysts' approach to post-natal depression suggests that women who become depressed after childbirth do so because of subconscious anger towards the baby and because of their rejection of the feminine role. The trouble with any definition that includes the word 'feminine' is that no one really knows what it means, and as a result psychoanalysts can pin whatever they like on the woman on the basis that she isn't 'feminine'. It is in this area of defining what 'feminine' might mean that we overlap with the third school of thought on post-natal depression – that which holds that it is purely a psychosocial phenomenon brought about by a woman's attitudes to motherhood and baby-rearing in the society in which we live.

Those of us with experience of mothers in the early months after birth are certainly impressed by the multitude of social factors that can go into the production of true post-natal depression. It has been found that women with housing problems, those who are unemployed, those who have a 'separate' parenting role from their husbands (that is, those who don't share parenting with their husbands), and those who know little about babies are most at risk.

84

The circumstances of birth are also socially important factors. Women who have medical intervention in their births are more likely to cry and feel low in the early days, as are those who have had had an epidural analgesic. It has also been reported that women who feel unsatisfactory about their birth experiences are more likely to be unhappy or depressed afterwards. In fact women who are most seriously depressed are more likely than others to be dissatisfied with the whole management of their births, even though they may not immediately volunteer this concern. Women who feel they lost control over their births and those in whom high levels of technology were used were also found to be more seriously depressed. Women who have had little contact with babies before their own birth experience are also more likely to suffer from depression.

But far deeper than any of these factors is an undercurrent in society that makes childbirth and child rearing (especially the rearing of young children) so likely to produce depression. And this is based on our whole attitude to children – who have become planned commodities of which the average women experiences 2.2 'units'.

These days, most families are fragmented and the young girl (and boy for that matter) is not brought up in a large extended family which gives her an opportunity to practise being a mother to other babies. An astonishing number of women reach adulthood with very little knowledge or experience of babies and the vast majority have never seen a baby breast fed, for example. Because most modern families consist of two children relatively close in age, they grow up together and miss out on the proxy parenting that occurs in large families. Similarly, since most women only ever have two children, they never really get practised at it. As one woman put it to me, 'Here I am at home with my third baby and it's the first time I've really felt relaxed about the whole thing'. Most women stop having babies just as they're getting good at it. This is a great loss, because to many women having babies is permanently associated with feeling insecure, anxious and depressed.

Research shows that most women, even in these enlightened times when women's magazines are full of frank articles on the subject, are literally shocked when they get their first baby home after the birth. Most women say that everything from the pregnancy and the birth to the social position of a young mother and the work involved in baby care is very different from what they had expected. Four out of five say that their expectations had been unrealistically romantic. It's this gap between reality and expectations that, in my opinion, is the greatest single factor in the production of true post-natal depression. In other parts of this book we have seen that loss is a key factor in depression and here is a loss of major proportions. The mother, possibly for all her teenage and early married life, cherished the notion of idealistic romantic motherhood, yet finds it to be something very different in reality. She loses her image of ideal motherhood and feels her loss very severely. I believe it is this loss that produces much of the post-natal depression we see today.

In some women this sense of loss is overcome by the sense of gain that they have from having the baby, but this is by no means universal and such a sense of gain can take time to develop. Few women fall in love with their babies at once and about three-quarters talk of their relationship with the baby being marred by tiredness in the early weeks. Unfortunately, too many women expect looking after a young baby at home to be a wonderful experience. Of course it can be, but often it is not in our society, because today's woman has to look after her children in isolation. This deprives her of the accumulated knowledge and wisdom of her relatives and means that she spends a great deal of time and energy caring for her baby's every need.

Today's woman who has been working up until her first baby will also have suffered another real loss – her independence. Almost all women, however independent, are pleased when they learn they are about to have a baby. When they find that the reality of looking after it isn't as marvellous as they'd expected, they become depressed because what they have gained doesn't seem to compensate for what they have lost. This produces considerable guilt feelings. After all, who can you talk to about such things? Who could you tell that you've made a mistake and that babies really aren't what you thought you'd bargained for at all?

86

Babies are certainly not all good news but it's very unfashionable to say as much and most women are incapable of saying it in the early weeks after the birth, however much they might think so. Instead, they battle on with little family help and then, if they have one of the vulnerability factors outlined above (no job, a 'no-sharing' husband, poor housing and know little about babies), they're likely to become depressed. Clearly, one way round post-natal depression is to educate women to have more realistic expectations and a better knowledge of childbirth and baby rearing, and to try to change society so that women are more at ease with the reality of motherhood.

Once a woman *is* depressed she should see a doctor who will probably use anti-depressant drugs or even ECT to cure the condition. Sometimes hormones or even B vitamins will be used. One study found that about half of all post-natally depressed women recovered without any treatment at all. Psychotherapy can be useful, but there is a danger in this because most psychotherapists are men and are likely to perpetuate existing traditional male-female role expectations (however subconsciously), and so run the risk of alienating a number of women who find that it is these very attitudes that are so unhelpful to them anyway. Ideally, women psycho-therapists or counsellors are what is needed, but there is only one place in the UK where such help is available (The Women's Therapy Centre, 6 Manor Gardens, London N7 6LA – Telephone 01–263 6200).

Almost all women with post-natal depression get better in time, but they can be greatly helped by a close friend, an understanding family doctor, or a self-help group. The Association for Post-Natal Illness, 7 Gowan Avenue, Fulham, London SW6 or Meet-A-Mum Association, 26a Cumnor Hill, Oxford OX2 9HA will be able to help.

Depression caused by success

We have been conditioned into thinking that depression is always caused by negative experiences, but this is not necessarily so. Some people become depressed as a result of their success.

The reasons why this happens are complex. Some successful

87

people see their success as undeserved and others feel guilty for having been so ambitious, often at the expense of those around them. Some people fear success and back away from it just as they are about to achieve it. Some successful people become ill at the height of their success, as if it were all too much for them, and others pay too dearly for success in the form of anxiety or feel that the results of their success 'turn to ashes in their mouths'. In a culture which is still influenced by the Victorian principles of hard work and striving, some successful people can't accept success for what it is and fear that they will somehow, someday, have to pay the price. Such people subconsciously believe they should suffer in return for being so fortunate and (quite unconsciously of course) think themselves into a depression.

Various psychoanalysts have expressed their theories on this subject but a commonly recurring theme is one of lessons learned in childhood. These, it is argued, teach the person that success produces a sense of rivalry in others and puts the successful person at risk through acts of vengeance. In adult life, the argument goes, similar mechanisms are in force and some people can't stand the idea of the possible outcome. For these people, depression is a way out of a seemingly impossible dilemma.

Medication only provides a temporary answer to those with such problems, but it is a valid treatment in the absence of any other. Such people really need psychotherapeutic help in coming to terms with their own personalities and their underlying fears.

Depression caused by mental or physical fatigue

In today's complex and often lonely society, large numbers of people are stressed by life's events to the point where they become so worn out either physically, mentally, or both, that it takes very little to tip them 'over the edge'. One way out of the stress can be to seek refuge in depression.

The key to this cause of depression is prevention. Far too many people drive themselves too hard in too many directions and then wonder why it is that one day everything gets on top of them. It can happen to any of us, but to be forewarned is to be forearmed.

A situation like this often comes about as a result of long-term grinding stress such as that of an unsatisfactory marriage, poor quality or unsuitable housing, too many children, poverty, a dislike of one's job, the helplessness one feels when one can't seem to get out of a rut and so on. Any or all of these can so wear a person down that depression occurs. In some cases this depression is valuable because it enables the person to 'phase out' of life for a while, but for most people it answers nothing because the same social injustices and troubles will be there when the depression lifts.

Treatment consists of curing the symptoms of depression followed by family help and help from social service agencies, if necessary, to make the sufferer's life more bearable. It is a sad fact of a modern industrial society that this is often not possible and that many thousands of people live, and will continue to live, in conditions which wear them down physically and mentally. Symptomatic relief may be all that these depressives can ever hope to enjoy.

Depression caused by the menstrual cycle

It has been known for centuries that women suffer physical and emotional problems in the days immediately preceding the onset of their periods, but very little research about depression and the menstrual cycle had been done until recently. As long ago as 1959, it was reported that half of the women admitted to mental hospitals for acute psychiatric illnesses were either menstruating or were just about to begin. It might have been expected that the admission rate would be high for those with depression (forty-seven per cent) and those who had made unsuccessful suicidal attempts (fifty-three per cent), because many women report that they feel low around this time of the month. What was surprising, though, was that illnesses such as schizophrenia (forty-seven per cent), alcoholism and neuroses were also prominent in women admitted at this time of the month.

Suicides are more common in women around their periods, as are shoplifting; motoring offences and crashes; child abuse; accidents at work; and a host of other events. Even the admission of children to hospital as emergencies is linked to their mothers' menstrual stage.

It has been estimated that up to ninety-five per cent of normal women experience pre-menstrual anxiety, lethargy, irritability and depression, but few studies have been done to show how important or severe any of these symptoms is. However, one large study using standardized tests to measure levels of depression in fifty women found that, although anxiety and depression were commonly present in the four days before a period, the changes were, on average, small and very different from those seen in clinically depressed women or in those with reactive depression. These researchers also found that the normal mood of a woman had little effect on whether or not she became depressed pre-menstrually.

Another study, though, found that women with pre-menstrual depression were twice as likely as a control group to have a history of serious depressive episodes and twice as likely to have a family member with depression. On following up this group of women with serious pre-menstrual depression, they found that seven per cent went on to develop true depression within the first year after the study, whereas none of the control group women did.

Depression caused by grief

We have already seen on page 52 that grieving over the loss of a loved one, a pet, or even a situation in life produces a depressive reaction in the vast majority of people. In fact depression is widely accepted as a normal part of the grief reaction.

Very early in life we become sensitised to loss. At first we fear the loss of our mother because it is she who supplies all our needs, both physical and emotional. Later, as we grow, we realize that the world is not there just to please us and that from time to time other people's actions result in our losing something.

Losses of many different kinds are at the heart of a vast number of depressions. Indeed, some experts hold the view that loss is the key cause of depression. Loss, it seems, can be important in at least two separate but interlinked ways. A loss in childhood may well make the person vulnerable to further loss and a particular loss in adulthood then completes the circuit which triggers a depression.

It was always said that reactive depressions were more likely to be preceded by some kind of loss in the nine months before the onset of the depression, but recent research has found that this is not so. Those suffering from endogenous depression were found to have had as many losses in the same time period.

Of all losses, those through death seem to be the most potent in producing depression. The death of a newborn baby has been shown to be associated with depression lasting a year or more. It is said, according to one study, that most of these women are not known to be depressed by their family doctors and so go untreated. As about ten per cent of the women who have had a stillbirth are still depressed six months after the death, this is a serious problem.

Mourning and bereavement are very like depression, but only rarely is there any loss of self-esteem. Grief reactions to bereavement vary in length and severity according to the individual and the culture in which he or she is grieving. Many cultures set traditional mourning periods, lasting from as little as twenty-four hours to a year in duration. Such set limits tell the person and the society that grieving is allowed (and even encouraged) during this time, but that at the end of the set time it must stop. In western cultures there is no such tradition and people grieve for very differing times in an informal and unstructured way. Some people, especially those with rigid, perfectionist personalities, are overwhelmed with guilt after a bereavement, especially of a spouse, and fare very badly, often becoming depressed as a result. Most people grieve for a few weeks or months and then the outside world reasserts itself and absorbs them once again.

About a third of widows and widowers experience true depression. It's interesting that there is no substantial difference in its incidence among men and women who lose a spouse; that age seems to make no difference; that a history of previous depressions doesn't seem to predispose to depression after widowhood; that neither the length of the terminal illness nor the place of death (home or hospital) seems to make any difference; and that neither the length of marriage nor the quality of marriage seem to predict the outcome either.

It seems clear that people respond to bereavement and other losses with unhappiness and sometimes even with true depression, but the relationship between the two is still not clear.

Depression caused by retirement, divorce and loneliness

I'm grouping all of these together because they are common life situations that can result in depression.

Retirement is a potent cause of depression and should not be underestimated because the most 'successful' group of suicides are to be found in this age group.

Most men retire at the age of sixty-five, yet they have on average nearly fifteen more years to live. The absolute numbers of the aged are growing, as we saw in chapter four, so the problems produced by retirement are there in greater numbers than ever before. Retirement is one of the major changes in anyone's life. It is a goal to look forward to, certainly, but is rarely everything that the person thought it would be. Enforced leisure isn't the fun a busy commuter dreams it might be, partly because retirement brings other problems, financial, personal and social, which the working person doesn't foresee.

Few people are as well off retired as they were when working. Moving to a less expensive home, reduced funds for luxuries, the cost of travel and many other things often seem to reduce the horizons of the retired and not to extend them as they had hoped. Most people think of themselves in their occupational role and, deprived of this, they find it difficult to accept their status. Doing odd jobs around the home really isn't the answer. Socially, too, things can be difficult, because most people have built their friendships around work friends and not being at work reduces their opportunity to socialize.

Failing health is an ever present worry or burden depending on whether you are fit or ill. Friends may be dying around the retired person and loneliness can be a real problem, especially if the spouse has died too. We will see later how depression can come on in old age so we will not look at it here (see page 137).

Some people with varied interests fare very well in retirement and a few see it as the start of a new life, but a common emotional reaction to retirement is depression. If ever you see a recently retired friend or relative becoming depressed, get help.

Divorce is now so common that it will soon affect one in four marriages. However unpleasant things become between a couple when they are still together, there are always considerable losses involved in divorce. The greatest sacrifice of all is losing one's children, or even seeing them only infrequently. In addition to this is the feeling of having failed at a major venture in life – the fact that the world is full of others who have also done so is no consolation to most people. The legal wrangles, the money worries, the children's feelings and the new role as a single person with all its loneliness and misery are all foundation stones on which depression can build.

Divorce isn't only the closing of one set of doors, but necessarily involves the opening of many others and this takes effort. After a divorce this effort can be too much for many people and depression can be the result. However one rationalizes divorce, it's mostly about loss. And loss is a key feature of depression. It is currently fashionable to accept divorce glibly as an everyday event of little importance; but in truth it is a time of real grief to most and of depression to many.

Loneliness is an increasingly common phenomenon in our society and it's not just the old that are lonely. Single people living alone, the divorced, the misfits and the outsiders of life are all lonely, some of them desperately so. Most of us feel a need to belong to a group or to be in a recognizable section of society. When we can't achieve this for some reason, we all too easily feel 'cast out' and suffer real pain.

This pain can be relieved in many ways. Go to people whom you can talk to about it. A good place to start is your general practitioner or a self-help group. A group called Contact is especially interested in helping lonely old people. Their address is 15 Henrietta Street, Covent Garden, London WC2E 8QA (01 240 0630). Other organizations that could be of help are Cruse and the National Association for the Divorced and Separated (see the list on pages 235-6 for addresses). The National Council for Voluntary Organizations (see page 236) has a voluntary social services directory and a handbook if you feel you'd like to overcome your loneliness by helping someone else. Getting details of adult education courses is a good start in combating loneliness and preventing depression. Find out what's available from your local town hall or library. You may not actually feel keen to learn anything, especially if you're on the way to getting depressed, but it'll make you feel a lot better simply getting out a couple of nights a week and you'll certainly meet people with similar interests. The National Institute of Adult Education will help you with ideas, and the National Federation of Solo Clubs is also very helpful if you are lonely (see page 236 for their addresses and telephone numbers).

Stresses causing depression

When someone becomes depressed it's tempting to try to find a specific cause or precipitating factor. There is often no one particular trigger that pushes people from a state in which they can just cope with life's problems into one in which they become depressed, but a large body of research does throw some light on the subject.

We have seen that there are long-term factors that make certain people more vulnerable to life's stresses. Studies have found that 'giving up' as a reaction to defeat after a reported (actual, threatened or symbolic) loss of something people valued is the key factor that puts patients in hospital with depression. Childhood relationships, recent relationships, health problems and employment are also stressed as key events in another study.

One study comparing 100 depressed patients with 100 people on ordinary medical wards found that the only significant differences in their life events were to do with change of dwelling, departure of relatives, infidelity, and discord at home and at work during the past year. All of these events were found more frequently in the depressed group, whereas there were more new friendships made in the non-psychiatric patients. Although many studies have found links between negative life events (usually those associated with 'exits' from life or relationships), it is impossible to say whether the affected people were depressed or not *at the time* of the loss or even before it. In other words, sub-clinically depressed people may *produce* 'exit' events in some way. Anyway, several research teams have been unable to find any precipitating factor at all for depression in about half of all depressives.

One large and well controlled US study asked depressed patients to select life events that had occurred in the six months before their depression from a choice of thirty-one. Overall, the depressed patients reported three times as many events as control patients, but this might have been because they were more motivated to think clearly about the problem and might also, because of their depression, have coloured recent past events a darker shade than necessary. The depressed group, though, did mention arguments with spouse, separation, death, serious illness, departure of an immediate relative, personal physical illness and change in work conditions more frequently.

Another survey of forty severe depressives admitted to hospital found that 'threat to sexual identity' was the most frequent stressful event within a year of being admitted for depression. Other key events were changes in marital relationships, physical illness, failure of children to meet parents' desired goals, increased responsibility, and death of an important person. This particular study found that substantially the same events were the precipitating causes in both endogenous and reactive depressions. This finding has also been confirmed in other surveys and has led many experts to say that a definition of endogenous depression as 'coming from within' is difficult to sustain. It is now almost certain that all depression has an external precipitating cause, if only it can be found.

Marital problems as a cause of depression

It has been known for twenty-five years that married people are more likely to enjoy good psychological and emotional health than their single, separated, widowed, or divorced counterparts. Why this should be is not known, but it is probably linked to the ability to share problems in a way that makes life's stresses easier to bear; the social acceptability of being married; and the possibility that a two-person team will tend to fare better in difficult situations than one person working alone. Single people, the divorced and the separated are at a social disadvantage, are more likely to suffer from loneliness and are often less well off materially than their married counterparts. Perhaps these things in themselves produce depression. Sexual problems, too, are very common in the newly single, and becoming unmarried is known to produce depression in some people.

Finally, it may be that the psychological problems of the unmarried are not a *consequence* of their marital status but a *cause* of it. This explanation argues that people who are depressed or who suffer from other personality disorders are relatively less able than others to marry or to stay married.

One large study of 2300 people in the US found that the currently married were most free of depression, the formerly married most plagued by it and that the never married fell in between the two. Among those formerly married, the separated were the most depressed and there was very little difference between the divorced and the widowed. Because there are important social changes that have to be taken into account when comparing the marrieds with the others, they examined various social variables in the 2300 sample. Financial hardship, social isolation and the problems of bringing up children alone were all greater among the unmarried, but these factors alone didn't account for all the differences found in the levels of depression. They found that the unmarrieds were very much more likely to suffer severe financial strain than the marrieds and that marrieds also said they were free from financial worries very much more frequently than did the unmarrieds. Regardless of marital status, the level of economic hardship was found to correlate very closely with the level of depression experienced. From this part of the study they concluded that the unmarrieds are more vulnerable to the effects of limited financial resources.

When it comes to looking at social factors, having lived in the same area for less than two years, not belonging to a voluntary organization and having only one or no friends close by, were found to be potential causes of depression. It was found that the unmarrieds scored worse on these factors, which fits in well with other research that shows that single people, especially the formerly married, have greater difficulty than couples in establishing a durable and extensive social life.

On the matter of child care, marrieds are more likely to have a greater burden in absolute numbers of children than are the unmarried. Even so, the burden of child care is in fact greater for the unmarried and is highly correlated with depression levels.

So, in summary, this large and well conducted survey found that marriage acts as a protective barrier against some of life's distressing experiences. It doesn't, of course, prevent adverse social circumstances, but helps people fend off many of the psychological and emotional ills that such problems would otherwise create.

But although being married or having a stable relationship protects people from depression, a very large number of such people still become depressed. In fact, one world expert concluded, after years of studies, that marital therapy might be the most useful psychotherapeutic approach for depression!

Recent studies suggest that poor marital relationships of all kinds often lead to the production and maintenance of depression. Most depressed patients are currently married, and depressed women of all marital states are more likely to have been married than their non-depressed counterparts. The highest rates of depression among women occur in their forties, a time when marital satisfaction is often at its lowest. One study of 146 women with depression and other emotional disorders, followed up for twelve years, found that the poorest outcomes were among those who had said on admission that their symptoms were precipitated by marital events.

Of course, there may not be a connection between being married and becoming depressed: it might be that the two simply occur together. Many theorists have argued about this and there are as many opinions as there are experts. It is possible, though, that one of the key depression-causing factors about marriage is the attempt at interpersonal control by the couple. Many couples fight a continuing battle (often not consciously) for control of life's events, goals, sex and hosts of other things. This can eventually lead the partner who continuously 'loses' to become depressed. Several studies have found that marriages in which one partner is depressed are characterized by their relative lack of communication. Verbal and non-verbal communication is reduced in such marriages and the spouses are more likely to be self-preoccupied, to show high levels of tension and to show more negative facial expressions than normal couples. Other studies have found that the way the depressed person reacts to his spouse and to strangers is entirely different. One UK study on this subject concluded that the couple often develops a social system which perpetuates the depression. They also pointed out how important it is for psychologists and psychiatrists not to draw conclusions about the patient's home life from what they find when they or outsiders talk to the patient, even in the presence of his or her spouse.

Other research shows that, in marriages with a depressed partner, the couples show less affection and a tendency to remark on fewer desirable attributes of their spouse compared with those same depressives after treatment. Lack of affection from a husband seems to play a more important role in the production of depression in women than does the reverse situation.

Depressed couples certainly argue more than do the non-depressed. One study of forty depressed women and forty controls showed that there was an increased amount of hostile behaviour towards their husbands among the depressed. Another study found that women when depressed are more negative and hostile towards their husbands than are depressed men towards their wives.

So, in summary, many changes occur within a marriage which contains a depressed person. There is generally a lower level of affection, a reduction of expression of affection, an increase in expression of criticism, and considerable evidence of a struggle for interpersonal control. Such marriages tend to be less cooperative than others and there is an increase of husband-dominated patterns, whether it is the husband or the wife who is depressed.

Of course, not all of these changes are necessarily the result of the depression – many may have been present beforehand and may even have brought the depression about in the first place. In either event, the repair of these disrupted relationships can bring relief to the couple, not only in the short-term but also in the long-term. Improved marital and familial relationships can greatly help cure depression, but both partners must be motivated to remedy the situation. Some spouses have a need, conscious or subconscious, to keep the patient 'sick', weak and depressed. A husband's feelings concerning his depressed wife include anger because of her clinging dependency, sympathy for the suffering she's undergoing and occasionally guilt in case he's contributed to the depression in some way. The 'well' partner experiences an enhanced level of self-esteem and feels important and relevant to the patient, perhaps for the first time. The patient often experiences a lot of guilt and self-blame and frequently speaks of the spouse in overpraising and laudatory terms. Other depressed people blame their spouses (though not openly to their faces) and are really very angry deep down. This often comes about because they feel they have to blame somebody and can't blame themselves.

Marriage then, when it works well and when the partners work as a team rather than as two individuals, is a real protection against depression. Many couples, however, don't have a close relationship based on equality and respect and so resort to interpersonal battling with a resulting loss of self-esteem in the one who constantly 'loses'. This atmosphere fosters poor relations both in and out of bed, until the couple find themselves living together in a state of armed neutrality. Such marriages appear normal and happy to the outside world and, indeed, survive quite well until a major stress or repeated minor stresses push it over the threshold of acceptability to one or both partners. It is at this point that depression begins and by then the couple have forgotten how to help each other, if indeed they ever really knew. At this stage professional help is essential. A family doctor can be good, especially if you have known him for years, or marriage guidance counsellors can assist you to find the way out of the maze. For many of those in a depressed marriage the answer to a cure lies within the marriage itself, but it often needs an outsider to be able to clear the accumulated cobwebs, to seek out the painful areas that have been pushed under the marital carpet for too long and to get the couple to be open to each other, perhaps for the first time. Once this process has begun, most couples experience a more loving and fulfilled sex life and are soon on the mend. Marriage guidance counsellors are at hand in most areas of this country. You can find out more about them from their headquarters (see page 235 for the address and telephone number).

CHAPTER 3

The signs and symptoms of depression and what to do about them

We have already seen in chapter one that depression has many faces and that each person with the disease has an individual profile of signs and symptoms. Before we go on to look at each of the commonest signs and symptoms and what we can do about them, let's define what signs and symptoms are, because I'll use the words in their proper medical way in this chapter. A *sign* of a disease is the visible or detectable evidence of the disease that can be perceived by an outsider. A *symptom* is what the patient complains of, which may not be evident to an outsider. So, for example, a rash on the skin is a sign and the itching it produces is a symptom. People who are depressed have lots of symptoms, which by their very definition are apparent only to them. They also have some signs, for example lying awake at night or excessive sweating.

Very few depressives have all the signs and symptoms described below; but these are all found at various stages of the illness in various people. In simple terms, the more serious the depression, the more signs and symptoms the depressive will have. This doesn't always follow, because occasionally an apparently happy depressed person can suddenly commit suicide as the first 'sign' of depression.

Depression, as we have seen, is difficult to define and many people who have some of the signs and symptoms detailed in this chapter will not necessarily be depressed. If you or a relative have more than two or three of these manifestations you should see a doctor, just in case it *is* depression. If you have a depressive in the family you'll know only too well how crippling the signs and symptoms of depression can be, not only to the sufferer, but also to the rest of the family. They get in the way of relationships, often render the sufferer socially unaccepted and unacceptable, produce anger and frustration in the family circle and generally cause domestic emotional chaos.

A normally cheerful man will feel distant from his wife, will want to sit around most of the time and become absorbed in himself and his ailments when he's depressed. All these things are very difficult for the family members to come to terms with. As a result, they often feel angry that the depressive can't get a hold of his emotional life, and they tell him to 'pull himself together'. We have already seen in chapter one that this is impossible and that in practice it produces the opposite result, because it convinces people of their worthlessness and the burden they are on the rest of the family.

There is fairly good evidence that we all come to adult life with a stock of acquired knowledge of what to do in certain life situations. Feeling depressed is one such situation and a recent study has found that people do in fact have reasonably effective learned 'recipes' for how to cope with such circumstances. In this study, fifty people aged from nine to sixty-eight years were asked, 'What's the thing to do when you're feeling depressed?' and told that there were no right or wrong answers.

After analyzing the responses, the researchers decided that there is a body of commonsense 'knowledge' about what to do when you feel depressed. The responses included both positive and negative suggestions: of maintaining and breaking away from routines; of shutting off from the world and searching out friends; of 'wallowing in it' (enjoying it); and getting help to relieve oneself of the symptoms. There are no magic answers as to what to do when you feel depressed as each answer depends on the person, the type of depression, the circumstances at the time, the seriousness of the condition, who or what happens to be at hand to help and a host of other factors.

Many of the answers the people in the survey gave related to a change of job, scene or activity, which suggests that change is in itself 'anti-depressive' in many people's eyes. Change is indeed at the heart of all depression treatment as something has to be done to make life acceptable for the sufferer.

Unfortunately, to people who are depressed such self-help suggestions often seem academic because their motivation is so low. If this is the case, family and friends will have to implement the suggestions in this section and even that may not be possible.

It's not easy to help the depressed because the very nature of the illness makes them unable to think positively. This can be very frustrating for those around them. The situation can be greatly helped simply by showing a serious and caring interest in depressives because this alone reduces their terrible feeling of mental and emotional isolation. Most depressed people won't have the symptoms and signs discussed below in unendurable quantities and will be open to gentle encouragement and the thought that someone close to them cares.

Sadness

This is probably the most common sign (and symptom) of depression. Depressives look sad, their faces are immobile, they express very few emotions, rarely smile, may complain of feeling sad, spend long periods gazing *through things* instead of at them and may look as though they're going to burst into tears at any time. There are varying degrees of this ranging from mild to severe sadness.

What to do: There really is very little either the sufferers themselves or their relatives can do about the sadness. Certainly, it is not helped by their families trying to cheer them up, because sad depressives, unless they're really severely ill (when they won't care what you do), see this for what it is and aren't amused. On the contrary, they feel that they're being treated like fools, which further confirms their low opinion of themselves. The sadness will lift as treatment progresses, but there is little the family can do specifically to combat it. Other self-help measures suggested in this chapter will tend to make depressives less sad, as they aim at relieving other symptoms.

Tearfulness (crying)

Along with sadness often goes tearfulness. This crying is all the more upsetting for those around because it is often done alone. Some agitated depressives also cry a lot and nothing will stop them, especially if they have a hysterical personality anyway. Some depressed people say that they'd like to cry 'to get it off their chest' but they just can't.

102

What to do: Few of us like to see people crying and in European and North American society crying is not acceptable social behaviour in men. This is by no means true of all cultures, many of which expect people to cry openly in certain situations.

It's very difficult for most of us to console someone who cries a lot, especially if we're being affected by the same event that has made the other person depressed. A good cry together is no bad thing and can amaze depressed people (who think they are alone with their misery) and even help them, if they are not too down in the depths. Crying is a safety valve that lets off the emotional steam and many reactive depressives feel a lot better after a good howl. Unfortunately, the beneficial effects are usually short-lived.

For all but this type of depressive crying though, persistent tearfulness is *not* helpful at all. Some people find that they simply cannot cry when staring someone else in the eye, but whether the use of such manoeuvres by relatives to prevent someone crying actually does any good, except saving handkerchiefs, is doubtful. Crying can be of positive value. It may well 'wash out' some of the emotions tied up in the depressive and many a useful heartfelt conversation has started with a good cry. When people are crying they are at their most vulnerable, so if you are a caring relative, you can build on this. Perhaps it'll be through a crying bout that you'll be able to get the person to disclose some hidden fear, guilt or problem that is really at the heart of things. Only then can you understand what's really going on and perhaps do something to help.

Persistent or repeated crying is wearing for everybody and is one of the signs of depression that needs treating.

Sleep problems

Almost all truly depressed people (especially those with endogenous depressions) experience some type of sleep disturbance. It has been claimed that reactive depressives have difficulty getting off to sleep and that the endogenously depressed get off easily but awake early in the morning. Some doctors also use early morning waking as a pointer that the person will benefit from electroconvulsive therapy (ECT), so the study of sleep patterns in the depressed can be valuable.

It's very difficult to assess just how real sleep loss is in depression because, strange though it may seem, it's difficult to know when people are asleep, unless you wire them up to an electroencephalogram (EEG) which measures their brain waves. This procedure is tedious and probably alters people's sleep patterns anyway, not because of the equipment itself but because they know they are being monitored and because they are often in a strange place as well.

In spite of all these difficulties, several studies have found that all types of depressives spend less time asleep, more time getting off to sleep and are more prone to early morning waking than are control groups of patients. Severely ill (psychotic) depressives sleep least of all. Factors such as age and social class are known to affect sleep and this makes sleep research very difficult indeed to interpret but, even so, it is now widely accepted that depressives *do* sleep less.

Subjective evaluation of sleep is very unreliable, as many studies have found. Generally, people tend to underestimate their total sleep time and overestimate their delay in getting off to sleep, as measured by EEG methods. Similar studies have found that as depression is treated, people actually do sleep more, but that as both reactively and endogenously depressed subjects recover, they take longer to get off to sleep.

People get very agitated about how much they sleep and feel they have to conform to a standard eight-hour night or some other 'natural' time span they've been brought up to believe is acceptable. Anything other than this is considered unusual.

In fact, perfectly normal, healthy people vary enormously in the amount of sleep they need. Eight per cent of the population sleep for less than five hours; fifteen per cent sleep between nine and ten hours and two per cent over ten hours. The numbers of hours spent asleep lessen with advancing age, so just because you're sleeping less at sixty-five than you did at thirty-five, this doesn't mean to say you're depressed. People over the age of sixty take more daytime naps, fall asleep earlier and awaken earlier anyway, so here again such signs should not be mistaken for those of depression.

Anti-depressant drugs have provable and predictable effects on sleep, their main action being to reduce REM sleep. This Rapid Eye Movement sleep occurs several times throughout the night and is thought to be associated with dreaming. ECT also reduces REM sleep. We shall see how sleep deprivation can actually be used to treat depression in chapter six.

What to do: Early morning wakening is especially unpleasant for the depressive. The world is still asleep and there is an eeriness about everything that can be unpleasant even for a perfectly healthy person. The minutes seem to go very slowly at that time of the day and depressives find themselves looking at the clock often at intervals of as little as a minute or two. There really is very little that relatives can do about helping depressed people over this, unless they (the relatives) reorganize their bed times so as to go to sleep earlier and, as a result, awake earlier as well. In this way depressed people aren't awake alone for too long. Another way of helping depressives is to go without some sleep yourself. This may seem like madness to you as you read this, but many people probably sleep longer than they need and can easily get up an hour or two earlier. You'll end up getting a lot more done in *your* day and will also be around to start off the day with the depressive. All this calls for some very selfless behaviour but you can make a virtue of it and enrich your own life a little, too.

Some slowed down (retarded) depressives want to sleep in the day. This can be very annoying for their families who have to watch them, knowing that they'll be up very early next morning and may wake them up.

Sleeping tablets can be helpful for the reactive depressive but the endogenously depressed need their depression treated. Successful treatment cures the sleeplessness.

Reduced appetite

Depressives are infuriating to cook for. They pick at food, complain about it, say they're not hungry and in fact eat very little. This leads to a loss of weight which worries them and their family still further. Some very depressed people go for days without eating and if this is superimposed upon a long-term poor eating pattern, it can cause nutritional deficiencies which need treating in themselves.

What to do: However annoying it is, it's still worthwhile

putting food in front of depressives even though they might not touch it. Never bully them to eat it because by forcing them to do so you're depriving them of their innermost desire to punish themselves and they'll feel even worse than before. Be firm and encourage them to eat by serving things they like. This can often mean preparing dishes that you wouldn't normally prepare, but this is just one of the many burdens that fall on the family of the depressed. When they have their favourite foods in front of them you can tell them that they need food in order to get better. Be pleased when they eat something but don't say anything harsh when they don't. Really depressed people may say, 'I don't know why you bother with all this for me, I'm not worth it'. This is just a part of the total picture of depression. Ignore this type of statement when it comes to food and continue to do what you feel is best, assuring them that you'd be making it anyway, so they might as well eat it. Never show disappointment if you've been to great lengths to prepare something special which they then leave. Tell them you'll save it for later, just in case they want it.

It's a slow and painful business coaxing adults to eat when they don't want to, but slowly and with perseverance as the depression lifts things will improve. If ever a depressive stops eating for more than a few days you should tell the doctor.

Loss of interest in sex

One of the key features of depression is that sufferers stop getting pleasure out of life. One of the first pleasures to go is their interest in sex. Sexual intercourse is an integral part of normal, happy life in most of us. It is, however, very easily knocked by emotional upsets and depression ranks high on the list of conditions that reduce sexual appetite. A woman who becomes depressed can submit passively to intercourse 'to please her husband', but a depressed man often cannot get or sustain an erection, becomes anxious about this and is soon completely impotent. This further adds to his depression. Such impotence is more often experienced by older men, who may well see themselves as 'less of a man' anyway as they become convinced that life has passed them by or that they will never achieve what they had hoped. If the wife of such a man has problems in her own life, she may not be able to be of much help and the couple will slowly develop marital problems.

What to do: The greatest problem is that of maintaining the depressed person's self-confidence. The man's wife can be most helpful by taking the initiative sexually, but it's often not easy for her to feel helpful when she may feel rejected and unloved as a result of the depression. In addition to the effects of the depression, the man also subconsciously rejects his wife because she makes him feel 'unmanly' and powerless – even in these days of women's liberation, most men intuitively feel they should be the powerful, motivating force in sexual matters. Some women imagine that their husbands are getting sexual satisfaction elsewhere and that this is the reason why they have gone off them. Such suspicion further adds to the already considerable problems and has to be fought against.

Most women treat their husbands' temporary inability to perform as a transient stage in their illness and are kind about it. Loving couples who have enjoyed a vigorous sex life often find ways other than penis-in-vagina intercourse in which they can make love, and mutual masturbation and oral sex can both play a part in arousing the depressed man into some sexual activity. Even if such approaches aren't welcomed by the man, the couple can still hug and kiss and be physically close. A woman in this situation may become sexually frustrated and find relief in masturbation. With luck, there should only be a temporary rift in the couple's sexual relationship.

A depressed person still wants to be loved and cherished, so even if intimate loving behaviour doesn't result in intercourse it can still be valuable and enjoyable.

Affection between the couple can be difficult to keep alive when the depression is severe, because there are so many annoying and frustrating things that happen all day that it's difficult for the couple to feel very loving at times. Depending on the severity of the depression, though, there are ways (often with expert help) around many of the sexual problems.

Loss of interest in other pleasurable activities

One of the main features of depression is a feeling of flatness and a loss of pleasure from hobbies and other activities that normally give people a 'lift' above the routines of everyday life.

Because the pleasure derived from these activities is lost, the drive to pursue them goes too, and in no time individuals become overwhelmed by their own inertia. Not only do world events, the performance of favourite football clubs and other distant events lose meaning and importance, but so also do pleasures nearer home. Friendships suffer and eventually close family relationships cease to be important. As the condition deepens, the family is rejected and depressives live in a world populated only by themselves. This can be one of the most upsetting faces of depression for the relatives because, for a reason which is not their fault and which they cannot understand, they, the ones who deserve the sympathy and understanding at having to put up with their relative's depression, are themselves rejected. It's difficult, but the relatives should try to remember that depressives aren't rejecting them deliberately – their illness controls them so totally that they couldn't behave differently even if they wanted to, and the very nature of depression is that they are *not* motivated to behave differently.

What to do: The only way around this or, preferably, to stop it happening in the first place is firmly to encourage them to do things they used to enjoy. Depressives will rarely initiate activities so it's up to you to do so. Unfortunately, they will often let you down at the last minute because of mental or physical symptoms and this can be terribly frustrating. Still, rather as with food, it is a matter of persisting, because if you don't it'll drag you all down. And this is what happens all too easily.

Depressives not only kill pleasurable activities for themselves, but also tend to ruin family pleasures, simply because many of their enjoyable activities were previously linked with those of their family. If your relative is depressed it's essential to keep up your own interests and pleasures or, before you know where you are, you'll be sinking into depression too. Anyway it's a good idea, if you possibly can, to get out of the company of the depressive from time to time, simply to keep yourself going. If his wife is depressed, a husband may feel that going out to work is enough of a change from the gloomy atmosphere at home. If a husband is depressed, his wife often can't get much outside stimulation because her personal interests and pursuits may be seriously curtailed as a result of her depressive husband. All too easily she finds that she is dragged down too unless she is careful.

Depression isn't contagious in the generally accepted sense of the word, but it does seem to affect those around the depressed person more often than would be expected by chance alone and it's scarcely surprising that this should be so. Why this occurs, no one knows. Certainly the low mood of the household rubs off on everyone, but perhaps this isn't all that's happening. Studies of healing energy in Canada have found some remarkable things which are of interest in depression.

Dr Bernard Grad, a biochemist working in Canada, did some exciting experiments in the late 1950s with a proven healer. Dr Grad gave three types of water to identical plants and watched what happened to their growth. The first bottle of water had been held by the healer, the second was untreated and the third was held by a non-healer. The plants grew significantly faster when watered with the contents of the flask held by the healer for thirty minutes than when watered with the contents of the other two flasks. Grad then repeated the experiment with the flasks being held by three different people: a healer, a person suffering from very severe (psychotic) depression and someone with mild depression. In addition, there was a control bottle of water held by no one. The people's reactions to being asked to do such a strange thing are interesting and shed light on the very nature of depression. The psychotically ill depressive stated that he didn't want electroconvulsive therapy when asked to hold the water bottle and needed considerable reassurance that it was not a way of giving him electric shocks. The reactively depressed woman wanted to know why she should do such a foolish thing and when it was all explained said, 'What a marvellous idea'. For the thirty-minute 'holding' period, she cradled the bottle in her lap like a baby.

The results showed that the healer's water made plants grow faster than did the control water and that those watered with the seriously depressed man's water grew substantially more slowly. The water from the reactively depressed woman's bottle performed better than that from the seriously depressed man's, but not as well as did the healer's. Somehow, then, the depressed people had 'transferred' something to the water that adversely affected plant growth.

At the moment we have no idea what it is, but research currently under way on natural body forces, thought by some to be diminished in depression, might provide some answers. Many people say that there is something intrinsically 'negative' about being with a depressed person. Perhaps whatever Grad's subjects were transferring to the water is also being transferred to those around depressives – but we're a long way off knowing the answer to this phenonemon.

Self-neglect

As depression deepens, so affected people often let themselves go, cease to care about their appearance and personal hygiene and generally become slovenly. Previously well-dressed women don't bother to do their hair or apply make-up and throw on any clothes that happen to be around; men will look dirty and unshaven. Bathing becomes one of the many areas of self-neglect and soon the person smells offensive and is unpleasant to be with.

What to do: Act firmly and insist that the person look after his or her personal hygiene. You have every right to act strongly in this area; after all, you have quite enough to put up with in other ways without having to put up with self-neglect too. Help him by laying out fresh clothes, because he won't be sufficiently motivated to search for a missing sock or the right trousers. Make everything easy for her so that she has no excuse for continuing with the neglect. Run a bath, put toothpaste on the brush, and in every way make it impossible for the affected person to ignore your efforts. Do this with kindness though, and don't bully. Remember that although some of the strange behaviour may seem manipulative (and it is), depressives cannot help how they are behaving.

Don't fall into the trap of thinking that depressives' appearance and hygiene don't matter – they do. They're certainly not life-threatening but they detract from your and their quality of life and generally drag the family down – so it's well worth the effort. True, illness makes them temporarily unable to look after themselves, but you don't want the outside world to think you neglect them. People might think that it was this kind of neglect which led to their depression in the first place!

When the disease is over and they are well again they'll want to hold their heads high and not be dogged by other people's memories of their previously disgusting appearance and behaviour. In short, it's well worth helping people retain their dignity when they're ill. They won't thank you for it at the time, but it pays dividends both during their illness and when they recover.

Fearfulness

There are two major fears that depressives have. They fear being left alone and they fear death. Previously independent people can very easily become housebound when depressed, simply because they have irrational fears which probably reduce the range of activities they can undertake. Those depressives whose condition is characterized by physical ailments use their complaints to curtail their outings until they effectively become housebound. Some depressives become afraid of driving or have panic attacks in crowded shops, in the underground or on crossing bridges, for example. They can't explain what it is about these situations that has made them afraid, but these irrational fears can cripple not only the affected individual but also his or her family. 'My husband hasn't driven since his depression set in', is a comment I frequently hear. This seemingly small change in lifestyle can dramatically alter the running of the family, as the wife acts as chauffeuse to her husband. If things get really bad, her problem is solved because eventually he won't go out in the car at all because he's so fearful.

This rather pathetic decline from a normal, capable person to a fearful social cripple is just part of the painful picture of depression and one which upsets the rest of the family a great deal.

What to do: The main thing to do here is to ensure that depressed people aren't alone, especially in the presence of one of their feared situations. Because the feelings are irrational but

111

the panic attacks they produce so real, it is cruel to let them get into a situation in which they panic. This means having someone present all the time, which inevitably throws strain on the immediate family or whoever provides the company. Understanding friends and relatives will probably help if asked. Even neighbours can take the pressure off the immediate relatives and ideally they should be understanding and have some insight into the problem. Being within phone distance isn't good enough, because it's actually being left alone that's so terrifying to them – knowing that someone can be there if really needed isn't good enough.

All this is very trying for the family and it's not surprising that they occasionally need a break away from the depressive. A short stay in a psychiatric unit can sometimes be arranged for the depressed person and there are specialist nursing homes that can help too. Having a relative to stay for a week or so while the rest of the family gets away for a break can also be a life-saver. Remember, you'll be of no help to your depressed relative if *you* too become depressed by the situation.

Fears of death are relatively common in depression, especially if it is a serious one. Don't forget that many depressives feel suicidal and some are totally overwhelmed with thoughts on the subject from time to time in their disease. We shall see in chapter nine that all suicidal threats in depressed people *must* be taken seriously, simply because many do in fact kill themselves. The vast majority of depressives don't really want to die, but they do want to end their suffering and that which they produce in others. Many become so wrapped up in their own misery that the idea of death becomes almost attractive.

What to do: The only thing to do in these situations is to be honest and say that it's not surprising that they fear death because their illness is making life unbearable for them. Don't make light of the situation or they'll get more desperate because they will think you don't understand or that you think they're enjoying themselves. Point out that they were never like this before and will get over these thoughts when they're better.

All these fears come and go sporadically and will need real

action on your behalf when they are at their height. Sometimes the fears rise to a fever pitch and people panic so much that they may beg to be killed to be put out of their misery. At this stage they have reached breaking point and must not be left at all. Attempted suicidal gestures are often carried out in front of someone, as we shall see in chapter nine, but seriously suicidal depressives almost never kill themselves in the company of someone they know.

Beware of being sent out for something, because when you get back a depressive in this state could be dead. If you have to go out, get someone else to stay with the sufferer. One man I know in this situation, despite all his family's careful watchfulness, was left alone for a minute. He threw himself out of the ground floor dining room window in an attempt to kill himself. He only suffered minor bruises and cuts and flattened his prize dahlias, but it put him in hospital where he could be constantly watched. We had a smile about it some weeks later as he showed me his ruined flowers, but at that moment of desperation he was completely out of control and needed help.

For more about suicide and what to do, see page 232.

Loss of self-esteem and self-confidence

We all have very different levels of confidence and self-esteem, even when we're not depressed, so when depression strikes we each have different reserves on which to draw. Highly confident people with lots of self-esteem may need to get *very* depressed before they begin to see themselves as useless, whereas others who had little to start with soon become wrapped up in self-pity and dejection. Endogenously depressed individuals lose all pride in themselves and feel that there's nothing of value or worth in them. They tell everyone who'll listen about their worthlessness and it is this negative self-esteem that is such a dominant feature of depression. Those suffering from a reactive depression tend not to lose self-esteem; they tend to feel that the *world* has lost its meaning and not that *they* themselves are worthless.

What to do: Be positive. Praise the person for those things he or she does do well, even though this can be difficult when you're feeling ambivalent at best and hostile at worst. Build up their confidence and play down their weaknesses, and if possible make up for them yourself. Once self-esteem is lost, such techniques might not work, simply because the condition has gone past the stage where being positive helps at all.

The job now is to fight the hopelessness with reasoned argument. Draw from the past to illustrate that life won't always be like this and give examples of what the sufferer used to do very well. Try to show the person that loss of self-esteem is irrational and that he or she is still the same person – a person who'll be well again in time.

Some people also overcome these problems by actually provoking the depressed person to think constructively and positively about a new problem. Many people have a hobby or interest that they feel 'expert' in to some degree. By encouraging others to seek the advice or help of depressed people in their special areas of interest you encourage them to see themselves as having some worth in the eyes of outsiders.

It's very easy for the family to live *around* rather than with the depressive, who will slowly and insidiously be left out of important decision-making processes. All of this helps confirm an already poor self-image and substantiate the feelings of worthlessness. However difficult it may be (and it often can be), try to involve depressed people in the important things of life. It won't cure their depression, but they'll see that you still value them and this will help. Redressing some of the negatives of depression is just as important as actually being positive.

Anxiety

As we saw in chapter one, very few depressives are entirely free from anxiety and many are anxious most of the time. For some, anxiety takes the form of panic attacks (with sweating, fast breathing, palpitation and dizziness), which may be provoked by one of the many obsessional fears we discussed on page 111. Other depressives suffer from a generalized anxiety in anticipation of events – events which may never happen. This is called anticipatory anxiety and is totally irrational.

People affected with such anxiety are uncontrollably upset by the thought of an activity that might be hours or days off. If they know they're going to be left alone, for example, even days ahead, they'll begin to worry about what might happen to them when they're alone. They build up these worries and fears to such a height that, well before the event, they find themselves crippled mentally (and even physically) with ailments they can't control.

What to do: Live hour by hour and day by day. Don't plan ahead (or if you do, don't tell the depressive about it). Spring things on them and they'll be all right. Don't give them time to prepare all their fears and obsessions. Very often the situation or activity they have so feared is quite innocuous anyway and could even be helpful to their condition. Don't forget that their disease makes them generally negative. This means that the harmless remark 'I've asked Auntie Flo to come and see us this afternoon' could fill a depressive with horror. Will I be well enough to see her? What will she think of me? What if I have one of my 'turns'? These and a host of other questions may fill the person's mind and completely ruin what could have been a pleasant visit. Other peoples' joys and pleasures, too, only bring forth a flow of negative remarks from depressives. If you're going to a party or other social gathering don't tell them until the last minute if they're given to anticipating anxiety or they'll find hordes of excuses for not going or ways of poisoning you against the whole idea.

Poor decision-making and poor judgement

One of the most frustrating symptoms for anyone, including depressives themselves, is their inability to make even the most trivial of decisions. It can be agony to watch a depressive taking minutes debating which socks or dress to choose. They are often totally baffled by a choice of even two options and end up choosing neither, opting to do nothing rather than to make a choice. Many normal people cannot make up their minds, but *their* problem is usually that they can see a great many options and possible outcomes to their decisions. Depressed people can see only negative outcomes of whichever decision they make and so do nothing. Depressives, because of the negative nature of their illness, will always tend to do nothing, given a choice.

Coupled with this poor ability to make decisions is their poor judgement. One of the dangers of depression is that if it goes unrecognized it can lead families into terrible problems. Depressives can't be relied upon to make sound judgements and this has to be faced early on in the disease. Depressed people will often have a convincing and compelling (to them at least) way out of their depression. For example, they won't ever be really suited to their wives or husbands, so a divorce is the answer to their depression; they never get on with their neighbours, so to sell house and move is the answer; the market for their goods or services has dramatically changed so they should sell their business, and so on. It's terribly sad to see the aftermath of such actions and those around depressives often kick themselves later for having let them do such things. It is impossible to judge how much business, national and even international chaos has been caused by people in responsible positions making poor decisions because of unrecognized depression.

What to do: In the kindest possible way, you have to protect depressed individuals from themselves. On the question of indecision, don't make them have to decide – do it for them. Don't give them choices. When it comes to serving a meal, for example, put a little of all the dishes on their plate or they could be ten minutes deciding whether or not to have cabbage and whether or not to have mustard. Put out their clothes for them and don't worry about appearing to bulldoze them along. The agony they go through having to decide for themselves is far greater than any small loss of self-esteem you may think they'll suffer as you impose your will on the situation. They'll be relieved to have the burden of decision-making taken off them.

On the subject of judgement, things are not quite so simple. Depressives who have been through it before know they can't trust themselves when they're depressed and so take no major decisions. But more usually it's the family who first realize the truth of the situation and have to take over. This isn't easy, because by doing so you are taking over the responsibilities of that person, and in the eyes of many people this is only one step away from having them 'put away' in a hospital where they won't have to make any decisions at all. The depressed person won't welcome this behaviour either and will probably be very difficult. You may need medical help or the help of friends in order to convince depressives that their desires are wrong, but there is no doubt that a lot of long-term misery is caused because of decisions wrongly made by depressed people who are in no fit state to make them. Such poor decisions occasionally render the affected person so ineffective or inefficient at work that he or she may be dismissed. This is sometimes the first obvious sign of depression and must be taken seriously.

Agitation

Depression has many faces, as we have seen. Some depressed individuals are very 'low' in their mood whereas some are very agitated. The latter are overactive and tense. They pace the floor, wring their hands, flit from one activity to another and are generally 'nervous'. This type of depression is extremely wearing to have to live with and you'll often feel like screaming. These people complain of physical symptoms and are exceptionally edgy all the time. They may talk a lot and bombard those around them with endless questions, the vast majority of which are centred on themselves, their favourite topic of conversation.

In addition to the physical agitation there may be mental agitation with flights of ideas, strings of disconnected thoughts and floods of emotions uncontrollably washing over them. Sometimes all this agitation can be so wearing for the affected individuals that they literally exhaust themselves and can see death as the only way out of the torment. Someone in this situation needs urgent psychiatric help.

What to do: As they ramble on and on, recounting the same fears, misgivings and regrets, it's easy to become frustrated and annoyed by it all. The things that so agitate depressives mean little or nothing to the outsider, although you can often see an element of truth in what is said. There's no arguing or reasoning with people when they are like this. Their state of mental health doesn't allow them to see your point of view. On a physical level, though, you can calm them and be reassuring. Spend time with them and persuade them to tell you about their reasons for being so agitated. This will do *you* no good at

117

all but will help them to see that you care, and this can be a lifesaver if they're about to snap. Perhaps a close friend would be better to allow them to unburden all their troubles and guilt on to. The friend won't have to live with them and so will be more tolerant and patient and anyway might be genuinely interested in what they have to say. Also, outsiders can tell the agitated person something of *their* lives and problems and that can often defuse the situation a little.

Agitated depressives don't simply calm down and get better. Most need treatment in the form of drugs or ECT as well as sympathetic therapy from a professional, family or friends.

Poor concentration and memory

These two symptoms are annoying and frustrating for people suffering from depression but are not dangerous or life-threatening. Poor concentration results in a very short attention span with depressives getting distracted from any given task after a few minutes. They find they can't think straight and that their minds wander, often back to themselves and their predicament. Coupled with this, their memory fails, especially for recent and trivial things. They forget where they put things, what they had for lunch and, more importantly, whether or not they took their tablets.

What to do: Take control of the important activities that depressed individuals cannot any longer control for themselves. When they can't concentrate, reassure them constantly of things they're insecure about, give them time to collect their thoughts and don't get into the habit of rushing them into replying to a question. Don't frustrate them by getting them to do jobs that you know they will be unable to concentrate on, as their inability to do the jobs will confirm their own poor self-esteem.

Memory loss is trying for those around depressed individuals, but do try to be easy on them as you recall the events they can't. Don't ridicule them or make them look small in front of others. This can do nothing but harm. Tell them that their memory will clear up as the depression gets better and in the meantime be their memory *for* them.

On a more practical note, if your relative suffers from a poor memory, keep all drugs safely away somewhere and give them out at the appointed times. If you don't do this, he or she may either forget to take them at all or take them several times over by mistake. You must protect the depressive from lapses of memory such as these.

Concern over bodily symptoms

Almost all endogenously and some reactively depressed people have bodily symptoms and signs, as we saw on page 28. Indeed, some depressions show up first in these ways. Many depressed people complain of a poor appetite and constipation and others complain about weakness, constant tiredness and generalized aches and pains. For a full list of the physical (as opposed to mental and emotional) symptoms that can be a part of depression, see page 40.

It's very difficult to understand why these things should occur and there is, as yet, no convincing answer. Many psychoanalysts argue that the underlying psychological make-up of the person can be used to predict which 'target organs' will be affected when depression strikes. So, they argue, in an 'oral' person (a term denoting an arrest of psychological development at a certain orally-centred phase of infancy) the signs and symptoms will be oral in nature. Thus over- or under-eating, stomach upsets and pains, peptic ulcers and constipation are likely to be manifest in such people. Just how valid such explanations are is difficult to prove, but the links between mind and body are well known and the study of psychosomatic disease is now quite legitimate. Somehow, depression affects the highest centres in the brain to affect in turn distant body organs. The person's predisposing personality undoubtedly plays a big part in determining which organs are affected and, indeed, whether they're affected at all.

Many depressives are wrongly labelled as hypochondriacs by the medical profession and their relatives alike. This is unfair because hypochondria is really something quite different. A preoccupation with bodily symptoms though *is* a common feature of depression. Researchers have found it difficult to compare those depressives with and without physical complaints, simply because they have found it almost impossible to find groups of depressives entirely free from physical ailments. One study compared depressed hypochondriacal patients from a general hospital with a matched group of depressed patients without bodily symptoms from a psychiatric clinic. The main differences were that the former showed poor sexual and marital adjustment; a fluctuating course of the depression, often precipitated by death or other external causes; a greater chance of the depression being long-standing; less disruption of family, social and occupational activities; a relative absence of depressed mood; and less anxiety.

Delusions about body function are particularly common in the elderly, in whom a concern over 'blocked bowels' is often seen. Some of the very severely depressed actually deny their bodies exist and a rare few even claim to be dead!

In certain depressive reactions to grief the bereaved can suffer identical symptoms to those of the dead person just before he or she died.

What to do: The frequency, intensity and conviction with which depressives complain of bodily symptoms are truly impressive and lead even the best physicians to persist in investigating the possible underlying cause. As we have already seen, depressed people aren't imagining their symptoms and neither are they 'putting them on'. Their minds take over control of their bodies and they really are experiencing what they say they are. Relatives often feel foolish when, after treatment of the depression, all these signs and symptoms go, because they assume they were somehow duped by such convincing stuff. It was convincing stuff because, to the sufferer, it was *real*.

The danger, once the family knows about the depressive's bodily symptoms, is that they'll put everything down to depression. Then one day he or she will get a terrible stomach ache and everyone will ignore a burst appendix. Having a mental illness does not preclude having a physical one too – a depressed middle-aged man is just as entitled to have angina as his non-depressed brother.

So what can you do? Once the doctor has put your mind at rest that the symptoms are caused by the depression, the best thing to do is go along with and help the person as if the symptoms came from bodily (as opposed to mental) sources.

Cruel remarks about it being 'all in the mind' don't help suffering depressives one bit. Love and attention are what they need and this is one time when you should give both. As you do so, and as the depression lifts, these previously crippling physical complaints lift as if by magic.

Tiredness and weakness

Many depressed people complain that the slightest effort exhausts them and that it's because of this that they sit around so much. The very nature of depression is that everything about them slows down. Their thinking, feelings, actions, emotions and so on are all dampened down – in serious depression to the point of complete inactivity. This tiredness, weakness and slowness may become so serious that they can't even chew their food. At this stage in-patient hospital treatment will be needed. This retarded state of depression is called *catatonia*. In its most severe form, the depressed person is in a stupor, doesn't move, stares fixedly into space, doesn't respond on being addressed and is barely conscious. If ever a depressed person you know gets like this, tell the doctor at once.

What to do: The vast majority of depressives never get as far as catatonia, but are nonetheless slowed down, tired and weak. They need understanding and help because they are so over-whelmed by their tiredness that they can't help themselves. Try to stimulate them by engaging them in conversation on a topic they're interested in. Don't bully them to express an opinion or an interest in something they clearly don't care for and be guided by what they want to talk about. Gradually, you may stimulate a spark of interest which can be built on.

A 'shut down' commonly occurs in depression caused by a loss of some kind. This is much easier to deal with from your point of view because it's so much easier to sympathize with someone who is bereaved, for example. But there's a danger of feather-bedding the bereaved person if your caring goes on for more than a few weeks after the loss. Some people wallow in their loss and let everybody else run around for them, when they really should be grieving the loss and coming to terms with it. Everybody takes a different time to come out of this slowed down, miserable period after a loss, so be guided by the individual's needs.

With people who are tired, weak and slowed down the onus has to be on you, the well one, to generate activities that will keep them interested. Try to create a daily routine and stick to it. This will give depressives a central 'core' to the day and fixed points to aim for. By making depressed people feel wanted and needed, you'll engage them in some useful purpose and they'll forget their tiredness for a while. The depressed person who feels needed and valued is less likely to be unacceptably incapacitated by weakness and tiredness.

Delusions

These are false beliefs which have no basis in reality. They are not common in depression, but when they do occur they can be very persistent and disabling. Delusions are a serious symptom of depression and need to be treated at once.

There are many kinds of delusions in depression. Some are paranoid delusions, in which people think that someone or something is trying to harm them. Beings from outer space beaming harmful rays, gas seeping under the bedroom door and radio and TV news items that are about them are not uncommon examples of paranoid delusions. Paranoid people can be very plausible and will link true facts of their illness to these obviously bizarre ideas. Such people often refuse medical treatment because 'it could be poison'.

Another form of delusion is one of guilt. Guilt is often an integral part of depression anyway, but in guilt delusions the original guilt content is not based on reality. Most normally depressed people have good reason (at least in their own minds) for interpreting certain past events in a way that produces guilt feelings. The deluded person on the other hand will, unconsciously, *create* sources of guilt. Such people are often very proper, moral and rigid in normal life and will invent some moral flaw in order to explain their illness. They need to feel they are being punished for past sins and will seek confirmation from you that they are wretched sinners, unworthy of your attention and love. Of course, you, your relatives and friends will realize that they are chastizing themselves unnecessarily and won't punish them in the way they want.

What to do: First of all, never try to talk depressives out of their delusions – you won't succeed. They are not in touch with reality, have become seriously mentally ill and will not be influenced by what you say. In fact, they actually gain some strength from their delusions, which provide them with explanations and anchorage points in their sea of depression. To depressives, their delusions are very real and if you try to remove them they may not be able to survive. Leave the handling of this difficult business to professionals: there is no room for kitchen table psychiatry at this stage of the disease.

Second, don't let them do anything about their delusions. Keep a careful watch whilst medical help is on the way. Most people who have delusions will need hospital in-patient care.

So much for the specific symptoms of depression and how to help someone over them. But what can one do for oneself, in general terms, for depression?

First, it is often advised (and people find it works) that depressed people involve themselves in some kind of social or physical activity. This can take them out of themselves and so help them become less self-absorbed. Clearly, this does nothing to cure the underlying depression but it *can* work wonders, especially in reactive depressions. Helping others is a good way of taking your mind off yourself and can often do the trick.

Most depressives have a considerable amount of inwardly-directed anger, anger that should have been vented elsewhere. Getting rid of this anger can be very valuable, but can be difficult to do. If you are depressed, simply telling someone about what makes you angry can be very therapeutic and many psychotherapists use this technique to allow their clients to let off steam, perhaps for the first time in their lives. Anger can also be channelled into constructive outlets and need not be turned inwards. A good therapist will have ideas specific to you and your situation as to how to achieve this.

Many depressives are riddled with guilt, often on matters over which they have little or no control. This guilt soon leads to self-hate. One of the most important things in overcoming depression is to learn, or relearn, how to love yourself again. Depressives feel unloved and unlovable and those around them have a difficult task making them feel worthy of the world. Forgiving ourselves is even harder than seeking the forgiveness of others, because we tend to set ourselves higher standards than others do. Until you can get back to loving yourself, you'll never be free of your depression.

Far too many Western people are intensely 'private', overly concerned about what others may feel or say – and as a result hardly ever open up, even to their closest friends. We all need to accept our emotions more readily, to accept that it's in the nature of people to lose sometimes, to grieve, to mourn and to be sad. We could all do with more of the emotional honesty that is found in many cultures around the world. This involves sharing our feelings with those we can trust. Simply sharing can be of positive value and it's often surprising how helpful the most unlikely person can be. It's difficult for most of us to admit that we're vulnerable, until, that is, we realise that everyone else is just as vulnerable as we are. Even loving, married couples spend most of their lives talking *at* each other and not *with* each other. It's a sad fact that it can take a major crisis like a depression within a marriage to get a couple talking on subjects of real importance, perhaps for the first time in their marriage.

When it comes to helping each other, don't underestimate the importance of the self-help groups. Depressives Anonymous (see page 235 for their address) have local groups all over the country which meet to give mutual support to depressives. Contrary to popular belief, members of Depressives Anonymous don't sit around telling each other how miserable they are; they are there to give positive, often very practical help from their wealth of experience. MIND also has local groups, the addresses of which can be obtained from their headquarters in London (see page 236 for the address and telephone number).

In addition to all that's been said in this chapter, professional help should still play an important part in the management of depression. Psychotherapy, drug treatment or ECT can all actively reduce the symptoms but won't necessarily *cure* the underlying disease. Only the person affected and his or her family and friends can do that. A bottle of tablets won't mend a marriage and a course of ECT doesn't bring a family together.

The 'cure' for depression, of both its symptoms and its causes, must lie in more love. A feeling of being loved and wanting to love in return can make up for all those feelings of emptiness and low self-esteem that so dog the depressed. We're all lovable in some way to some people. Love is the great protector or, as Freud so aptly put it, 'In the final analysis, we must love in order not to fall ill'.

CHAPTER 4

Depression at certain times of life

Depression can, of course, strike at any age. There are, however, certain times when it is common, yet may not be recognized for what it is by doctors and lay people alike. The times of life when this is most likely to occur are during childhood, in adolescence, in middle age and in old age. Let's look at each in turn.

Depression in childhood

This is a very difficult subject and is one which causes great conflict among those who deal with or study depression in children. On the one hand there are those who feel that there's no such thing as childhood depression and, on the other, there are those who are convinced that it is common. One of the problems is that children don't have the same signs and symptoms of depression as do adults. But as the distinguished British paediatrician Dr John Apley has said, 'childhood can neither be understood nor taught by extrapolating back from adults', and nowhere is this more true than when dealing with depression. The other problem is that, even among children as a group, depression manifests itself differently according to the child's stage of development, age and degree of attachment to its mother.

In the first few weeks of life the baby's emotions are mainly expressed in a negative way – it cries when things go wrong. As the months go by the baby continues to let its mother (or mother substitute) know when things aren't going the way it wants, by crying. At some time in the first six months, a baby becomes capable of distinguishing its mother from other people and from this time it becomes anxious if she isn't there. Such anxiety is often accompanied by obvious sadness and misery. As the infant becomes increasingly more demanding of its mother's attention it also gets frustrated and angry when she doesn't respond. This anger is often accompanied by sadness and anxiety.

All through their development, children are very greatly influenced by their mother and her moods. A considerable amount of research has shown that young children of depressed mothers are more likely to become depressed as children and that depressed adults, when asked about their early childhood, are more likely than average to report poor parenting because of mental ill health in their parents (usually the mother). It's easy to understand that small children could 'model' themselves on their depressed mother and to see how a slowed down, apathetic, apparently non-caring mother could deprive a young child of emotional warmth. Some children reared in a normal family, but with a depressed mother, end up behaving just like those reared in an institution. They want a lot of body contact, are very inhibited socially and can't form lasting relationships. Studies have shown that depressed mothers have a profound effect on their children, so it's not surprising that such children are more at risk emotionally. One major study, for example, found that depressed women were excessively involved in their children's daily lives, had difficulty in communicating with them and were only too aware that they had stopped being affectionate towards them. Over half of the children of such mothers had school behaviour problems. Even quite small children become depressed if their mothers are depressed, often because they feel somehow responsible for their mother's low mood and can never please her. The depressed mother is also given to extremes of unpredictable mood-swings which further perplex the child.

A quarter of a century ago, Bowlby's research on children separated from their mothers set the scene for our modern understanding of childhood depression. He found that infants separated from their mothers in institutions became miserable, expressionless and withdrawn, all symptoms close to those of adult depression. But although this has been widely recognized and accepted as a type of depressive reaction, just how depression manifests itself in later childhood cannot be agreed upon. There is no accepted definition of childhood depression; the diagnosis is usually made from the clinical impression the doctor gets when talking to the child and family.

Overt depression is extremely rare in children, but many experts think that a kind of 'masked' depression is very common. Signs and symptoms of such depressions in very young children are thought to include irritability, a short attention span, sleep difficulties, colic, temper tantrums, bed wetting, certain allergies, clumsiness and fretfulness. The classical adult-type signs and symptoms of depression, including sadness, are often not present.

Later on in childhood, depressive illness may first show itself as a refusal to go to school or in the form of other misbehaviour such as aggressiveness, stealing or truancy. At this age, though, bodily symptoms tend to predominate and poor appetite, headaches, excessive crying, loss of weight, sleep difficulties and abdominal pains are very common symptoms of depression. Just how important these physical symptoms can be is shown in a pair of research studies, each of 100 children with recurrent abdominal pains. In only eight per cent and six per cent respectively was any physical cause ever found for the pains.

Conduct disorders can be difficult to distinguish from emotional disorders in children, but do differ in a number of ways. Conduct disorders are very much more common in boys, whereas emotional disorders occur with equal frequency in both sexes. Boys with conduct disorders have a high rate of educational problems; those with emotional problems don't. Children with emotional problems usually become socially well-adapted in later life, whereas those with conduct problems don't. Both groups of children are equally miserable and sad.

Sadness in children is a difficult emotion to assess, for both the parents and doctors. Several leading researchers in the field see sad children as very different in important ways from normal ones, but whether or not they are depressed is difficult to say. Very tense, miserable children may lash out when provoked and may find themselves in a lot of trouble as their behaviour becomes increasingly antisocial. Such children can end up in custodial care of some kind if their depression isn't recognized. Having said this though, it isn't unusual to find depressive symptoms and sadness in children with disorders that are not depression. Children with learning problems, hyperactivity and even behaviour problems are known to have poor self-esteem and to feel sad a lot of the time.

Quite often, depressed children are 'loners' who can't enjoy playing and doing things with other children. Sometimes these children are profoundly miserable and at other times they tease and behave sadistically towards their peers. In some children an abrupt shift in behaviour may suggest depression. A previously alert child who suddenly becomes withdrawn, apathetic and unable to study may be getting depressed. Some depressed children are hyperactive (overactive), but whether this is a parallel to adult mania (see page 36) isn't known.

Bereavement, separation from the parents, or illness in a parent can cause depression in children in a parallel way to that experienced by adults. Separation from other members of the family and from the peer group can also adversely affect a child emotionally. Some children are depressed when they move away from a close friend. As we have seen, depression or mental illness in a mother can also separate her from her child. In many cases, there is a long gap between the loss of the key person in the child's life and the onset of depression.

Just how depression in childhood should be treated is not known. Some experts are convinced that anti-depressant drugs are of use and others feel they should be absolutely forbidden for children.

Almost certainly, the best treatment is family therapy of some kind. Most of these children need more love and attention within the family and a general practitioner, child psychiatrist, psychologist or paediatrician can often try to get something moving in this direction. Very often the problems lie with parents who are unable to give their children the support and love they need and, as with so many family problems, the child may never really develop to full potential as long as he or she remains at home. Temperamental and personality incompatibilities occur in families just as in other groups and, very often, these are not capable of resolution. It has been shown that excessively strict and uncompromising standards give a child a feeling of hopelessness and helplessness because she or he can never match up to parental standards. Repeated tellings-off reaffirm the child's feeling of being unworthy of parental love and that whatever he or she does will be a disappointment to them. Some children respond to this type of upbringing by becoming excessively industrious 'goodie-goodies', but deep down they are often depressed and feel inferior. Others interiorize their guilt and sense of unworthiness and carry it with them into adult life, when it can be triggered to a full-blown depression.

Even being a favourite child can backfire in emotional terms. Such children are often unconsciously fearful of arousing envy and jealousy in others and even develop a pattern of behaviour that involves drastically underselling themselves. The conflict between carrying the family banner and having to make everyone like them, at whatever personal cost, plays havoc with the child's emotions and this will often come out as depression eventually.

Perhaps the most encouraging finding in the context of 'crazy, mixed-up children' is that, even after a thirty-year follow-up of children attending a child guidance clinic, one researcher found that fewer than one per cent developed depression in later life.

Of course, children, just like adults, can become depressed because of an underlying physical disease process. Leukaemia, infectious diseases (the common childhood infections), diabetes, disorders of the pituitary gland, nutritional and vitamin deficiencies and serious physical disabilities can all produce depressions.

For a discussion of childhood suicide see page 215.

Depression in adolescence

Although depression can occur at any age, as we have seen, it is very frequently missed in adolescence or misdiagnosed as a physical, emotional or behavioural disorder. As a consequence, individuals continue longer in their suffering than necessary and are at a constant suicide risk. Suicide rates are rising among adolescents at a time when they are falling in other age groups, so this is clearly a serious problem. But having said this, the depressed adolescent can often be very difficult to recognize.

A family history of depression can often be helpful in bringing the diagnosis to mind at all, but it's usually a physical symptom (or many of them) that takes the adolescent to his or her doctor when depressed. Feeling tired, weak and run down are among the commonest complaints but insomnia, loss of appetite, abdominal pains, weight loss and constipation follow close behind.

Depressed adolescents complain of fatigue that isn't related to effort and they feel worse in the morning. Early morning waking is a problem but, rarely, oversleeping can also be a sign of depression. Noises in the ears, dizziness, flushing, visual disturbances, dryness of the mouth, numbness and tingling of the fingers and toes also occasionally occur as part of the picture.

As well as these varied physical symptoms, there are the emotional ones. Most depressed adolescents feel miserable, unconfident and have irrational phobias. Anxiety, fears, guilt, crying and desperation are not uncommon. Depressed adolescents often have difficulty expressing themselves and those around them realize that they're under par a lot of the time. Anxiety is almost always a feature of adolescent depression and many young people early on in the disease say that they feel something serious is about to happen to them.

All these emotions combine to make the adolescent irritable, hyperactive, aggressive and at times even delinquent. Depressed adolescents frequently become hostile to, or express hatred of, their parents and exaggerate their faults. Because of this clinical picture, some depressed adolescents are wrongly diagnosed as being schizophrenic and because some of them turn to drugs or alcohol as a way out of their misery they are labelled as 'alcoholics' or 'druggies'.

As their depression deepens, so adolescents find it increasingly difficult to concentrate and become very slow mentally. As the weeks go by, they lose interest in their hobbies and friends and don't feel it's worth doing anything. Everything becomes an effort until they can't be bothered to dress or keep themselves looking tidy. Eventually they have to force themselves to think and act. Slowly, they realize that they have become socially unacceptable and so withdraw from the family – often staying alone in their room for hours on end. Once things get this bad, the only way out of such a serious depression seems, to them, to be suicide. In the US, suicide is the second commonest cause of death among adolescents, with about 80,000 young people attempting suicide each year.

The classical clinical picture of depression as seen in adults is rare in adolescence, but as young people experience the biological changes of puberty and the stresses involved in growing away from their parents, pressures build up to predispose them to the adolescent type of depression. Ambivalent feelings can be very strong at the best of times in adolescence. They know deep down that they have to break away from childhood, yet they feel insecure with their new-found freedom and sense of power. It's often difficult to give up the security of childhood and its pleasures and many psychoanalysts theorize that it is the mourning for this lost childhood that is at the root of much adolescent depression. Many adolescents feel abandoned by their parents (though in fact they are not), and the hostility this arouses is reflected back, not on to the parents, whom they do not want to hurt, but on to themselves. This hostility may take the form of aggressiveness towards others or the seeking out of dangerous situations. Any activity, no matter how dangerous and potentially destructive, is seen as being preferable to facing an unacceptable self-image. Girls will sometimes become sexually promiscuous, tempting fate in relationships with men. Such depressed girls have problems with pregnancies and abortions, but adolescents of both sexes rebel against authority in ways such as these when they're depressed because they confuse obedience with a loss of selfhood. Cheating, lying, gambling and sexual roulette are all defences against their feelings of inferiority, and are an attempt to build up self-esteem at a time when it is very low.

Sexual activity in depressed adolescents can often be a frantic search for someone to care for them, but endless unsuitable partners eventually result in an even poorer self-image and, almost inevitably, a sense of loss at repeatedly being let down. It is in these circumstances that the depressed adolescent frequently tries to commit suicide. A failed interpersonal relationship is nearly always at the heart of teenage suicide attempts.

Treatment can be very successful once the condition is recognized for what it is. If a first-degree blood relative has been depressed and has reacted favourably to a particular anti-depressant drug, then the chances are that the adolescent will too, so it's worth trying this first. Some psychiatrists stop depressed girls taking the Pill while they are on anti-depressant drugs because the Pill accelerates the metabolism of tricyclic anti-depressants. If your doctor ever suggests that you come off the Pill, don't forget to take other precautions (if your depression hasn't completely killed your sex drive), because the last thing you'll want is to get pregnant.

Because depressed adolescents have so many social and family problems, it is often necessary for the doctor treating them to see the parents too. Once they realize that depression is the trouble they can frequently be of more help. This can be difficult because depressed adolescents so often have antagonized their parents by their extraordinary behaviour over months or years. Outside guidance from a clinic or a family doctor can often help teenagers re-integrate their lives and, with support from family and friends, they usually get better. There is some evidence that keeping adolescents busy and encouraging them to vent their normal adolescent aggressiveness in harmless pursuits can be useful. They'll also need practical, day-to-day help with difficulties at school, home and with friends of both sexes.

Adolescence is a difficult enough time for anyone going through it, but to be depressed as well is a real, additional burden. Experts dealing with depressed teenagers are impressed by their insatiable need for love. Unfortunately, rebellious teenagers often don't make themselves instantly lovable; so the onus is on adults to make even greater efforts than normal, and this can take some doing.

Depression in middle age

Middle age is an eventful time for most couples, and indeed for single people too. It's a time when we take stock of ourselves and our achievements, as well as being a time of hormonal changes.

In women, the menopause occurs on average about the age of forty-nine, but the cessation of periods can occur at any time from the early forties to the mid-fifties. Menopausal symptoms such as hot flushes, palpitation, sweating and psychological changes are common and a small fraction of women become depressed as a result of or as a part of them. This is also a time when many women have their uterus removed (hysterectomy), and this in itself can cause depression.

Whether men have a similar menopause is not known. Certainly men undergo psychological and emotional changes at this time of life, but there is little evidence that these are caused by hormonal changes as in their female counterparts.

Women are most at risk of suffering from middle age depression between the ages of forty-five and fifty-six; whilst men tend to be at greatest risk in their early and mid-sixties.

A lot of changes are going on in middle age, and it's a tough time for many people. Many of those who reach their forties and haven't got married, for example, see themselves as unlikely to do so and begin to fear a life of loneliness and self-centredness. Up until this time they could make all kinds of excuses to themselves about 'work coming first' and so on, but in the forties reality begins to hit them and this can produce a depressive reaction which can eventually become a full-blown depression.

Some people reach middle age without really having 'got their act together', and the realization that they haven't come to terms with their own personality, their sexuality and their role in life, for example, can come very hard – particularly when they realize they're on the downhill slope of life. Most of us experience feelings like this at some time in middle age, but additional trigger factors can tip any of us into a full blown depression.

For married couples (and that's most of us in our society), middle age can be a difficult time of readjustment. Children are usually in their adolescence by this time and this is a trying period for parents, especially in today's society which has so changed in its values compared with when they were teenagers.

Many men find that after having battled for years to make their way in the world they are often at their most successful in middle age. Ironically, this can bring domestic uneasiness because children who saw little of their father as they were growing up resent him suddenly being interested in, and having time for, them in their adolescence. This produces pressures on the father who had, in his eyes, been doing his best for them all along.

Middle age is also the time when children leave the nest and this can be especially painful for their mothers. Unfortunately, today's society makes this process more unpleasant than it need be, because when children leave home they don't go to live down the road. Most parents lose their children in a very final way the day they leave home. Today's youngsters often go to college or university a long way away, feel the pressure from their peers to live in flats and digs and rarely stay at home until they get married as was the case a generation ago. Today's mother knows that the chances are higher than ever that her child will marry someone who'll 'take' her child far away from her and, indeed, very large numbers of young people are actually emigrating, both before and after marriage. All this makes middle age a time of loss for many parents – and loss is a key factor in depression.

Middle age can also be a time of trial for a couple's marriage. Some couples are just as much in love in middle age as they ever were, and others, who are not, have settled down to a stable relationship that has few ups and downs. After twenty years together most couples have got to a stage in which they can happily co-exist, but as their children leave home many couples find that they have little in common and that it was the children who had cemented their relationship for years. The realization that this is so can be very depressing, especially if they now find their spouses relatively unattractive for some reason. It is at this time that some men begin to flirt or experiment with extra-marital relationships for the first time. Not only do they feel that life (and in particular their attractiveness to women) might be passing them by, but they also resent that, because society is now so much more liberated, they didn't have such opportunities in their youth – and so try to capture a little of it for themselves. This often happens at a time when the wife is going through the menopause and isn't feeling at her most capable in the attractiveness stakes. Thus the scene is set for marital disharmony and depression.

It's an undeniable fact that a couple who have striven for years to buy a house, to set up a home, to get on at work, to bring up a family and so on, begin to have time to themselves in middle age, often for the first time since they were in the intoxicating throes of 'being in love'. Because so many middle aged couples have spent the last twenty years slowly growing apart, they cannot easily enjoy this new-found freedom together, since their relationship has badly deteriorated. Sexual boredom, too, can set in or become more obvious at this time and this, coupled with all the other negatives, reduces the quality of life of many middle aged couples in a way that lays them wide open to depression.

For a few successful men, middle age can be a very stressful time at work. Even if a man has been highly successful, he can become depressed (see page 87) as he questions his success and what it cost him in personal terms to get there. This is a period when men see their children growing up and wonder where their childhood went. They have missed it all because they were working so hard and now regret the loss. Some successful men can't cope with too much success because they feel insecure. After all, if you're at the top at fifty, where can you go but down over the next fifteen years until retirement? This can produce stresses and strains which, combined with domestic unease, can produce depression.

Most people, though, have the opposite problem. They suddenly realize that the world is *not* their oyster and that they've reached their natural level in society and are likely to stay there until they retire. Dreams of their own business, of a directorship, or whatever, fade fast as younger men are promoted over them and the next twenty years in the same job with little to excite them looms up. In today's cut and thrust society, a lot of middle aged men find themselves retired prematurely or made redundant by their companies. This can be a very bitter pill to swallow for someone who thought he would be productive for many years to come. Early retirement is not everyone's idea of heaven, as we saw on page 92.

So middle age can be a difficult time and one when a couple is thrown back together on what they see as the downhill run to ageing and death. Middle age can, and should be, a wonderful, fulfilling time but for many it doesn't turn out to be so and because of all the changes that are going on depression is very likely to occur. When it does occur, it may not be in a 'classical' form that everyone recognizes. This is a problem, because the depression may be missed and the person may die by his or her own hand.

Depression in middle age manifests itself in many forms, especially in men. Women tend to go down with emotional and psychological symptoms which are recognized and treated with varying degrees of success by the medical profession. Depressed middle aged men, though, often take to drink, gambling or extra-marital sex as a way of deadening the mental pain. In fact, I'd go so far as to say that any middle aged man who starts gambling, drinking or entering into promiscuous sexual relationships around middle age needs medical assessment to see if he's really depressed underneath it all. The drinking, gambling and sex can all bring very real problems in their own right, and all too often the family gets wrapped up in the outcome of these pursuits. Very rarely does anyone look for a cause – often until it's too late. So, if a middle aged relative of yours ever shows signs of any of the activities mentioned above *for the first time*, take them seriously and get help.

Depression in old age

A healthy man's natural life potential is probably around 110 years according to some experts, and today many of us are getting near that as average life expectancy reaches the 80 mark. Of the three thousand million people on the earth today, approximately 200 million are over the age of sixty and people over sixty make up 13 per cent of the population of Europe, for example.

Psychiatric illness in the elderly is common and is becoming more so. During the first half of this century, a four-fold increase in the number of people over fifty-five (in the USA) was associated with a nine-fold increase in first admissions to mental hospitals in this age group. Why this should be the case isn't known, but social changes that increasingly exclude the elderly from the mainstream of family life and society cannot be helping the situation.

From about the age of eighteen we all start ageing. But ageing isn't a disease, and produces no symptoms as such. It's disease processes that produce symptoms and disabilities and by no means everyone gets diseases – at least outside the western world. The old music hall joke about 'wanting to die healthy' produces a laugh because we erroneously associate death with disease. Many millions of old people die each year all over the world, not of diseases but of old age. In the West we have become so disease-ridden, partly because of our lifestyle, that it is rare for old people to live out their full life span, simply because disease prevents them from doing so.

Normal, healthy elderly people are sensible, have no symptoms, get about on their own and live happily until they die from old age. The fact that this picture is increasingly rare does not detract from its validity.

As the elderly brain ages, cells are lost at a rate of about 100,000 a day. This may seem a lot but in fact isn't, because there are billions more left, even at death. The death of these cells does not cause mental disease in the elderly. All psychiatric illness in the elderly is caused either by circumstances that would make the rest of us depressed, or is produced by diseases that affect the normal working of the brain. There is no room here to look at all the possible mental and emotional disorders that occur in old people, so let's confine ourselves to depression.

Depression is very common in old age. In fact, just as in younger people, it is the commonest emotional disorder. About one in ten people over sixty-five will suffer from depression at some time. Usually, it's because of a build up of circumstances. Old age is a time of compounding losses. Loss of job (retirement), loss of friends or spouse through death, loss of companionship, financial loss and loss of faculties (eyesight and hearing especially) can all add up to produce a genuinely depressing situation. Of course a fair proportion of those who become depressed in old age bring with them their personality problems, marital disharmonies and other longstanding difficulties, that might just flare up under the stress of the commonly experienced 'losses' of old age. Old people complain of exactly the same things when they're depressed as do younger people, but the explanation is often slightly different.

The problem for doctors and relatives is that most old people in the West have degenerative disease of their arteries, a condition that affects the blood supply to their brains. This reduced blood supply produces signs and symptoms that are labelled as 'senility', and the mental, emotional and physical changes that go hand in hand with this condition can confuse or mask an underlying depression. This is at the least a pity, because depression in the elderly can often be treated very satisfactorily, and at the worst a tragedy, because many of the depressed elderly kill themselves.

The majority of elderly depressed people feel at their worst in the early morning. They can't get up, feel the world isn't worth getting up for and that everything is gloomy and hopeless. At this time of the day everything seems pointless and time appears endless. Most old people do not, however, say they are depressed.

Another common depressive symptom in the elderly is that they slow down. They complain that everything is an effort, find that they spend increasing amounts of the day sitting in the same place, can't even be bothered to go to the lavatory (and so appear to be incontinent when they in fact are not), and can't be bothered to exercise their minds either. Their mental activity becomes so slowed that they may not even know what day of the week it is, and anyway usually couldn't care less.

Feelings of guilt and unworthiness are also very common. They wonder what they could have done to have brought such a thing upon themselves, blame themselves for past events and omissions, imagine that they have done awful things to others and eventually may even try to kill themselves in a fit of worthlessness.

But it's the bodily (hypochondriacal) symptoms that often predominate in depression in the elderly. These can be a worry to the rest of the family because they can't imagine what's happening. A depressed old lady is filled with the dreadfulness of life and spends a lot of time brooding over things that seem to indicate to her that there is a general 'deterioration of her body'. She'll complain of stomach rumbling, constipation, poor sleep, poor appetite, headaches, pains all over the place and many other things. The weakness and endless tiredness she experiences confirm to her that she's 'going to pieces'. Because of our conditioning in the western world, which makes us forge an unreasonable link between old people and disease, we are only too willing to ignore many of these symptoms and to put them down to 'old age'. Such old people sometimes get labelled as demented (a condition that can be caused by degenerative disease in the brain), though just because twenty per cent of those over eighty *are* demented, it certainly doesn't mean that everything that goes wrong with anyone over sixty can be put down to dementia.

To be realistic, though, old people today tend to have several diseases and it is these that complicate both the diagnosis and treatment of depression. Degenerative changes in the arteries cause them to 'silt up' with atheroma and to harden. This produces angina when it affects the heart's arteries, pain on walking when it affects the legs' arteries and mental changes when the brain is deprived of blood.

When it comes to the treatment of depression, the elderly present special problems because their bodies aren't functioning quite as well as those of a younger person. Kidney and liver function slows down with ageing and degenerative disease in the arteries all over the body can produce other problems with treatment.

Some old people are forgetful, they may be deaf or blind and even mild degenerative brain damage makes it difficult for them to understand what they are being asked to do. All this means that drugs are often not taken properly by the aged and that, as a result, their depressions don't respond as well as they should. Relatives and friends can be of great help here in ensuring that any prescribed drugs are taken regularly and in the correct dose. As many old people are on several drugs for various other conditions, there is an increased risk of interactions occurring between the anti-depressant medication and other things they're taking. For a discussion of the interactions of various drugs with the anti-depressants see page 149.

Some side-effects of anti-depressants are especially troublesome in the aged, possibly because they are more sensitive to the drugs. Dryness of the mouth is a common complaint, blurring of vision is not uncommon and a build up of urine can occur in old men who have an existing enlargement of the prostate. Constipation occurs fairly frequently and a low blood pressure on standing (or getting out of the bath) is not uncommon. The heart rate and pulse can be affected, producing dizziness, but this is not related to posture. The amount of body fluid in the tissues can increase, causing swollen ankles and a bloated abdomen. Difficulty in focussing the eyes can be a nuisance and excessive sweating can be unpleasant. Some men find they don't ejaculate normally. If ever you have any of these side-effects it's best to tell your doctor, because the blood pressure, heart rate and urine ones need treating.

In ill old people, dehydration is always a risk, and depressed old people are especially at risk because they sometimes can't be bothered to eat or drink. This can produce an acute onset of confusion resembling dementia.

Anti-depressant drugs and ECT are the mainstay of the treatment of depression in the elderly, with drugs usually being tried first. They are most effective in severe depression and can produce dramatic results. ECT acts more quickly than drugs but, two months after the start of the treatment, both are seen to be equally effective. ECT can produce confusion and memory loss in the elderly (see page 184) and because of this some psychiatrists think it inadvisable to use it unless drugs haven't worked, or unless the person is in danger of committing suicide.

But drugs and ECT are only a part of the treatment of depression in the elderly. Depressed old people need a lot of help and backup from their family and friends. Unfortunately they rarely get it. Their friends have often died and their family may be far away. This throws a tremendous burden on to the health and social services. Poverty, bereavement and isolation are all powerful causes of depression at any age, but are especially so in the elderly. Any and every helping agency should be enlisted to ensure that at least some of the underlying causes of the depression are sorted out if at all possible. Drugs and ECT don't cure loneliness or a feeling of being rejected by one's family, but there *are* other ways of overcoming these problems. Voluntary organizations, meals-on-wheels, old people's outings and local geriatric day centres can all be of practical help as the worst of the depression lifts.

Having a depressed elderly relative is never easy, but as we have seen, there are a few ways of easing the load for you and your relative. Unfortunately, many depressed old people are treated very badly by their relatives and health professionals.

141

There is no reason to assume that because someone is depressed he or she is suddenly reduced to the level of an idiot. Take the trouble to explain what's happening and make sure that what is being done to help the depressive is clearly explained to him or her. Drugs and ECT produce fears and problems enough for the younger person, but the elderly depressed person needs even more reassurance. The subjects of drugs and ECT are discussed in detail in chapters five and six respectively. Help the depressed person to take the prescribed drugs regularly and keep an eye out for side-effects which the sufferer may be too depressed to report. Never hesitate to contact the person's doctor if you are at all worried.

Explaining the old person's condition to the rest of the family and to friends is also helpful. There's no reason why people should get the wrong idea about what's happening, or that the old person should be 'written off' by friends and relatives simply because he or she is depressed. Take a sympathetic but firm line, letting them run their lives along substantially the lines they want, but always encouraging them to do just that little bit more to help themselves and to see the world in a positive way. If the person is deluded (has convincing but unrealistic false ideas that won't leave them), don't go along with them and pretend that they are right. This is cruel. Either remain neutral or quietly restate the facts as they are, without getting into a battle over the matter.

Depression can be crippling at any age, but is especially so in old age when people's resources are depleted and they are fighting a losing battle on many health and social fronts. Old people with mental illness are often thought of as beyond help. This is generally untrue, but is especially so in the case of depression which can, if anything, be more effectively treated in old age than at other times.

CHAPTER 5
Drug treatments for depression

Drugs for the treatment of emotional and psychological
problems are not new – they have been used for thousands of
years. In the early days most were, of course, of herbal origin
but today's medicines are almost all synthetic.

The history of really effective synthetic psychoactive
(acting on the brain) compounds is very short, as the majority
of them were introduced in the mid-1950s. The first drug to be
used for mental illness was the tranquillizer chlorpromazine
(Largactil), which was first used in the early 1950s. This
spawned a new group of tranquillizers called the phenothiazines and it was this group of drugs that very largely resulted in
the Mental Health Act of 1959; because once patients could be
calmed and the most alarming signs of mental illness
suppressed, mental hospitals were transformed from disturbing 'institutions' into places more like other hospitals. Their
discovery also meant that many people for whom mental
hospital would have been the only answer were able to live
near-normal lives in the community. The physical restraint
needed to control the more bizarre behaviour exhibited by
some patients disappeared virtually overnight, as the tranquillizers did for mental illness what the antibiotics had done
for infections.

Since the 1950s, the drug treatment of mental illness has
become one of the major growth areas of the western
pharmaceutical industry. It has been calculated that five
million people in the UK receive twenty-five million
prescriptions annually between them for psychiatric drugs, at
a cost to the country of over twenty-five million pounds. This
may well have got out of hand in the treatment of various
emotional states, but in this chapter we'll confine ourselves to

the drug treatment of depression itself.

Once a doctor has made the diagnosis of depression there are three families of drugs that he can prescribe. Within each family there are many different members, each with its own advantages, disadvantages, cost, safety and so on. The three families are the tranquillizers, the sleeping tablets and the anti-depressants themselves. Let's look at each in turn.

Tranquillizers (sedatives)

These drugs, as the name suggests, make the person calm. They reduce nervous tension and relax the person, both of which can be valuable properties in the treatment of depression – a condition often accompanied by anxiety, fear and anger.

If a powerful sedative is needed for severely mentally disturbed people then chlorpromazine is still the most widely used. Its calming effect comes on very quickly (in about half an hour) and lasts for about eight hours. The treatment should be continued as directed by the doctor and should probably not be discontinued abruptly, but gradually tailed off.

The most commonly used drugs in this group of powerful tranquillizers are:

Generic name	Proprietary name
Chlorpromazine	Largactil
Trifluoperazine	Stelazine, Amylozine, Expansyl, Stelabid
Thioridazine	Melleril

They are usually given in the form of tablets or syrups but, since 1961, long-acting (depot) versions of this group have been available as injections. These injections are used once the acute phase of the illness is over and consequently people can go home quickly and don't have to remember to take tablets. Because they have to return to the clinic or hospital to have further depot injections, they also keep in contact with the doctors looking after them and this can be helpful in itself.

This phenothiazine group of drugs is used only in the most acute and severe stages of depression and none of them has any anti-depressant activity in itself. Side-effects include stiffness

144

of the neck and limbs, drowsiness and lethargy, weight gain, loss of sex drive, skin sensitivity to light and, rarely, jaundice.

Depression isn't usually so severe that major sedatives or tranquillizers are needed, but the *less powerful tranquillizers* are very commonly used, especially for the treatment of reactive depression. The drug treatment of depression should depend entirely on making an accurate diagnosis, because experience has shown that endogenous depressives (see page 26) fare very much better than do reactive depressives when treated with anti-depressant drugs. Because of this, many doctors never use true anti-depressant drugs in reactive depressions, but rather give the upset, anxious and depressed person a tranquillizer to help patients over their immediate problems. As reactive depressives account for about three-quarters of all depressives, the tranquillizers are very widely used indeed. They are also used in the treatment of all kinds of stress and anxiety reactions, as well as for true reactive depression. Because of the wide availability of these tranquillizers, most people with mild and reactive depressions never need to go any further than their general practitioners for satisfactory treatment.

The commonest drugs in this group are:

Generic name	Proprietary name
Chlordiazepoxide	Librium, Calmoden, Libraxin, Limbitrol, Tropium
Diazepam	Valium, Atensine
Lorazepam	Ativan
Medazepam	Nobrium
Oxazepam	Serenid-D
Chlormethiazole	Hemineverin
Meprobamate	Equanil, Equagesic, Milonorm, Miltown, Tenavoid

They all produce relaxation, reduce or abolish fear and anxiety and are also useful in treating obsessions, tension and phobias. Some have a particular advantage when treating certain symptoms and the doctor will try to prescribe the most appropriate one for any given condition. As anxiety is so commonly a part of depression, these drugs are very widely used, sometimes in combination with anti-depressants.

Side-effects are many, but are often not a problem in practice. They *can* produce troublesome side-effects though if taken in combination with tricyclic anti-depressants or alcohol. The more minor side-effects include constipation, confusion, headaches, rashes, nausea, drowsiness, dizziness and apathy. Many experts are concerned that with prolonged use Valium, for example, can be addictive. This is occasionally a physical addiction (as with heroin or other 'hard' drugs), but is more commonly a form of psychological dependence – the person finds it difficult to cope with life without the drug.

Tranquillizers such as these should only be used as a short-term emotional crutch to tide people over a difficult period in their lives. Unfortunately, this is the counsel of perfection and many hundreds of thousands of people take them regularly, partly because their life, in their view, is one long problem or because, having become used to them, they find them hard to give up.

Properly used though, tranquillizers can be the only drug treatment that's necessary for the vast majority of people with mild depression. The drug's action produces calmness and serenity at a troubled time and, together with emotional support from family, friends and even perhaps the family doctor, should be enough to set the person back on a normal path. As long as this is how tranquillizers are used, there is no harm in them at all.

Sleeping tablets

Because sleep is disturbed as a part of the clinical picture of depression, many depressed people go to their doctors for sleeping tablets. Often, a tranquillizer (which does not in itself induce sleep) will calm people enough to let them sleep. Because of this, many doctors suggest that the daily dose of tranquillizer already being taken by such depressed patients be taken at such a time as to relax them in the evening so that they can sleep. It might also mean taking a dose before going to bed, but be guided by your doctor on this.

Sleeping pills, unlike tranquillizers, are designed to produce sleep. The danger with them is that once people have got used to them, they find it increasingly difficult to give them up. They feel they won't sleep properly without the pills and soon become fearful of lying awake. This in itself produces a vicious circle of fear of insomnia leading to actual insomnia. The other danger with sleeping pills is that of overdose. Not only are they dangerous when taken deliberately, but they can easily be taken by accident too. It is not generally known, but sleeping tablets produce confusion before they induce sleep and in this confused state many people have reached out to their bedside tables and taken another dose of the tablets, sometimes with serious results. Because of this, it's wise to take your sleeping tablets and then to lock the rest away safely, away from children and away from the bedside table.

The following are the most commonly used sleeping tablets:

Generic name	Proprietary name
Nitrazepam	Mogadon, Nitrados, Remnos, Somnased, Somnite
Flurazepam	Dalmane
Dichloralphenazone	Welldorm, Midrid
Glutethimide	Doriden
Barbiturates	Tuinal
	Amytal
	Nembutal
	Seconal
	Soneryl

Insofar as any sleeping pills are 'safe', Mogadon is the safest with Dalmane coming a close second. Barbiturate sleeping tablets are not prescribed as frequently as they used to be, because of the danger of addiction, their side-effects, and the complications that can follow their withdrawal. They are also very dangerous when taken in overdose or in combination with alcohol.

Anti-depressants

These are the drugs that most people think of as 'real' cures for depression. In fact, unless the right type of depression is being treated with the right drug, the results are quite disappointing, as we shall see. This group of drugs is of proven value in treating endogenous depression and manic-depression.

Tricyclic anti-depressants

This is a family of drugs, the 'parents' of which were discovered

147

in the late 1950s. They are called tricyclic because their chemical structure has three rings in it. More recently, tetracyclic compounds have been found to have some advantages over their tricyclic brothers. Because they have a chemical similarity, they all behave similarly in the body but each has individual properties that can be used with advantage in patients with particular problems.

The first of the family was imipramine and it was soon found to be useful in endogenous depression.

The most commonly used drugs in this group are:

Generic name	Proprietary name
Imipramine	Tofranil, Berkomine, Norpramine
Amitriptyline hydrochloride	Tryptizol, Lentizol, Domical, Saroten, Limbitrol, Triptafen
Clomipramine	Anafranil
Trimipramine	Surmontil
Dothiepin	Prothiaden

There are many others, but they are all similar to or modifications of the drugs on this list.

All tricyclic anti-depressants take one to three weeks to produce their anti-depressant effects and can take even longer in some people. Because of this, it's absolutely essential to continue the medication until your doctor tells you to stop. If you cannot tolerate their side-effects (see below), tell him and he'll try another drug in the same family. The same problem exists when discontinuing these compounds. The side-effects can take nearly as long to disappear as the positive effects did to build up.

Amitriptyline closely resembles imipramine in its activity, but also has mild tranquillizing properties (imipramine has stimulant properties). Occasionally amitriptyline is given by injection.

Nortriptyline (Aventyl) is one of the metabolites of amitriptyline in the body and has similar effects. *Desipramine* (Pertofran) is a metabolite of imipramine and, like it, is also a stimulant. *Protriptyline* is relatively rapid in onset but again is stimulating and thus not very good if the depression is accompanied by anxiety and tension.

148

Trimipramine has the advantage of being able to be given by slow intravenous infusion in a drip to control severe depression promptly. *Doxepin* (Sinequan) and dothiepin are useful because they also have tranquillizing effects.

Side-effects are a major problem with tricyclic anti-depressants. At least one patient in five suffers with them and this is probably the main factor which leads up to sixty per cent of people to stop taking the drugs altogether, or to take them in a reduced (and often ineffective) dose. Any tricyclics can produce dryness of the mouth, drowsiness, fuzzy thinking, low blood pressure on standing, blurred vision, constipation, weight gain and sexual disturbances and in large doses they can produce strange tremors, shaking and other involuntary movements. Some people also become sleepless on these drugs. Some of these side-effects can be countered with other drugs, but it's usually thought wise to try another tricyclic compound.

A more serious side-effect, especially in the elderly, is that on the heart. Tricyclics can produce odd heart beat rhythms, but they are generally not serious. If you have a heart disease or have ever had any abnormality of heart rhythm, it's safer to tell your doctor before he starts you on any anti-depressant. If you have recently had a heart attack, you should definitely not take them. Old people are far less tolerant of the side-effects of the tricyclics and experience problems at far lower doses than do younger people. Faintness on standing up, disturbances of vision and urinary obstruction (especially in elderly men with prostate trouble) are not at all uncommon and should be reported to the doctor at once if they occur. Tricyclics should not be given to people with glaucoma.

As far as we know, very little of these drugs gets through into the milk of a breast-feeding mother but if long-term therapy is necessary some centres would monitor the drug's blood level in the infant just for safety. Tricyclics seem to be perfectly safe when taken in pregnancy, except perhaps in the earliest months. It is generally agreed that children under the age of eight should not receive tricyclic anti-depressants.

Drug interactions are increasingly being recognized as a potential hazard with this group of drugs and, partly because of this, the early enthusiasm which surrounded the anti-depressant drugs is being modified. Because they reduce the mobility of the bowel they can affect the absorption of other drugs. A drug such as digoxin, for example, is better absorbed, while phenylbutazone absorption is delayed or reduced.

Tricyclics enhance the effects of anti-histamines and thyroxine and can produce toxicity with phenothiazine tranquillizers (see page 144).

They can displace anticoagulant drugs from their blood proteins and so produce bleeding in people taking these blood-thinning tablets. In epileptics who are taking anticonvulsants, tricyclics are liable to induce seizures, so calling for an increase in anti-epilepsy therapy. They produce effects antagonistic to the blood pressure-lowering drugs methyldopa (Aldomet) and guanethidine, even though the tricyclics themselves have blood pressure lowering effects. Smoking and big doses of vitamin C both reduce the effectiveness of the tricyclics while vitamin B6 does the opposite.

Ordinary doses of tricyclics can potentiate the effects of certain adrenaline-like substances. This is important for those who take proprietary cold preparations containing these substances, or for those having an adrenaline-containing local anaesthetic at the dentist.

There has been a lot of medical debate as to whether tricyclics should (or indeed can safely) be used in combination with another group of anti-depressants called mono-amine oxide inhibitors (MAOI's), but current opinion is that the dangers have been greatly overestimated. Some psychiatrists regularly use the two together in combination, with good results.

But the most important drug interaction is that occurring with alcohol. Alcohol in any form enhances the calming of the nervous system produced by tricyclics and so should not be taken at all. The combination of alcohol and these anti-depressants can change people from being totally capable and rational to being a danger to themselves and others, especially when driving.

The most dangerous disadvantage of the tricyclics is their slow speed of onset. Because it takes at least two weeks, and sometimes much longer, for the results to be felt, depressed people sometimes despair, stop taking them at all or alternatively take a large number of tablets at once. Anti-depressant tablets are now commonly used for committing suicide.

Some newer, quicker acting anti-depressants that are claimed to overcome many of the problems connected with the other tricyclics are:

Generic name	Proprietary name
Mianserin	Bolvidon, Norval
L-tryptophan	Pacitron
Maprotiline	Ludiomil

More experience is needed with these to be sure that they are a meaningful improvement on the tricyclics, but early trials and clinical experience seem hopeful.

Symptom relief with the tricyclics varies greatly from patient to patient and large numbers of people get no relief at all. Assuming they do work in a particular individual (and this will usually be someone with endogenous depression), anxiety and insomnia seem to disappear within a very few days of starting the treatment. Normal sleep patterns don't return for weeks, though. During the second or third week, the depressed person has more energy and at the same time there is less concern over bodily complaints. The depressed mood is often the last thing to go and can take three weeks or much longer (especially if, as is often the case, the dose of the drug has been inadequate). Disturbed sexual functioning also takes several weeks to get back to normal.

It's interesting that if one member of the family responds well to a certain drug then close blood relatives will probably do so too. It's a great help, therefore, to tell the doctor if any of your close family has had any good (or bad) experiences with a particular anti-depressant drug. It is a fact that men seem to respond better to anti-depressant drugs, but no one knows why.

The length of treatment varies considerably from patient to patient. If the depression seems to respond well to the therapy, then the drug can be withdrawn after a few weeks or months. If, as a result of this withdrawal, the depression doesn't return, the person can remain off drugs until the next episode of depression, if indeed there is one. On the other hand, people

151

with several episodes of depression behind them already, especially if each succeeding episode is more severe than the last, should probably go on long-term preventive drug therapy.

Doses for long-term prevention can be about half of those used in the acute stage of depression, but it is difficult to know how justifiable very long-term anti-depressant therapy is in many people. One survey among general practitioners' patients found that some of them had been on tricyclics for over ten years, often receiving repeat prescriptions and totally un-reviewed by the family doctor. Clearly, someone on long-term preventive lithium therapy cannot be ignored in this way (see pages 153-4), because the drug needs much more careful monitoring. Long-term therapy with anti-depressant drugs does not cause addiction.

It is unreasonable to assume that a tricyclic is ineffective in the treatment of endogenous depression, unless the drug has been given in a full dosage for at least three weeks. Far too many patients (and doctors) reject a drug because of its supposed failure, when in fact they haven't given it a chance to do the job. If the level of side-effects is so high that the person can't tolerate the drug, then another related compound should be tried.

Mono-amine oxidase inhibitors (MAOIs)

Even though MAOIs have been in continuous use for over twenty years, their role in the treatment of depression is still confused. Some doctors see them as a panacea, others as too dangerous to use. They only make up about three per cent of all drugs prescribed for depression.

Although they are used so little, they do seem to have a special place in the treatment of certain psychiatric conditions. These include some reactive and atypical depressions; depressive anxiety states, phobic anxiety, and certain phobic anxiety syndromes. Studies have shown that severely depressed out-patients do better on MAOIs than do similarly depressed in-patients. In spite of these and many other encouraging findings, many psychiatrists still see MAOIs as a last ditch therapeutic effort when other drugs have failed. It is usual to try tricyclics first, before starting on treatment with MAOIs.

The drugs most commonly used in this group are:

Generic name	Proprietary name
Isocarboxazid	Marplan
Phenelzine	Nardil
Nialamid	Niamid
Tranylcypromine	Parnate
Tranylypromine and Trifluoperazine	Parstelin

The main reason that these compounds haven't caught on is probably that by interfering with the enzyme that breaks down monoamines within the body, these build up and can then react dangerously with the amino acids in some common proteins. The most serious effects produced by this interaction are high blood pressure with severe headaches, breathlessness and even brain haemorrhages. The foods most likely to contain the amino acids that could precipitate such attacks are cheese, meat extracts, Marmite, beans, some pickled fish and alcohol. Cards are supplied to be given to each patient who is prescribed these drugs, but many people ignore the instructions because they don't understand how serious the outcome could be.

If you are on MAOIs you may find that other foods and drinks give you headaches. Should you ever make such a link, tell your doctor about it and then keep off that food or drink for the duration of the treatment. Always be sure to tell the admitting doctor or the anaesthetist that you are on MAOIs if ever you have to have an anaesthetic.

Lithium carbonate

The story of lithium is one of the few pieces of good news in the drug therapy of psychiatric illnesses. It is an effective cure for manic-depressive illness and can be used to prevent certain other types of depression.

Lithium carbonate is an inexpensive substance related to common table salt, but which acts very differently in the body. Its discovery by the Australian psychiatrist J F Cade in 1947 marked the start of a very remarkable treatment. Cade noted abnormalities in the elimination of uric acid in the urines of certain types of psychiatric patients. In order to study the possible effects of this substance on the body, he gave lithium urate (the most soluble of the salts of uric acid) to guinea pigs. He used a control substance, lithium carbonate, in his experiments so that he could tell whether it was the lithium part or the urate part that was causing the abnormal effects. To his amazement the animals which received the lithium carbonate became 'lethargic and unresponsive to treatment' in his own words, and were easily handled. After a few hours the animals became normally fearful again. Cade then gave lithium salts to several agitated and excited psychiatric patients and found that many improved dramatically. Several of his first series of ten patients had been hopeless cases. After lithium they were able to leave hospital.

At first these findings were greeted with enthusiasm, but it soon became clear that lithium salts were very toxic. Reports started circulating of heart patients who had substituted lithium chloride for common salt in their diets and had subsequently died of lithium poisoning.

It wasn't until the 1960s that lithium made a comeback and then it did so only because it became possible to measure the blood levels of the substance and so to prevent toxicity. Today, with careful monitoring, lithium salts are safely used in the treatment of agitated, hyperexcitable patients (those with mania) and there is good evidence to support the claim that they can delay or even prevent the recurrence of severe depressive episodes. If and when such episodes do occur when the person is taking lithium, they are of shorter duration and are not nearly as severe as would have been expected. *However*, they do not have any effect on existing depression – they prevent depression but don't cure it.

Just how lithium works is not known, but a great deal of research suggests that it probably makes people less responsive to external influences and stimulation. Lithium seems to 'switch off' people from their surroundings, so that they react in a more detached way to their environment. People on lithium treatment do indeed complain of 'feeling remote' from their surroundings in such a way that 'events don't seem important any more'.

154

Some psychiatrists researching into depression claim that many depressed people are over-anxious and agitated about things in their environment, things that don't affect others as seriously. Their 'thermostat' for irritation and depression is set too low. We probably all have a built-in 'switch-off' mechanism like this but in certain individuals it lets too many unhelpful environmental stresses through.

It is possible to continue breast-feeding if you are on lithium, but the baby should be monitored for its blood lithium levels to ensure that toxicity doesn't occur.

Lithium has revolutionised the treatment of manic-depressive psychosis in a way which is the envy of the whole of psychiatry.

Some psychiatrists, especially in the USA, are using tricyclic anti-depressants to treat acute depressive episodes and are then putting their patients on lithium to prevent subsequent attacks.

If you have to go on lithium, you'll have to have regular blood tests to ensure that the lithium level is just right so that you won't suffer from any toxic effects and you'll be asked to continue eating and drinking as normal so that the body's lithium levels don't fluctuate too widely. The early stages of stabilization on lithium often require such frequent blood samples to be taken that it is easier to be in hospital. After this though regular visits to the out-patient clinic are sufficient.

In the early days of the treatment there may be a tremor (shaking or trembling) of the hands, a loss of appetite and nausea. If the blood levels of lithium ever climb too high then more serious toxic effects occur. If you have any of the following when you are on a lithium compound, tell your doctor *at once*. The list of toxic effects includes an increase in those already mentioned, ringing in the ears, blurred vision, diarrhoea and drowsiness which can lead to coma.

Most patients can manage their own drug dosages so as to keep an effective blood level yet never have symptoms of toxicity.

Be sure to tell the doctor who intends prescribing lithium for you if you are on water tablets (diuretics) and remember to swallow the lithium tablets whole and *not* to take them with hot liquids.

Drugs commonly used in this group are:

Generic name	Proprietary name
Lithium carbonate	Priadel, Camcolit

Lithium has so changed the outlook for manic-depressive psychosis that previously hopeless people whose lives were wasted in emotional agony and crippling damage to friends, family and themselves are now normal again within two or three weeks. There are very few such dramatic treatments in the whole of medicine.

The problem is in deciding who to use this effective drug on. It has been proven beyond any doubt that manic-depressive illness responds, but unfortunately not everyone with this condition has a manic phase of the illness first. Some start off with a depressive episode (or indeed have only depressive episodes for years before a manic phase distinguishes the illness from endogenous depression) and are treated with tricyclics first. These people are apparently endogenous depressives, but are really manic-depressives in a depressive stage. In one series of patients who had had three episodes of depression with no sign of mania (they were therefore confidently labelled as endogenous depressives) it was found that one in seven subsequently had a manic attack. This put them firmly under the manic-depressive disease label and explains why it is that some depressives with apparent endogenous depression are cured with lithium. Remember that we saw in chapter one that manic-depressive illness is a very different condition from ordinary depression and has, for example, a strong familial element to it.

For a discussion on how anti-depressant drugs are thought to work, see page 66.

Do anti-depressant drugs really work?

There is little doubt that lithium carbonate works, as many controlled trials have shown, but even though this is wonderful news for both patients and their relatives, because manic-depressive illness is so uncommon, the question is not one that will concern most depressives. MAOIs are the subject of much more controversy, but they too are prescribed only for a minority of those with depression.

So the question that needs to be answered is 'Do tricyclic anti-depressants work?' Surprisingly, the answer is very difficult to come by, even though many careful trials have been carried out on the topic in excellent centres around the world. A large number of lay people and indeed large sections of the medical profession actually believe that modern drug therapy is the answer to depression. Many of the learned papers on depression start off with statements such as, 'now that the pharmacotherapy of depression is so effective . . .', and then go on to discuss some other facet of depression as if drugs have dismissed the major problem – that of curing the condition.

Alas, nothing could be further from the truth. Depression, as we saw on page 25 falls into five main groups. One (very uncommon) group, the manic-depressives, respond well to lithium salts, it is true; the larger (about twenty to thirty per cent of the whole depressed population) endogenously depressed group often respond to anti-depressants; but the vast majority of depressed people (those with reactive depression) certainly don't.

The power of suggestion is enormous in any therapeutic situation and it has been proven that about thirty-five per cent of the population will respond to placebos (dummy tablets) for almost any condition. When it comes to emotional and psychological disorders, this figure jumps to forty or fifty per cent. This means that the assessment of any therapy for depression is very difficult, but should make us all, doctors and patients alike, concerned about the over-prescription of anti-depressants. Many patients get better simply after talking their problem over with their doctor. Indeed, some don't allow the doctor to get a word in edgeways and yet feel improved for having 'got it off their chest'.

Unfortunately, too many people seem to want medicines today and will go to almost any lengths to ensure that their doctors prescribe them. It's a pity that too few doctors realize that what the patient really wants is not necessarily a drug (although this has become a tangible sign that the doctor takes one seriously in our society), but some other indication of care and concern.

A leading British psychiatrist, Dr Colin Brewer, maintains, and I agree with him, that most people with depression should

157

have a placebo as their first medication. This would not, of course, apply to those who were seriously depressed or suicidal.

The advantages of this approach are many. First, the patient would be spared many of the side-effects associated with certain of the tranquillizers and anti-depressant drugs (sixty per cent of those given anti-depressants stop taking them themselves within four to six weeks because of adverse side-effects). Second, the country would be saved a great deal of money; and third, the diagnosis could be made more accurately. If everyone in whom a diagnosis of 'depression' is made is given an anti-depressant, then those who improve will be labelled as depressives and they'll be stuck with that label in their medical notes for ever. In truth, of course, up to half of those suffering from all but the most serious forms of depression will improve simply by being given a placebo; thus sparing them the unpleasant and even potentially harmful (in terms of future employment, etc.) label of 'depressive'.

If the person improves on the placebo, so well and good and nothing has been lost; if not, anti-depressants can be prescribed subsequently if the condition still seems no better. More important though is the follow up of the placebo responders, to whom it can be explained that it was the patient, and not the tablets, that effected the cure. This can only do good in a society in which people's threshold of helplessness is so low that they run to doctors for help at the slightest setback. The more that the public at large feels that doctors have a magic answer to every emotional and psychological knock in life, the better chance there'll be that the medical profession will be inundated with trivial complaints which distract their attention from those who really do need help. A combination of placebo use and an increase in self-reliance could greatly reduce not only the country's drug bill, but also the very real suffering caused by the side-effects of those potent chemicals that act on the brain.

Giving people drugs for unhappiness suggests that they are suffering from a disease, when in fact they have simply had a setback in life. Labelling the unhappiness as a 'disease' puts it firmly into the lap of the doctor, who then feels bound to do something about it. This in turn encourages the patient to do

158

little or nothing (because it's doctor's job to cure disease) and before we know where we are we have a society in which doctors are responsible for the nation's unhappiness – a task which is clearly beyond them and for which they have neither the training nor the stomach.

The irony is that it's very difficult for doctors to prescribe placebos; but this is a problem which could easily be overcome with the help of the pharmaceutical industry. Drug companies are naturally unhappy at the thought of millions of patients being given placebos, even though they could still make a substantial profit and do so in the knowledge that they're causing no harm. In fact, there's probably a fortune to be made by some enterprising pharmaceutical company if only it had the sense to go into placebo production.

In theory, patients who know they're being given a placebo ought to be pretty annoyed about it, but experience proves quite the opposite. One major American survey, for example, found that people responded very well to tablets they were told were inert. One of the patients in the trial felt so good on his placebo that he refused to believe that it was a placebo and insisted that it was a new, highly effective pill.

But all of this talk about an alternative to tricyclics isn't just academic or amusing – it's deadly serious. Over 100,000 people deliberately took overdoses in the UK last year, and two-thirds of these used prescribed drugs. Of these attempted suicides, ten per cent used tricyclic anti-depressants. In the period 1965-73 in Britain tricyclic suicides rose at three times the rate of the increases in prescribing. In practice tricyclics are now becoming an important suicide method, yet many of those who try and even succeed should never have been given them in the first place.

So all in all there is very good evidence that rather than being helped by anti-depressant drugs, large numbers of people are actually being harmed by them. If anti-depressant drugs were really as effective as they are made out to be, surely hospital admission rates for depression would have fallen over the twenty years they've been available. Alas, this has not happened. A leading British psychiatrist has pointed out that between 1958 (the year before the introduction of the tricyclics) and 1966, the number of patients diagnosed as having endogenous or reactive depression and admitted to psychiatric wards had almost doubled. This considerable increase can hardly be explained by the increased willingness of people to go into psychiatric hospitals after the reforms of the 1959 Mental Health Act, because although the total number of psychiatric admissions rose during this time from 94,000 to 164,000, the proportion admitted with depression actually barely increased. Over the same period the number of anti-depressant prescriptions *doubled*.

Perhaps, then, if the tricyclics have had no real effect on depression rates they may have reduced the suicide and attempted suicide rates since their introduction. Unfortunately, the reverse is true. The number of suicides reached a peak in England and Wales in 1964 when tricyclics were being readily prescribed. Since then, the fall in suicides has been almost entirely due to the loss from the statistics of domestic coal gas suicides. The number of suicides from drugs *doubled* in the decade 1959-69 and we have seen that tricyclics are taking an increasing share in this particular 'market'.

Many trials have found that tricyclics are only marginally more effective than placebos, and some have even found that they are not as effective as dummy tablets. If we take 100 people with all types of depression, about half will get better because of the placebo effect of the drug, another twenty per cent will get better because of the drug itself and the other thirty per cent will not respond at all and will need other treatment (ECT, for example). I think a twenty per cent response rate is too high a price to pay, both economically and in terms of side-effects, and that we all, doctors and patients alike, ought to find other ways of coming to terms with unhappiness in society. There is certainly a place for tricyclics in the treatment of provable endogenous depression; but such cases are relatively few compared with the numbers who are reactively depressed.

It's a pity that most general practitioners, when faced with patients with depression, do little or nothing other than prescribe tricyclics and that when they do prescribe them they give too small a dose for too short a time to have any real effect. So under these circumstances, they are neither giving the patient the benefit (if any) of the drug, nor the benefit of consulting a doctor in the form of emotional support or other psychotherapy. In this way, depressed people often lose out all round, then are 'left' to get better with time alone which, for all but those who are suicidal, is good medicine. Most depressives cure themselves, given enough time.

The majority of people suffering from 'depression' don't need powerful drugs; they may simply need a mild tranquillizer to tide them over a life crisis. Even this has been shown to be less effective in terms of long-term well-being than emotional or psychotherapeutic support from a doctor, family or friends.

Drugs do have a place in depression, which in my opinion is a real disease like any other. It is, however, a much less common condition than is generally supposed. Unhappiness, is, unfortunately, very common and always will be, but it doesn't need the blunderbuss drug therapy it currently receives. Such indiscriminate therapy belittles both doctor and patient, and does nothing but harm to the opinion of both in each others' eyes. Anti-depressant drugs should only be used for the truly depressed and even then there may be other answers.

Someone, somewhere, has to break this cycle. Perhaps it could be you.

CHAPTER 6

Psychological treatments for depression

Psychotherapy – What is it?

There can be few terms that are as confusing to the general public as the word 'psychotherapy'. Many, quite understandably but erroneously, assume that it means psychoanalysis and naturally fear the thought of years of lying on couches talking about, for instance, their sexual feelings towards their mothers!

Psychotherapy is a hotch-potch word for a type of mind (psycho) treatment (therapy) which involves other human beings, instead of drugs or physical treatments. It is a way of using people to treat people. Psychotherapeutic sessions help people examine their values, needs, aspirations, fears, behaviour and judgement and help them see how to use their new-found understanding of these things to resolve their difficulties, anxieties and conflicts in life. Ideally, work done during (and between) psychotherapeutic sessions helps people adapt better to their environment and so reduces their need for drugs or other supportive therapy.

There are over 140 different kinds of psychotherapy available in the western world today, but they all share certain things in common. In any form of psychotherapy there is a confiding relationship and a two-way dialogue between the person giving the treatment and the person receiving it. Some people call it 'talk-therapy' because talking is usually all that is done.

What it is not

Psychotherapy is *not* the same as psychoanalysis. Psychoanalysis is a long-term (two or three years) method of treatment, in which an analyst interprets what the patient says

162

in the light of classical psychoanalytic teaching as propounded by Freud and others. However, most psychoanalysts would agree that it is too prolonged and too intensive a therapy to be used for the vast majority of depressives, especially those who are agitated, anxious or suicidal. Some psychological approaches to the treatment of depression use psychoanalytic principles, but this is not the same thing as having psychoanalysis.

Can I give psychotherapy to a depressed relative?

The answer to this is far from simple. The well-proven fact that married people suffer less from depression than do unmarrieds and divorcees points to a therapeutic role played by the person's spouse, but most of the time a close family member cannot be really helpful. This seemingly paradoxical situation arises because so often the depressed person has become ill *because* of a close family relationship problem. This makes a close family member the last person to discuss it all with. It's also a sad fact that depression so changes a person that immediate family members often become angry and frustrated at being manipulated and are thus very unlikely to *want* to dissect the problem, even if it does not involve them personally.

Certainly there are occasions when heart-to-heart discussions within the family can work wonders, but they are rare. Most depressives look outside their families for help and the first port of call is often a close friend. This can work, but can also be disastrous to the outcome of the depression or to the friendship or both.

If people seek you out to be their helper (therapist) it shows they respect you and hope you'll be able to help. If you listen empathetically, resist the temptation to compare yourself and your troubles with theirs and can coolly assess the pros and cons of the problem, then you *might* be able to help. Having read this book will have given you a lot of insight into the problems of depression and you'll have something of a head start already. The difficult bit comes next, because with little or no experience of dealing with depressed people (who by definition can't see what to do for themselves), you'll come up against the problem of not knowing what to do to help. If the

163

depressive isn't too badly depressed you can draw out suggestions and then help by encouraging him or her to make some decisions, even if in your heart you know they're not the ideal ones. With time, depressives will become more enthusiastic and, if you're clever enough about it, you can build on this so that they go away happier than when they came.

Unfortunately, most of us who have no training and experience in this kind of therapy find it almost impossible to keep our feelings and ideas out of the dialogue. In short, we cannot be objective. We try to push solutions that have worked for us in the past and all too soon depressed people feel they're being told what to do. This approach *can* work, but most often does not. This is where professional therapists have the advantage; they see so many people that they cannot relate personally as individuals to each one, and certainly wouldn't impose their personal and intimate solutions to life's problems – if only because they know from experience that each individual is unique, and that opinions based on subjective experiences rarely supply the right piece of the jigsaw.

So, it is unfortunately true that some kind of professional outsider is usually better at sorting out emotional and psychological problems than is a friend or relative. I say 'unfortunately true' because many people would rather not share their deepest thoughts, fears and anxieties with an outsider, preferring rather to chat it over with their spouse or a friend. I hope I have shown why this can't work most of the time.

Secondly, it's 'unfortunate' because, whilst there are lots of friends, relatives and spouses around, there are very few psychotherapists in the UK and most of the professional full-time ones are private and therefore cost money. People in the UK have not yet become used to paying for this sort of treatment and often begrudge spending the money. In reality it probably *is* worth being able to sort out your life's problems for the cost of a washing machine, but most people don't see it this way. It's strange that people will happily spend far more money having their varicose veins fixed than they will on fixing their emotional or marital turmoil. There are, of course, a lot of people who couldn't afford private psychotherapy at all.

In the US, psychotherapists abound and many people

consult them at the drop of a hat. In the UK the picture is altogether different. There are very few independent (private) psychotherapists outside central London and most people will have to go to some kind of doctor for this treatment. Research in the UK shows that psychotherapy carried out by family doctors is often very skimpy, if it is available at all. Thus in practice this leaves psychiatrists and psychologists working within the National Health Service as the largest group offering psychotherapy and there are simply not enough of them to go around. This means that most courses of psychotherapy are short (up to six sessions) and are often combined with drug therapy to make the patient more likely to benefit from the talking.

What types of therapy are there?

There are five main types of psychotherapy that are useful in treating depression. They are cognitive therapy; behavioural therapy; interpersonal psychotherapy; group therapy; and marital therapy.

As we have seen, none of these is psychoanalysis and indeed many of the therapies are not carried out by doctors at all. A large proportion of psychotherapists the world over are not doctors and there is no cause for concern over this. Many depressed people feel they should see a doctor for psychotherapy, but experience has shown that trained non-medics get just as good (and often better) results as do doctors. Doctors are trained to think in a rather restricted way about disease and it isn't until a doctor becomes very experienced in psychotherapeutic skills that he can be really useful to many of his patients. His training makes him think of drugs and other forms of intervention, whereas the essence of psychotherapy is a one-to-one non-judgemental approach to a person's problems. Doctors are brought up to think that they have to provide answers to those who are ill. Psychotherapy demands a much less simplistic approach and many doctors are not good at adjusting to it.

Social workers and psychologists, on the other hand, very often come to the subject with a very different viewpoint, have no social pressures to 'perform' as doctors do and so are able to be more empathetic with the patient.

165

Let's look at each of the major therapies in turn.

Cognitive therapy

This is based on the assumption that the low mood of depression results from the way individuals structure their thinking. As a result, they misinterpret and distort events and end up with a pessimistic view of themselves and the world in general. Treatment is directed at persuading patients to adopt a more realistic approach and results in several studies have been good. Such therapy has been shown to be more effective than either no treatment at all or treatment with imipramine (a proven anti-depressant drug).

Behavioural therapy

This is based on the finding that depressed people derive less positive feedback and pleasure from life than do others and that they enjoy the good things they do less than do others.

Various studies have been done in which people were asked to increase the number of pleasurable things they did in carefully controlled ways. Several therapeutic techniques have been developed based on these concepts. They are: social skills therapy, which encourages increased assertiveness, verbal skills and social judgements; pleasant events, which focus on increasing pleasant and rewarding experiences; and self-control, which emphasises self-monitoring, self-evaluation and self-reinforcement to correct the depressed person's problems.

Behavioural techniques have been proved to be better than no treatment in depression and, specifically, self-control methods have proved more effective than social skills methods.

Interpersonal psychotherapy

This treatment works on the assumption that depression develops in a social and interpersonal context and that correcting these relationships will cure the depression. The depression is seen by these therapists as having three separate components – symptom formation, social adjustment and personality. Interpersonal psychotherapy claims to intervene in the first two, but has no effect on personality. The idea is simply to improve the quality of the people's relationships and

166

social functioning so that they have an increased ability to cope with internal and external stresses. This sort of therapy has so far proved most useful for those depressed as a result of bereavement, grief and loss and those with marital problems.

It has been proven to be more effective than doing nothing and is improved by anti-depressant therapy given at the same time.

Group therapy

In this kind of treatment a trained psychotherapist and a group of patients exchange ideas and feelings in an effort to change the attitudes and behaviour of the members of the group. This sort of psychotherapy is relatively widely used in hospitals in the UK, partly because it is not as demanding on staff as is one-to-one psychotherapy. There are very few studies on just how useful such therapy is, but it is probably not as good as one-to-one treatment. Some people feel they can 'open up' in such a setting, while others get good ideas and insight into *their* problems simply by listening. Still others, with different temperaments and personalities, find group work intimidating, destructive and not at all helpful.

Marital therapy

One world expert has said that in his opinion marital therapy is the most effective type of psychotherapy. It is certainly true that many depressions arise from marital disharmony, or the inability of the spouse to understand the depressed person. A strong marriage in which there is total openness and understanding is less likely to produce a depressed person, but even in the best marriages external events can trigger a depression which then needs to be treated by outside help.

Marital therapy aims at altering the interaction between the married partners. It is based on the assumption that interpersonal relationships within a marriage affect thoughts, feelings and behaviour (both inside and outside the marriage), and that by putting the relationship to rights many depressed people can be cured. There are many different kinds of marital therapy but the most effective has been found to be that in which each partner is first seen separately and then both are seen together. In this way, both parties can openly put their

167

views and express their innermost thoughts without being inhibited by the presence of the other. Such an approach often highlights completely different (previously unrealized) attitudes between the partners on subjects of importance to them both. A clarification of such things often helps the depressed person enormously. Indeed, it is a sad fact that many couples open up to each other for the first time in their marriage during therapy – they have often never really talked to each other for years about things that matter to them.

Do they work?

This is a difficult question to answer because so few controlled studies have been done and, even when they have been, the numbers of patients have been very small and the types of depression from which they were suffering very different.

There are nine studies which have tested the efficacy of psychotherapy against a 'no intervention' control group, and all nine showed psychotherapy to be more effective than doing nothing.

When psychotherapy is compared with drug treatment the results are difficult to interpret. Five studies have compared tricyclic anti-depressants with psychotherapy. One study found cognitive therapy superior to a drug (imipramine) in the treatment of acutely depressed patients. One study found drugs and psychotherapy to be of about equal use and the other three studies found drugs to be superior to psychotherapy (interpersonal, group or marital) in the prevention of recurrent depression and the reduction of symptoms. These three studies did, however, find that psychotherapy was better in producing improved social functioning.

Five studies have looked at combined drug and psychotherapy treatment. All five showed the superiority of the combined treatment over either treatment alone or no treatment at all.

With the exception of cognitive and behavioural treatments, there are very few studies comparing the psychotherapies with each other. In those studies that do exist there has been a tendency for the type of therapy usually used by the researchers to come out more favourably than the others being tested. This undoubtedly relates to their greater experience in using that particular therapy.

There are, of course, more therapies than the five listed but many are frankly odd, most originate from the USA and the vast majority are untested or untestable. One of the dangers of a system in which anyone can set himself up as a 'psycho-therapist' and treat people with his own brand of therapy is that strange therapies will emerge, many of which will be useless and possibly even harmful. The above five therapies are widely available in the US in responsible medical and para-medical hands and are becoming more commonly used in the UK.

The average depressed person going to a psychotherapist in the UK will probably receive therapy that falls between (or combines the best of) two or more of the therapies I've described. Most general practitioners for example, who have experience of and a feeling for elementary psychotherapy, will have developed their own methods, many of which (although they don't realize it) will include the salient features of one of the five main types outlined above.

Are there any conditions that do or do not respond to psychotherapy?

Yes, there are. It is generally accepted that patients with organic (physical) brain damage, acute manic-depressive psychosis and schizophrenia, severe personality disorders, drug and alcohol addictions and certain forms of sexual deviation do not respond to psychotherapy, although they may respond to other types of psychological treatments. Any patient who is too disorganized mentally, too distrustful or too disturbed cannot have a rational relationship with another person and so cannot benefit from psychotherapy. Really severe depressions do not often do well with psychotherapy alone.

Some experts think that depression of more than five years' duration also responds badly to psychotherapy.

Are there any particular depressive symptoms that seem to have a good outcome with psychotherapy?

Yes. Several studies have shown that very anxious patients and those who are angry or acutely depressed can best be helped. The most promising candidates for psychotherapy are dissatisfied with themselves and yet are not too ill to be able to benefit from the treatment. Severe mood changes respond well, but those depressed people who have many bodily complaints seem to do rather badly.

Can psychotherapy alone ever work for depression?

Yes, provided the depression isn't too severé. Most reactive (as opposed to endogenous) depressions can be helped by psychotherapy alone and even many of the endogenously depressed get considerable benefit from treatment. Severely depressed and suicidal people can be helped over a crisis with psychotherapy alone, but will usually also need other treatment to cure the underlying condition.

Do I have to believe it'll do me any good for it to be useful?

Not really, but you have to be sufficiently highly motivated to take the whole thing seriously. Many therapists feel that patient motivation is the single most important factor in predicting the outcome of the treatment. There is plenty of evidence to show that therapists prefer highly motivated patients and select them whenever possible.

Having said this studies have shown that the patients' expectation of the outcome has no effect on the actual outcome. Those who felt therapy would be a waste of time but were prepared to go along with it usually had good outcomes and the reverse was also found to be true on occasions. People's ideas of what psychotherapy involves are often far from the truth and these 'unrealistic' expectations can get in the way of the therapy. Therapists, for their part, assume that the patient knows what to expect, but several studies have shown that they are wrong to do so. When comparisons were made between those who dropped out of psychotherapy and those who stayed the course, it was found that those who dropped out had all thought that they would play a passive role and be told what to do in their first interview. These were expectations not shared by their therapists.

Preparing a patient for therapy seems to be extremely valuable. This preparation should explain the role of the therapist, the way he or she behaves, what is likely to happen and so on. Research using patients who had such preparatory information found that they did better than those who did not receive it.

Any psychotherapeutic treatment calls for the patient to be alert, introspective and in touch with reality. You don't have to be highly intelligent, but very unintelligent or uncommunicative people don't benefit much because they can neither express their feelings adequately nor benefit from the therapist's remarks.

Is age a barrier to successful psychotherapy?

No, but it is widely accepted that young patients do rather better than old. (Freud, for example, claimed that the upper limit for psychoanalysis was fifty.) Many therapists have thought it more sensible to confine their efforts to younger people, because older patients are less likely to benefit from insight-oriented therapy, and have less life in front of them to act on the new ideas and benefit from them.

Young people are probably more pleasant for therapists to treat (so they'll tend to find reasons to justify their choosing to do so), because they're more flexible and have a greater capacity and willingness to learn and to experiment with new behaviour patterns. It's an exceptional person aged much over fifty who is willing, or indeed able, to change his or her behaviour dramatically. Older people may well perceive this lack of flexibility for the first time during psychotherapy and yet be unable to do anything about it. This can make them even more depressed.

Do middle class people do better with psychotherapy? –It seems a very middle class idea.

Yes, middle class people do get better results than other groups, though it's difficult to be dogmatic about social class because factors as different as income, occupation and education levels come into it.

Working class patients tend to refuse the offer of treatment more than the middle classes, and they tend to drop out of treatment prematurely more often. They also generally get the less experienced therapists and receive less intensive therapy.

Most therapists are themselves middle class, of course, and can all too easily have prejudices and misconceptions about the working class – perceptions that are not helpful in the therapeutic environment. It can be very difficult for a words-oriented person to empathize with someone less articulate of any class, and this is a major drawback to the value of psychotherapy generally.

Social class is often closely linked to educational attainment, which in turn is linked to intelligence. Intelligent people of whatever social group do relatively better in therapy because psychotherapy is a learning process and intelligent people learn faster. Those who have had an education above school level will also be used to more abstract, conceptual and verbal thinking and this too helps in the difficult matter of sorting oneself out.

However, intelligence, whilst helpful, isn't essential and many moderately intelligent people, given that they're told what's expected of them and what to expect of the therapy, do very well indeed.

How many treatment sessions will I need?

This is impossible to assess and will depend on the severity of your depression, your age, intelligence, the amount of 'work' you're prepared to put in between sessions, the frequency at which the therapist can see you and your general state of mental health. Assuming one session per week, most therapists would hope to see sufficient improvement within six or eight sessions to be able to discharge you. Some therapists use an open-ended approach in which both patient and therapist decide between themselves when they think they've got all they're likely to out of the sessions, but therapists are increasingly going for defined 'contracts' with their clients. This involves telling their patient at the end of the first session just how many more they'll need if all goes well. This can be good for many people because it gives them a goal to aim for, ensures that they put in lots of work between sessions, encourages them to come out with their thoughts and feelings sooner than they otherwise would have and takes away the uncertainty of how long it might all go on. Even at the end of a contract like this, the therapist might suggest another session or two and will certainly see you again if you think you need it.

What can I expect to get out of psychotherapy?

There are several levels at which psychotherapy works and a good therapist will try to give the depressed person many or all of them over the course of treatment. None of them is more important or meaningful than the others – they all have a role to play in your recovery.

When you're feeling anxious, down in the dumps and generally unworthy of anyone's attention, the psychotherapist can give you *emotional support*. This will give you the strength to go on with life and shows that someone cares how you feel. This is often accompanied by a sense of relief that someone else is sharing the burden of your worries, uncertainties and inferiority, someone who won't judge you and is there to help. This produces an intense bond between you and 'your' therapist, and 'yours' he or she certainly is. For that forty-five minute session you will have the therapist's entire attention, training and empathy to yourself. During that time all the therapist thinks about is you and being listened to so intently can, in itself, have a wonderful effect. It might be the first time in your life that anyone has given so much time and single-minded thought to you and your problems.

Many people experience a sense of emotional and psychological release or *catharsis* in their therapy sessions. All the self-punishing thoughts, all the things you can't say to your loved ones, and all the closed doors you couldn't have possibly opened alone because of your depression are set free and the result can be amazing. Some people leave their therapist walking on air, so 'cleansed' do they feel. At last the burden of it all has been shared and, as we all know, trouble shared is trouble halved. This letting loose of your feelings and innermost thoughts is what therapy is all about. Nothing you can say will hurt or upset the therapist: he or she has heard it all before and no doubt will again. If the therapist annoys you by saying something you can't agree with, say so. Their role is not to teach you anything, but to enable you to come to terms with yourself and your problems. If you feel guilty about something, talk about it – your secrets won't be spread around. Your therapist won't tell your spouse about anything you say unless you are in marital therapy, and even then it won't be mentioned without your permission and the therapist is more likely to get you to tell your spouse yourself.

As you peel back the onion skins of your emotions and get to the heart of yourself the sense of relief is almost overwhelming and many patients talk of being 'reborn' – they feel like new people. Not infrequently, such a catharsis is accompanied by a reduction in the bodily symptoms of depression, much to the amazement of everyone (except the therapist!).

As time goes by, the therapist will start to introduce other techniques. Even as early as the first session, the therapist may start making more positive suggestions of things to do to reduce anxiety and guilt. A good therapist will make practical suggestions as to how to organize one's life, how to cope with previously stressful or unbearable situations and so on. This *directive therapy* is the result of a lot of experience on behalf of the therapist. It's not guesswork when he or she tells you where to go for domestic help, to get financial advice or whether or not to have a holiday. Experience tells the therapist what works for a person like you at your stage of the depression. If he or she doesn't know all the answers, they can tell you who will.

Depending on how well you progress, the therapist will start to *explain what is going on*. This will not happen at the first session, because you'll be in no fit state to benefit from it, but as you improve you'll want to know 'what hit you'. So many depressions are caused by perfectly explicable things or combinations of things: all of which will have been seen before by the experienced therapist. It comes as an enormous relief to most depressed people to realize that there *are* explanations and that other people have experienced the same things and lived to fight another day. When one is depressed it's difficult to imagine that anybody could ever have been through such hell and anyway, you couldn't care less if they had because you're so wrapped up in it yourself. As the depression lifts a little under drugs, psychotherapy, or preferably a combination of the two, it's comforting to know it has all happened before to other people.

Gradually, as soon as you can accept them, the therapist will start to suggest new ways of looking at yourself and your problems. These are ideas that you can work on in between sessions and put your own personal stamp upon. Some of the

174

suggestions will give you pointers for dealing better with yourself, with your spouse or children, will help you understand why it is that your boss has never got on with you or whatever. These suggestions will have worked for others, so don't reject them out of hand. What seems stupid during the session can often, days or weeks later, shine out as a real truth and something you're glad to make your own. There's nothing wrong with this. The therapist isn't taking you over just because you build some of his or her ideas into your life. It's just like taking advice from any other expert: therapists do not necessarily give you advice that they'd follow in the same circumstances – they know that they are themselves and that you are you. The advice you receive is chosen and put forward to work for you. If, after you've had a chance to think over these suggestions (or even, preferably, to try them out), you feel they're impractical or useless, say so because you can gain a lot from discussing this.

All of this will be the backdrop, the common denominator, to the psychotherapy. On top of this general approach, the psychotherapist will superimpose a particular therapeutic approach (probably based on one of the five outlined above). This complex mixture, plus everything you, the patient, contributes, is what psychotherapy is all about.

Although one always hears what doctors and other therapists think of their treatments (and indeed of their patients), we rarely hear from the recipients of the treatment. This is especially so in the realm of psychological therapies. It is reassuring, therefore, to find that a study has been done to see what patients felt about psychotherapy. This survey interviewed forty-nine patients who had been through some form of psychotherapy. Interestingly, the patients thought that by and large the therapy had helped them, but in a rather different way than the psychotherapists thought. They commented that it was not the specific technique that the therapist had used that had done the trick, but simply the good relationship that formed between themselves and the therapist. It was 'support and encouragement' that they rated most as valuable and which had been most helpful in relieving their symptoms.

This is not new in itself. Many therapists would agree that it is the relationship with the therapist which *is* the therapy, but

175

this is unlikely to give therapists the job satisfaction and intellectual stimulation that *they* need. After all, many people can supply warmth, confidence and support and therapists hope they can supply rather more.

How do I find a psychotherapist?

This depends on what level of therapy you want. If you are prepared to try what your general practitioner has to offer, then this is fairly easily come by and is free. Simply ask the doctor to see you for a talk for half an hour one day and see how this goes. If you want further advice you can contact the British Association of Psychotherapists (see page 235 for their address and telephone number). Other psychotherapy services can be contacted locally through your general practitioner, local psychiatric hospital, your psychiatrist or local advice and counselling services. The Marriage Guidance Council (see page 235 for the address and telephone number of their national headquarters) provides a wide range of counselling, mainly, but not exclusively, related to interpersonal problems. You do not need to be married to use their services. Although the name 'Marriage Guidance' is rather stuffy and forbidding, the organization is not at all like this and will give counselling help to the single and married; to one or both partners; to the homosexual and the heterosexual. The counselling you're likely to receive from such organizations is not nearly as intensive as that which a professional psychotherapist will give, but is often enough for many depressed people and, to be practical, is often all that's available. There's no harm in trying something simple and inexpensive first before progressing to professional psychotherapy. Most of the counsellors at MG clinics are women and this can be a pleasant change for women who are uneasy about sharing their problems with men. (Most psychiatrists and psychotherapists are men.)

If you decide to go to any of these sources of psychotherapy you do not have to get permission from your general practitioner or psychiatrist, but it is probably courteous to inform them of what you are doing.

If you are very depressed and need help immediately, try your family doctor first or phone the Samaritans. The

Samaritans' number is in the local telephone directory. They offer simple counselling facilities over the phone and in an emergency when things look very black this can be a real lifeline.

CHAPTER 7

Physical treatments for depression

Right through history people have believed that depression is caused by an evil force which, if it could be overcome or let out, would result in relief from the distress it brought about. Holes were bored into the skull of a depressed person to let 'poisonous vapours' escape; depressed people were beaten to release the evil spirits; or their blood was let to remove 'bad blood'.

Physical, as opposed to drug, treatments have been few in number and even fewer have stood the test of time. In 1933 Dr Ladislas Meduna of Budapest used intravenous stimulants to produce convulsions that induced mental improvements. About the same time Dr Manfred Sakel discovered that insulin, when injected, produced a coma that improved brain function, especially in schizophrenia. Ten years before that Dr Jakob Klaesi had used barbiturates to induce prolonged periods of sleep in the treatment of emotional illness.

But sleep therapy, insulin coma and chemical convulsive treatments have all lost favour because they are either ineffective or too hazardous, leaving us with only three physical treatments for depression today.

By far the most commonly used is electroconvulsive therapy, in which an electrical current is passed across the brain, but sleep deprivation therapy looks interesting and psychosurgery is used for a tiny minority of severely depressed people who can get relief in no other way. Let's look at each in turn.

Electroconvulsive therapy (ECT)

A well-proven and highly effective way of treating some people with depression and especially severe depression is ECT. It is a procedure involving the passage of a low voltage electric

178

current through the brain. This current produces a fit, rather similar to that produced in epilepsy, and this indeed is how it first came to be used.

In 1934 Dr Meduna observed that epilepsy was very uncommon in schizophrenics. He then deduced (for no good reason that we know of today) that these two conditions must therefore be virtually incompatible. This led him to suggest that epileptic fits might be used to cure schizophenics. It soon became clear that artificially-induced fits did nothing to cure schizophrenics but that, quite by chance, certain depressed patients *did* improve.

Fits were first induced by injecting very powerful chemicals into the muscles, but in 1937 the Italians Cerletti and Bini passed an electric current through the brain to achieve the same results and this became the basis of modern ECT.

Why is it used?

ECT is usually used for specific groups of depressives who cannot be managed in other ways. The main indications are for:

1. Depressives who fail to respond to a proper trial of anti-depressant drugs
2. Depressives who cannot tolerate the side-effects of anti-depressant drugs
3. Depressives who cannot or will not take their drugs as prescribed
4. Depressives who are plagued with suicidal thoughts
5. Depressives who are so severely ill that they will not even eat or drink

How is it done?

ECT can be done as an in-patient or as an out-patient, but in either case a general anaesthetic has to be given so there are special precautions that have to be taken beforehand, as for any other general anaesthetic.

The clinic where the ECT is to be done will give you a leaflet or will tell you what you need to do by way of preparation. On the day of the treatment you should have no food or drink for at least four hours before the time of your ECT treatment. If you are going to be treated in the afternoon then you can have a light

179

breakfast before 9.00 am, and that's all. It's important to adhere to this instruction because there's a danger that under the anaesthetic you could vomit and inhale the fluid. This could be lethal. Doctors can sometimes prevent this complication and can certainly treat it if it occurs, but it only creates problems so don't tempt fate. Don't succumb to the odd cup of coffee, thinking it'll do you no harm: it might!

If you eat or drink anything the anaesthetist could refuse to anaesthetize you and your treatment will be put back, to your and your relatives' disappointment. This is a nuisance because it simply prolongs the course of treatment and delays your recovery.

It's a good idea to have somebody to go along to the clinic with you, someone with whom you feel safe. Some moderately depressed people, and those reaching the end of their treatment course, can go alone, but it's always more pleasant to have company if you can. Most people experience very few after-effects and are quite capable of getting home again alone, but company is preferable because there is always a small danger of a delayed after-effect of the anaesthetic (nausea, dizziness or anxiety).

The treatment itself is very simple. You'll be asked to remove your false teeth, your glasses, shoes and any other removable objects. If the procedure is being done with you as an out-patient, you'll stay in your outdoor clothes. You may or may not be given a pre-medication (pre-med) injection, depending on the anaesthetist, who will then get you to lie on a couch and will give you an injection into a vein (usually in the back of the hand). Within seconds you're asleep. Once you're asleep the anaesthetist injects a special substance that paralyses the body's muscles so that when the electric current is passed through the head it doesn't cause muscular contractions throughout the body. In the earliest days of the treatment, when paralysing drugs weren't used, patients used to convulse as the electric current was given. These convulsions were sometimes so strong that bones were broken. Today's patient hardly twitches, the convulsion is so small. For the short duration of the anaesthetic, the breathing muscles are paralysed (along with all the other muscles), so the anaesthetist will pump air into the lungs using positive pressure. This ensures that the tissues of the body are fully oxygenated throughout the procedure.

The electric shock is given via either one or two electrodes placed on one or both sides of the head. As soon as the action of the muscle-paralysing drug has been reversed, using another injection, breathing returns spontaneously. The person is allowed to recover from the anaesthetic and is watched carefully by a nurse until he or she is fully awake again. The actual ECT procedure itself takes about two or three minutes and you'll be fully conscious in ten minutes. You feel nothing at all.

As the anaesthetic wears off you'll become conscious but remain sleepy. Right from start to finish the whole procedure will have taken about an hour. You're then ready to go home or back to your hospital room.

Everybody reacts differently after ECT and the response can be different in any one individual at different stages of the treatment. Most people are drowsy for a few hours after the first few ECT treatments, but others become more alert and relaxed. A very retarded patient may experience a sense of exhilaration which will encourage the belief that further treatments will be useful. A few people feel worse after the treatment but if this happens to you, don't worry, because it soon wears off.

Most people feel sleepy after ECT and in many clinics they'll let you sleep for a while before going home. A few people have a headache or complain of a loss of memory, but these symptoms usually disappear very quickly. If you are accompanying a friend or relative for ECT treatments, don't fuss around them afterwards. Let them recover quietly in their own time and then take them home. Don't expect miraculous 'cures'. If you're agitated and keep asking questions 'to see if they've improved', they'll sense your anxiety – and that won't do them any good at all. There's no way of telling how successful ECT has been (or will be) after any one treatment, although there should be a general trend towards improvement as the course proceeds.

Does it really work?

The effectiveness of ECT has been the subject of research

almost since it was first introduced, but until recently there were no properly controlled studies of ECT, mainly because of the ethical limitations of psychiatric research of this kind. Recent trials do seem to confirm that ECT *is* effective in severe depressions and that a larger proportion of depressives show a response to ECT than to anti-depressants. The advantage that it definitely has is that its results are seen very quickly. Although a course of ECT treatment may last for twelve sessions spread over several weeks, most of those who are going to respond show a marked improvement after the first few treatments. Drugs, you'll remember, take two or three weeks to take effect and can take even longer. Some severely depressed and suicidal patients are dramatically improved after one ECT treatment.

Studies have now been done giving patients dummy ECT (an anaesthetic and a muscle-paralysing drug yet no shock), which showed that they did less well than those receiving the electric shock. This answered the critics who said that ECT simply had a super placebo effect, or that the general anaesthetic somehow produced some beneficial effect. Also, one study carried out in Edinburgh found that, although patients didn't positively enjoy ECT, most believed it had helped them and found it less frightening or unpleasant than going to the dentist. What some patients *did* find unpleasant was hearing other patients being treated while they were waiting their turn. But this is purely a practical and organizational problem, which should easily be overcome by sensitive medical and nursing staff.

Until as recently as 1978, very little hard research had been done into ECT and even today only a tiny amount of money has been spent in this area. We still don't know why or how it works. There are many theories, but certainly the convulsions (which the early workers in this field thought were beneficial) are nothing to do with its effectiveness, because today's patient doesn't have convulsions. In fact, electroconvulsive therapy is a bad name for it. The Americans more properly call it electroshock therapy.

ECT has become a controversial subject within the medical profession and some members of the general public are worried that it may be being used too freely on patients who haven't given their consent. Opponents of the treatment point to the lack of knowledge of how it works, the loss of memory it can induce and the 'big brother' image of patients being treated against their wills; but all these criticisms can be levelled equally well at the drugs used in the treatment of depression, drugs used with gay abandon by millions of people in the western world every day. We certainly don't know how *they* work, they cause enormous problems with side-effects and are prescribed indiscriminately far too often.

ECT works and can be shown to do so, but it is not a panacea for mental illness. Nor is it the bogey it has been made out to be. Further research may help explain how and why it works, but in the meantime thousands more depressed patients will undoubtedly get relief from their symptoms thanks to ECT.

How many ECT treatments are needed to produce results?

Usually about six, but more may be needed if the person doesn't show signs of responding. It is usual to have two or three treatments per week, though 'emergency' treatments may be given in the early weeks in very severe cases of depression. There is no limit to the number of treatments that can be given, though very few psychiatrists would give more than twenty. The number of treatments needed is gauged by the psychiatrist in charge of the patient, who will have to balance the observed improvements in the person's depression against any side-effects of the ECT itself (memory loss or confusion, for example). This takes experience to judge and varies greatly from patient to patient.

Is ECT dangerous – could I die as a result of it?

ECT itself is not dangerous but there is a small mortality risk from the anaesthetic. Don't forget too that some of those having ECT are so severely depressed that they'd probably kill themselves without treatment. In other words, the underlying condition for which ECT is used has a considerable mortality rate in itself (see chapter nine). The death rate from ECT has been found to be fewer than 10 per 100,000 treatments. Even pregnant women can safely be treated with ECT with no harm

183

to the foetus. Many experts would rather use ECT than drugs in such women.

Is it safe to have ECT if I'm taking drugs?

You should make sure before you have your first treatment that the psychiatrist or the anaesthetist knows what drugs you're taking. There are no problems in having ECT if you're taking any anti-depressant drugs. Mono-amine oxidase inhibitors potentiate the action of barbiturates and the anaesthetist will use a short-acting barbiturate intravenously to get you to sleep. This makes it especially important to mention if you are taking one of these (for a list of trade names see page 153). Some clinics will tell you to omit your morning drug on the day of your treatment, but don't do this unless you are asked to.

Don't forget to tell the doctor about other drugs you're on, even if they have nothing to do with your depression. Also tell him about any drug sensitivities or allergies you have.

Are there any side-effects of ECT?

Yes, there are. Short-term side-effects include headaches and muscle pains, but these usually disappear in forty-eight hours. There may also be short-term confusion and memory loss. The memory loss runs from before the treatment and continues afterwards. Memory impairment seems to get worse with increased numbers of treatments, but is rarely serious except in elderly patients. It often starts after the fourth or fifth treatment, but can occur at any stage, and usually disappears after the last treatment. In those who complain of persistent memory loss, it is thought that it is the continuing depression or anxiety that is producing the trouble and not the ECT itself. This goes for all but the old and those with pre-existing depression of brain tissue, in whom the memory loss can be permanent. Here, the ECT has probably accentuated an underlying problem rather than created it.

People often worry that ECT might be damaging their brain in some way but there is no evidence of this. As judged clinically, people show no signs of brain damage after ECT and studies of psychological and intellectual function after ECT show no deterioration.

184

Are there any physical disease conditions that could produce problems with ECT?

Yes. People who've recently had a heart attack or those with a cerebral aneurysm need to be treated with extreme care, but even then they can still have their treatments. The only absolute exclusion from treatment are people who have a brain tumour because ECT often exaggerates their existing disorientation and confusion.

What should I do when I get home after ECT?

Do whatever you want to do. Most people feel like a sleep, especially after the first few treatments, but if you want to sit around and watch TV that's perfectly all right.

Is it all right to leave someone alone at home after ECT?

Yes, it is, if they seem well but it is preferable to stay with them – not because of the ECT, but because they're depressed, even though they may seem improved. Just because they've had a few treatments doesn't mean they're miraculously cured of depression. However, if they seem rational, relatively improved (from the depression point of view) and are wide awake, they could be left for a short while. In the two or three week treatment period the person may be confused and in a state of flux so you'll probably find that you're happier staying nearby anyway. If any of the signs or symptoms become worrying to you, the relative, talk to your family doctor and tell the hospital doctors at the next treatment.

Can I eat and drink as usual after a treatment?

Yes. Indeed you will be more hungry (especially as you'll have missed a meal and won't have had a drink for some time). Having said this though, there's no need to eat, so don't force food down. If the ECT is having its desired effect you'll notice that your appetite (previously poor because of the depression) will start returning.

Is it all right for me to have ECT if I'm having a menstrual period?

Yes. Some women miss a period or two as a result of the ECT, but this doesn't matter. Other women whose periods have been irregular or even absent *because* of their depression will find that ECT regularizes them again as the depression clears.

Can I drive during my ECT course?

No – it is definitely not safe to do so. You will certainly not be able to drive home from the hospital or clinic after a treatment and you shouldn't drive in between treatments either. Depression serious enough to need ECT will make you an unsafe driver and a danger to yourself and others. Talk to your psychiatrist about getting back to driving when the treatments are over.

How quickly does ECT produce results?

Very quickly compared with the other treatments for depression. Within three to five treatments, your relatives will begin to notice changes for the better but the effects of the treatments are cumulative, so don't miss any appointments. Each person reacts differently and uniquely to ECT and progress rates vary enormously. It can take six or seven treatments before the average person feels confident that real improvement is occurring. After a long or serious depression it's often difficult for the patient to be the best judge anyway because, by its very nature, depression makes the depressive less sure about such judgements. When this is the case, it is the relatives who first notice the improvement. Some people show no signs of improvement until the tenth, eleventh or twelfth treatments and a minority need even more treatments than this. With two or three treatments a week, the average person will be very much better within three weeks.

When can I go back to work?

This varies greatly from person to person but, if the result of the ECT has been good, most people can go back about two weeks after the last treatment. Of course, if the depression is still present this time scale will have to be reviewed.

It's probably wise not to rush back to work unless you feel really right again. If you go back too soon, the associated pressures and the desire to catch up on the time you've lost could well prove too stressful and set you back several steps. If

186

at all possible, go back part-time at first to see how you get on. You are the best judge. If you feel well and think you can cope, work may be just the thing you need to help you on the road to recovery.

Can I be forced to have ECT?

No, you can't, unless you are admitted to a psychiatric unit or hospital against your will (see also page 197), when you could possibly be given ECT if the doctors feel it would save your life (if, for example you are a danger to yourself because you've tried, or said you'll try, to commit suicide). Other than this, you can refuse to have ECT at any time, just as you can refuse any other medical treatment. Just because you are mentally (as opposed to physically) unwell doesn't give doctors the right to take over and do what they want. However, if you repeatedly refuse to have ECT and the doctors honestly feel that they can't do anything else for your depression, they may ask you to leave the hospital or clinic, and you have no right in law to stay.

Are there any special 'types' of depression that do well with ECT?

Yes. Depressed people who fall into the endogenous group (see page 26) fare best. Those with many bodily (as opposed to psychological) symptoms and those with hypochondriacal symptoms do especially well. ECT is not as good for reactive depressions. It is claimed that three-quarters of those with endogenous depressions can be helped or cured by ECT – a substantial improvement on drug therapy, with fewer side-effects and with a far quicker onset of action.

Sleep deprivation

We saw in chapter three that depression causes many different kinds of sleep disturbance and that it most commonly causes an overall loss of sleep. This led some researchers to consider whether this might not be the body's answer to the depression; that in some way the body might be healing itself, as it does in so many disease states. The original observation that three depressed patients who stayed awake all of one night were dramatically improved was made by a West German professor in the early 1970s and the first therapeutic trials of sleep deprivation were carried out in the same clinic in 1971. In these, endogenous depressives were kept awake for a whole night and a whole day (thirty-six hours). The subjects weren't told what was really going on, but were informed that it was part of an eye examination. All the endogenously depressed patients felt better after their sleep deprivation, but a group of reactive depressives varied in their response (some were better and others worse) and normal subjects used as controls were unchanged or felt worse. Of those who did improve, most only remained so for a few days. Repeated sleep deprivation did, however, repeat the improvement.

Over the last few years, many other psychiatrists have duplicated this study and the general view is that over half of those with endogenous depression improve with sleep deprivation, albeit for a short time. Most of the research shows that improvement begins towards the end of the first sleepless night, but some people, it seems, don't feel any better until after a night's sleep following the treatment night. Some patients seem to benefit from a single night's sleeplessness and others need a course of sleep deprivation. Twice weekly sleep deprivation has been found to be very effective.

So here then might be a simple yet effective method of curing some cases of depression. The trouble is that depressives, by definition, are poorly motivated and it is not easy to keep them awake. In hospital research programmes this can be done with plenty of staff, tact and initiative; but in a domestic setting it becomes more difficult to implement, simply because the healthy person who stays up all night to keep the depressive awake (and company) will soon become bad tempered as the days go by. In hospital trials, though, only one in ten of the depressives dropped out because it was too unpleasant being up all night.

Just why sleep deprivation should work isn't known, but it is known that about thirty per cent of depressives respond to any medication or therapy, however useless it is, so a placebo effect in sleep deprivation therapy cannot be ruled out. It is even possible that the placebo effect is especially powerful with such a novel treatment. It's also difficult to separate the actual sleeplessness from the fact that this, by definition, means more personal contact and increased levels of attention from caring staff. Perhaps it was the interaction between the staff and the group of patients that had the desired effect.

It is possible that sleep deprivation works by interrupting the body's disordered diurnal rhythms (see page 103), so allowing the normal patterns to assert themselves. This theory is supported by the finding that severely depressed people kept asleep for long periods with narcotic drugs also awake less depressed.

As yet, sleep deprivation is a research tool and raises more questions than it answers in terms of the day-to-day management of depression. If you feel you want to give it a try at home you can do no harm, but only try it if you fit into the endogenous depression category (see page 26 for details). A recent trial shows that people who are depressed and slowed down by their depression or anxiety are particularly good responders. If you find it works for you it's probably worth trying twice-weekly sleepless nights, if you can readily find a way of keeping awake without disturbing the rest of the household. It's a simple enough thing to experiment with and might just be the answer for you. Research shows that it could take a few nights' trial before you get results. In one study, half of those who eventually responded had not done so after the first sleepless night. However, no research has shown that sleep deprivation is a *total* treatment for depression and even the most enthusiastic of its advocates still recommend a combination of drugs (albeit in reduced dosage) and sleep deprivation.

Brain surgery (Psychosurgery)

The treatment of the chronically depressed patient is still a very real problem for doctors and patients alike and, however successful other treatments are, there is always a core of 'untreatable' depressives. Many of these severely ill depressives are incapable of living a normal life and are in hospital for very long periods.

In 1937 it was first postulated that emotions were controlled by a part of the brain called the hippocampus and since then it has been found that by altering another part of the brain, the cingulate gyrus, one might be able to alter a person's emotions for the better.

189

Leucotomy, a procedure in which some of these personality and emotion areas are destroyed, was discovered almost by accident. Doctors noticed that naturally-occurring brain disease or brain damage following a head injury, for example, could produce a change in personality – often for the better.

As long ago as 1936 Egon Moniz, a neurosurgeon, made controlled surgical cuts in specific parts of the brain to affect severely depressed and anxious patients. Even with such crude efforts he produced beneficial results, but today's operations are highly sophisticated procedures by comparison.

Leucotomy or other operations in which specific areas of the brain are cut or deliberately destroyed are, however, rare operations today and are only done if the depressed person is self-destructive and untreatable by other methods. One large survey found that seventy per cent of such patients could be cured or improved by brain surgery, so it's well worth doing. After the operation, some patients respond for the first time to drugs or to ECT and go on to lead substantially normal lives. In good hands the operation is safe and successful and has probably received too much negative publicity. The public, and indeed the medical profession, has come to think of a leucotomy as a dramatic, almost fictional, Dracula-like operation; but experts around the world are producing good results, albeit on a very small scale. It is possible that with the refinement of operative techniques and the better localization of the affected parts of the brain, leucotomy could become a more widely used method of treating really severe depressions, but this would seem to be at least a decade away.

CHAPTER 8

Psychiatric hospitalization

Even with modern drug therapy and a mental health system that puts its emphasis on out-patient treatment, some depressed people are so seriously ill that they have to be admitted to hospital, if only for a short time. Unfortunately, the thought of this sometimes fills not only the patients themselves but also their relatives with dread. We can all remember the time, not all that long ago, when people were taken into mental hospitals never to be heard of again. This has now completely changed and the majority of psychiatric in-patients are out in the community again within a few months.

But it's impossible to change public attitudes to psychiatric hospitals in a decade or two and most of us still think of mental hospitals as 'loony bins', 'asylums', or at best 'institutions' where people are 'locked away'. As long as people feel this way, the thought of a relative having to be sent to one is likely to arouse anxiety and concern. 'All right', I can hear you say, 'if my relative were mad, I wouldn't mind him being locked away in one of these places but he's only depressed – surely it can't be necessary to put him away with all those people'. The hard fact is that a very large number of 'all those people' will be suffering from depression too, because it accounts for more psychiatric bed occupancy than any other condition.

Today's psychiatric hospital, whilst often not the most prepossessing architectural edifice, is more enlightened than it has ever been and as a result the stigma involved in having to be admitted for treatment has been greatly reduced. This is hardly surprising, since one in twelve of all men and one in eight of all women will be a psychiatric in-patient at least once in their lives. We no longer regard mental disease as a moral issue, a divine punishment or an expression of evil, so the

191

general stigma of psychiatric illness is also diminishing.

However, to be fair, the thought of having to go into a mental hospital is not one that is likely to fill any of us with joy. Many are overcrowded, understaffed and under-financed. Although over one-third of all National Health Service beds are filled with psychiatric patients, they only get thirteen per cent of the total budget. Most are very big (with between 1,000 and 2,000 patients), are situated well out of city centres (and thus difficult to get to) and undoubtedly exude a feeling of long-term hopelessness that one doesn't get when walking into the average hospital filled with medical and surgical patients. A survey of patients leaving psychiatric hospitals shows that most of them have been in there for three months or less, so the impression one might get of nobody ever leaving is, in fact, erroneous. However, on the other side of the coin it has to be pointed out that two-thirds of all psychiatric hospital admissions are re-admissions, which tends to suggest that life in the community isn't the perfect answer for many of them.

Because relatively little money is available for caring for the mentally ill – £3,000 million a year – the hospitals seem to lack the modern facilities and staffing levels one associates with acute hospitals. This fills the average relative with despondency, and I am not pretending that for many relatives the thought of a loved one having to go into a psychiatric hospital is anything but upsetting. Even the sparkling new units attached to many district general hospitals still have 'an air' about them – mainly, to be fair, because of our own preconceived ideas about mental illness, ideas which we've inherited in folklore.

Today's psychiatric hospital is primarily a treatment centre – it is not a long-term custodial institution. Certainly, you'll see patients there who are disturbed or behaving oddly, but you will also see physically disturbed and sick people if you go on a surgical ward. Someone coughing or limping would evoke compassion from the average visitor, yet parallel signs and symptoms in mental health are somehow more difficult to bear. This is an irrational fear that is soon dispelled when you find that many of those around you are just like you: ordinary people who need a special kind of care, often for a relatively short time.

192

So if you (or a relative) have to go into a psychiatric hospital, remember that it will usually only be for a few weeks, while you are in the most acute phase of the disease. There is as little chance of being left there and 'forgotten' as there is of leaving someone who has just had an emergency appendicectomy on a surgical ward for months on end.

When you get to the stage that the doctor advises admission to a psychiatric hospital or unit, it's best not to fight medical opinion over it. The doctor is only too aware of people's feelings, knows that the pressure on psychiatric beds is great (they no longer have large institutions with empty beds waiting to be filled) and would not suggest it if there was any other way out of the situation.

Why go into hospital?

Hospital care for a psychiatric emergency, such as can arise in severe depressions, is just as essential as hospital care for any other medical emergency. Many people feel that because the person isn't running around berserk or bleeding to death the condition they're witnessing can't be a real emergency. This is not true. We shall see in the suicide chapter that depression is an alarmingly fatal condition, far more so than many medical and surgical emergencies that we're all happy to watch disappear in an ambulance.

Once in hospital, care is tailor-made to suit the patient. It would be unthinkable to turn up to have a baby on the average medical ward: they're not prepared for it and naturally wouldn't have any midwives. So it is with mental emergencies. Units and hospitals specializing in these conditions are staffed by specialist nurses and doctors, and the hospitals themselves are equipped rather differently from the usual acute hospital. After all, most psychiatric patients are physically well and are up and about doing things most of the time. The average length of stay in a surgical ward is a matter of days, but in mental hospitals it is weeks or months. This calls for different facilities for socializing and *living*, as opposed to recovering from an operation and going home.

In addition to these special facilities, mental hospitals have to have areas in which really unwell patients can be closely supervised for their own good. There's very little point taking severely depressed, suicidal people into hospital if they could kill themselves as easily there as they could at home. This kind of supervision takes care and skill, as you will be able to appreciate if you have lived with a severely depressed or suicidal person. This kind of facility is only really available in psychiatric units. A general medical ward in an ordinary hospital cannot cope with such patients, however much you'd rather see your relative there instead. Such a safe environment is also far better than anything you could offer at home. True, it'll mean he or she has less 'freedom' for a short while, but if it's freedom to kill themselves that they're after, they're better off without it. You can never make your home suicide-proof to protect your severely ill relative, but in the secure parts of the hospital the windows will be 'leap-proof' and there'll always be someone to watch discreetly from a distance. You simply cannot offer this kind of supervision at home for twenty-four hours of the day – you'd need several friends or relatives, and that is usually impossible to arrange in either practical or emotional terms.

When dealing with cases of deep depression there are many things that need to be taken care of around the clock and only a hospital can manage this.

It's ironic that many acutely distressed people, who fight their doctor's decisions to send them to a psychiatric hospital, are often much happier the following morning once in the hospital (even without drugs), simply because they *know* in their heart of hearts that they're in the right place. Many people, and indeed their relatives, put up a token resistance to going into a mental hospital although deep down they know it's for the best. If you are really disturbed, you're worried what you might do to yourself and realize that you need help to protect you from yourself. Even a few hours in a caring environment, away from the family, can work wonders.

People tend to play down the services that a psychiatric hospital can offer, but often forget that it is staffed by doctors and psychiatric nurses who not only care for the patients, but also, like other medical staff, make diagnoses and treat people. This then is another reason for going into hospital. Whilst it may seem obvious to you that your relative is depressed, he or she may in fact have another physical or psychiatric condition

194

which needs diagnosing and treating. This can only be done in a specialist unit. Remember, too, that many depressed people have problems with drugs or alcohol, problems which can only be treated effectively by experts in specialized centres.

Lastly, a psychiatric hospital provides relief for the family of the ill person. For many of us, having a mentally ill relative is such a strain that we wonder if we too might not 'crack up' one day under the pressure. These strains reflect on to the patient and can actually have a detrimental effect on the depressive. Not only does having your relative in hospital free you to re-charge your emotional and physical batteries, but it could even mean that you can go back to work, take a holiday or pursue other pastimes that you'd suspended. It's all too easy for the relatives of severe depressives to get bogged down in the day-to-day problems of the illness, especially when the condition is characterized by hypochondriacal or manipulative behaviour. These relatives find that they simply haven't done anything for months, or even years, and that they too are being dragged down. A hospital stay for the patient can be a 'life-saver' for the relatives.

Two main questions come to the minds of those about to 'let' their relatives go into a mental hospital for the first time. The first is, 'Won't they resent being sent to a mental hospital?' and the second is, 'Won't all the mentally ill people there make the condition worse?'.

The answer to the first question is a definite 'NO'. As I've already pointed out, most depressed people are only too relieved that someone has taken the load off their shoulders and soon settle down to ward life quite happily. Being in hospital also convinces them that at least someone considers them to be *ill* and is taking their problem seriously. This again can bring a considerable sense of relief. Even people who have been committed to hospital against their will (see below) rarely resent it, even though they won't look back on their hospital stay as one of the enjoyable highlights of their lives. Many patients later actually thank the doctor who insisted on their admission, difficult though this may be to believe if you're in the throes of the early stages. Don't forget, as we saw in chapter three, that hopelessness is a major feature of depression and the hospitalized patients are being given hope – a precious gift – at a time when they most need it.

The second worry is a very real one, but can also be answered in the negative. Severely depressed people, especially in the early days, don't see themselves as different from the others in the ward. You, the relative, would notice differences and might be upset by certain behaviour in other patients, but people in the midst of their own problems and distress don't concern themselves with those around them. I've never heard emergency patients complain about the patients next to him when they are both extremely ill – on the contrary, very sick people tend to show compassion and understanding for one another. As depressed patients get better, they'll remark on the other patients around them and will slowly realize that their place is not in their midst. This is a sign that they're back in the real world, that their powers of discrimination are returning and that they're responding to treatment.

Getting the depressed person into hospital

People don't just turn up at mental hospitals and automatically get admitted as they do for medical emergencies; in fact persuading people to go into a mental hospital can be a real problem. For a start, they'll inevitably assume that they're being 'sent' there compulsorily, even if the suggestion comes from a relative or a friendly family doctor. That this is patently not the case can be seen from the statistics, which show that the vast majority of psychiatric patients go into hospital voluntarily. Such an admission is usually arranged by the family doctor, the psychiatrist the person has been seeing at the out-patient clinic, or by the social services department. Many patients put up a token fight, as we have seen, but it must be remembered that depression, by its very nature, makes people negative and unable to see the advantages of hospital care. Suggestions concerning going into hospital could be just another trigger to make them angry and anxious and you may well not be able to persuade them to go. Deep down, you know that they need special in-patient help, and there eventually comes a stage when you'll have to be tough and really insist that they have to go. There's a skill to this though. Don't choose a 'good' day, but wait until evening or for a 'bad' day, when they themselves are more likely to realize that they need help. If the depressive has worse periods of depression in the morning, suggest going into hospital then, and your chances of success will be higher.

If they're rational enough to listen to an explanation, tell them about the advantages of such a hospital (see page 193), but whatever you do, don't bargain with them. It's tempting to 'do deals' with people whose trump card is 'I'm not going to let you put me away'; but this is a dangerous move because it's unfair and unrealistic to play games with someone who is emotionally disturbed. Depressives can too easily misinterpret something you say and you could precipitate more trouble than you bargained for. In general, leave the arguments as to the advisability of admission to the professionals – they're used to handling such situations.

The legal side of mental hospitals

Although most people imagine that psychiatric hospitals are filled with people who've been 'sent' there, this is not the case. Most patients are there of their own free will and are called 'informal' patients. If you are an 'informal' patient you have the right to discharge yourself, even if the doctor thinks you should stay.

The group of patients who have been admitted 'under section' ('sectioned', 'detained' or 'compulsory' patients) may not discharge themselves and may be kept in hospital by law. They are a small proportion of those in psychiatric hospitals and units.

There are several different 'sections' (of the Mental Health Act of 1959) as we shall see, but they are not to be compared with prison sentences. For example, if you are admitted under Section 25, which lasts for up to twenty-eight days, this doesn't mean that you'll *have* to stay in hospital for this time. If the doctor in charge of your care thinks you are better, you'll be discharged sooner. You can also be allowed to go home on leave for weekends, or can be regraded to become an 'informal' patient.

If you are concerned as to whether or not you are under section, ask a senior nurse or a doctor. They should tell you and also explain which section you are under.

There are two types of section under which you can be

compulsorily admitted to a psychiatric hospital. One is civil (ninety-five per cent of all sections are of this type) and the other is criminal. Here is an explanation of the commonly used civil sections.

Section 29 (Admission for observation in psychiatric emergencies): This is a short-term section lasting up to seventy-two hours. In order to be sectioned under this category, a doctor (usually your family doctor), has to examine you and then fill in a form which states that you are suffering from a mental disturbance and that you require emergency admission for observation. Another form is then completed (usually by a social worker or a relative).

After seventy-two hours in hospital you become an informal patient unless a psychiatrist has examined you in the meantime and regraded you to Section 25.

Section 25 (Admission for observation): This is a short-term section which lasts for twenty-eight days. It requires two medical signatures (usually those of a general practitioner and a psychiatrist). The two doctors should not be on the staff of the same hospital. The original application for admission can be made by a relative or by a social worker. If after twenty-eight days it is thought that you still need to be compulsorily detained in hospital you can be regraded to section 26.

Section 26 (Admission for treatment): This is like Section 25, except that your relatives can object and can write to the local social services department to say so; the doctors signing the forms then have to state that you are definitely suffering from a specific mental illness and give reasons why they think so. This section can be renewed at the end of the first year. Your nearest relative can order your discharge by writing to the Hospital Managers (the Area Health Authority), saying that he or she wants to discharge you and giving them seventy-two hours notice. If your psychiatrist thinks you are a danger to yourself or others he can stop this discharge, but your relative can still get you out by applying to a Mental Health Tribunal. If you are over sixteen years of age, you can apply to a Mental Health Tribunal anyway to ask for your discharge from Section 26.

Section 136: This is a short-term (seventy-two hour) section, which applies if you have been found in a public place by a policeman who thinks you need to be taken to a 'place of safety', whether you are willing to go or not. This place of safety is almost always a police station or a hospital and you can be held there against your will for up to seventy-two hours to be seen by a doctor or a social worker.

Section 30: Under this section you can, if you are already in hospital as an informal patient, be detained against your will for up to three days.

These then are the main civil sections. I mentioned Mental Health Tribunals above. These are tribunals or committees consisting of three people (a lawyer, a psychiatrist and a lay person) to whom you or your relative can appeal if you are under a long-term section. The tribunal can get you discharged from your section. Unless you are under a retention order (Section 65 – a long-term section for criminals), the tribunal can override the advice of your psychiatrist and order your discharge. There are various times and circumstances under which you can apply to a tribunal, and details of these and other information can be obtained from MIND's Legal and Welfare Rights Service (see page 236 for address). Basically, you need an application form which the hospital should give you. This form should be filled in and sent to the local tribunal.

The form asks whether you want a 'formal hearing' or not. It is better to say 'yes' to this, because in a formal hearing you can stay and hear more of the evidence and because formal hearings result in a discharge more often than do informal hearings. You can also apply for a public hearing at which anyone can be present. Public hearings are, however, rarely granted. It is advisable for your nearest relative to apply for you, because if he or she applies for a 'formal' hearing it cannot be refused. You can withdraw your application for a hearing at any time before the hearing, but it may mean that you forfeit your chance to apply again for up to two years.

Most people appearing before a tribunal fare better if they are represented. This representation can be in the form of a lawyer, but a friend or relative will do. If you do use a solicitor he can claim legal aid and expenses for preparing the case, but not for appearing at the tribunal hearing itself. The tribunal will want to be sure that you have somewhere to live if you are discharged and it will help if you have someone at the hearing who can vouch for this.

At the hearing you will put your case and call your witnesses and the psychiatrist will put his case (probably that you should stay in hospital). You may not be allowed to hear your psychiatrist's medical evidence, but your representative will (a good reason for having one).

The tribunal will usually let you know its decision by post within seven days.

If you are in hospital under any section you should stay there. However, if you leave without permission you are not breaking the law, although it *is* illegal for anyone else to help you leave. If you do leave, you can in law be taken back again against your will at any time up to twenty-eight days after the day you went absent without permission. This applies even if your section would otherwise have expired. If you haven't returned to the hospital within twenty-eight days the section will usually expire.

When you become a patient in a mental hospital you do have various legal restrictions placed upon you, whether you are under section or not. Many of these are for your own safety and protection (both physically and legally).

The Mental Health Act of 1959 allows hospitals to withhold *letters* to and from psychiatric in-patients, for example, in certain circumstances. This is very rarely used unless you are in a criminally-oriented special hospital, but the law is there nevertheless. Any letters or parcels addressed to you at the hospital may in law be opened, but this rarely happens in practice. If, on opening a letter, your psychiatrist thinks it would upset you or hinder your progress he or she has the right to withhold it and should return it to the sender. Outgoing mail can be stopped too, if your psychiatrist thinks that it is offensive to the person it is going to or that it is defamatory or likely to prejudice your interests in any way. However, no psychiatrist is allowed to open your outgoing mail unless he or she feels you are suffering from a mental illness likely to make you write such letters.

200

You are ineligible for *jury service* if you are living in a mental hospital or similar institution as a result of a mental disorder, if you are being treated regularly for such a disorder by your doctor, or if you are under a Court of Protection.

If you have a *driving licence* you are bound to let the Licensing Authority know as soon as you realize that your mental state could affect your driving. If you wonder whether you should or should not tell them, ask your doctor. Notifying the Licensing Authority of your mental illness doesn't necessarily mean that they'll suspend your licence, although this is usually the case.

Voting is a complicated subject. If you are in the psychiatric wing of a district general hospital, your name should be included by the hospital if you are not already registered to vote from your home address. If you want to vote, your name must be on the electoral register somewhere. You can have your name down in two places, but you can only vote once. Patients under section cannot vote, but if they are not actually receiving treatment they can vote if the consultant in charge gives them permission.

Your personal belongings may well be searched for anything that might be able to harm you as soon as you go into hospital. They will all be carefully kept and given back to you when you are discharged or when you discharge yourself (if you are an informal patient).

If you are an informal patient, you can go home on *leave* at any time the doctor agrees. If you want to go home for a weekend, for example, ask the nurse in charge or the doctor. Even if you are under section, you can still be allowed to go home if it is thought that you'll be all right.

If you are mentally ill, you're not allowed to make a will, sell property or act as a trustee. This does not depend on whether or not you're in hospital, or whether or not you are under section, but on whether you are capable of making rational decisions on important matters – in or out of hospital. Many severely depressed people are really in no fit state to make such decisions and the court may have to appoint a 'receiver' to run their affairs for them. This receiver is usually a relative, but can be a court official. This person can sell your home, invest your money or make a will on your behalf, for example. The court that deals with all these matters is called the Court of Protection and is situated in London.

Treatment decisions are, just as in any other hospital setting, in the hands of the doctors. You have no right to demand any special treatments. However, it makes sense to suggest things you think might be helpful. For example, there is a considerable genetic component to drug sensitivity reactions and to a person's response to drugs; so if a member of your close family has been depressed and responded to (or reacted adversely to) a particular drug, the chances are that you will too, so tell the psychiatrist.

If you are worried about a treatment planned for you, ask the medical and nursing staff about it, about the side-effects and whether it is necessary. You will almost always have the right to refuse the treatment, but you can be asked to leave the hospital if you don't let the doctors carry out treatment they think will cure you. This goes for ordinary general hospitals too. It is illegal for doctors to treat you against your will and you can sue the hospital for assault if this happens. If you are an informal patient you can refuse any treatment and they may not force anything on you *unless* it is to save your life.

If you are under section your rights are not clear. It is best to contact the Legal Department of MIND (see page 236 for address) if you are in this situation. They can give advice and have access to lawyers with a special knowledge of this area.

Complaints are not often necessary, but when they are it's helpful to know what to do. Remember that a relative or even a visitor can make a complaint on your behalf.

Every hospital has its own complaints procedure and you or a relative should ask what to do. The booklet about the hospital that you'll have been given on admission usually tells you how to go about complaining. Most complaints are dealt with locally to everyone's satisfaction, but if you are not satisfied you can get your Community Health Council (the telephone number of which can be found in the local directory) to advise you how to proceed.

As a last resort, the Health Service Commissioner (the Ombudsman) can be approached to investigate the complaint himself. He has the powers to investigate widely, but cannot intervene on matters of medical management. He will only take the matter up if you have had no success with the ordinary channels of complaint. He can be contacted at the office of the Health Service Commissioner (see page 235 for the address and telephone number).

If, after all of these approaches, you're still not satisfied, your local MP or MIND's Legal and Welfare Rights Department may be able to help.

Your depressed relative in hospital

Unfortunately, space doesn't permit a detailed discussion of all the things that will pass through your mind the day your relative has to go into hospital, so I'll confine myself to those things that are of particular importance.

Most hospitals have a helpful booklet for you and your hospitalized relative to read. If the depressive is too distraught to bother, and this will almost always be the case with an emergency admission for depression, be sure to read it through yourself. It will tell you about what you should take in, about visiting, the rules and regulations of the hospital and a host of other useful facts. Don't forget to ask the nurse in charge if you have any questions. Even after the reorganization of the health service and a new system of grading nurses, ward sisters are still called 'sister' and their male equivalents (very commonplace in psychiatric hospitals) 'charge nurse'. All day-to-day enquiries should be made to these people, but specific medical enquiries can be discussed with your relative's psychiatrist.

Whilst on the subject of psychiatrists, don't get carried away with the idea that because the depressive is in a psychiatric hospital, hours will be spent daily in deep consultation with a psychiatrist, because nothing could be further from the truth. For all kinds of reasons (and mainly because it wouldn't be valuable), patients in a mental hospital are not seen every day for psychotherapy. A consultant psychiatrist (the head of the treatment team) will come round at least once a week, but most of the time junior doctors in training to be psychiatrists will look after the daily routines.

Just what will routinely happen in hospital when your relative has been admitted with depression will vary greatly according to the hospital and the psychiatrist in charge. Much good day-to-day therapeutic work is done by the nurses and

203

trained psychiatric nurses are very skilled at this. Some hospitals will use group therapy and others will have clinics or get-togethers for those with special problems. The amount of psychotherapy (talk therapy) your relative receives will often be minimal, and the mainstay of hospital treatment will be drugs and careful nursing.

Visiting is one of the most difficult parts about having a relative in a psychiatric ward. Hospital visiting is never easy, even in an ordinary hospital ward, but it's doubly difficult in mental hospitals. Here are some tips.

Don't stay too long. Make repeated visits for short periods rather than the other way round. Just because you're 'allowed' a certain visiting period, don't feel you have to use it all up. A short get-together is less tiring for the patient and less stressful for you. Never forget that your relative is in this particular type of hospital because he or she can't cope with the outside world for a while, so don't regale them with all the domestic problems they're escaping from. Part of the reason for being in hospital is to get away from all of life's troubles for a time.

It's up to you to protect your relative from other visitors, however well-meaning. Make sure that all visiting is coordinated through one person, preferably the ill person's spouse. In this way, three or four people won't turn up at the same time and be disappointed if the hospital allows only restricted numbers of visitors per bed. It also gives you the opportunity of putting people off for a day or two if your relative is going through a bad patch or a setback in treatment.

Try to be yourself. Don't be self-conscious about the other patients and their visitors, worrying in case they're thinking 'How could a nice woman like that have a husband in here?', or conversely 'Why did she drive him to it?' All the others are in the same boat and all but the toughest have exactly the same fears, guilt and reservations as you have. Never try to cheer the depressed person up by telling jokes, silly stories or other 'amusing' anecdotes. The patient will want to see you because you're you and not as a source of entertainment. By all means be as pleasant as possible, but if you force the jollity the patient will begin to wonder what on earth has come over you and whether you suspect that they've lost their wits since being admitted. It's not easy being a patient at the best of times, but if people go out of their way to 'cheer you up' artificially it all becomes very wearing.

One of the greatest pitfalls of psychiatric visiting is getting involved with other patients. Many people have very few visitors and it's tempting to befriend those who approach you when you visit. Beware, because you may unwittingly find yourself getting involved in all kinds of problems. Unless you're really used to psychiatric patients, getting involved with them can be disturbing, especially if you then worry about what sort of people your relative is with. Don't forget that the occupants of the ward are not emotionally or mentally normal or they wouldn't be there. Befriending other patients can lead to gossip, false accusations or requests for food, drink or drugs that you'll feel awkward about.

Keep your conversation as positive as possible and stick to subjects that you know will hold your relative's interest. Be encouraging, tell them if they look better and listen attentively to any hospital stories or accounts of treatment. Never forget that everything a patient says is tinged by depression, and so it is likely to be over pessimistic and critical. It's easy to get upset by accounts of the lousy food, terrible patients and uncaring staff, but remember that until the time of admission you were probably the butt of similar negative thoughts.

As time goes by and the drugs begin to work you'll begin to notice some of their side-effects. If these seem to be too unpleasant, discuss the matter with the senior nurse on duty or even ask to see the doctor. Psychiatric patients, and especially depressed ones, are very quick to grumble about their treatment (or lack of it) and there is always, in their eyes, reason for improvement. They are in no fit state to remember that it took months, and even years, to get that depressed and that overnight cures are unlikely, so be patient. Psychotherapy sessions will never be long enough, nor the therapist understanding enough; drugs will always be 'useless'; ECT an unwelcome intrusion with or without side-effects. The difficult thing is that there is often more than a grain of truth in what patients say, but it is up to you, the well person, to talk to the doctor or nurses to see how true it is and, if so, what could be done. Armed with some realistic facts from the staff, you can then encourage your relative to be positive about the

205

improvements. And improvements there will be, if only you can see them for what they are. Walking down the corridor and talking to a new person can be a real milestone on the road to recovery. A flicker of enjoyment from a game of table tennis or a job well done in occupational therapy can seem unimportant to the insensitive visitor, but can be the signal that things are on the mend. Build on these little things and take pleasure where it is to be found.

Life for the depressed person in hospital can't be very pleasant, however good the surroundings and however nice the people. Very often, the central point of the day will be your visit, so don't make rash promises about when you'll come or how often. Only promise what you can live up to because if *you* start letting your relative down, he or she will go back a step or two in their treatment. Having said this, beware of being manipulated. Many experts see the manipulation of others as one of the most distressing features of depressive illness, so be warned. If you're not careful they'll have you complaining about everything, getting them moved to another bed or ward, getting new neighbours to replace the existing ones, and so on. The staff will be used to this, but you won't and it'll all be very worrying. So be warned.

Perhaps the greatest manipulation you'll be open to is that of getting the patient back home. Many depressives, knowing that the staff and the other patients are only too aware of their ruses and manipulative techniques, would rather be at home where they can control the environment better. This is not a malicious remark but, alas, a realistic one. It is part of the illness and a well-recognized one. Certain types of depressed patients will try to shock you and unsettle you by their stories, in the hopes that you'll be so upset that you'll withdraw them from the ward at once. It's upsetting for any relatives to learn how pleasant the patient can be so soon after the visitor has left. Visitors (especially the spouse) often see patients at their worst and hear from staff and other patients what ideal patients they are. This doesn't square with the complaints and manipulative treatment the visitors get and, not unnaturally, they wonder why. I'm afraid part of the answer is that this is what some depressed people do. Such relatives have been the unwitting butt of this type of behaviour for months, or even years, before

206

the admission of the depressed person to hospital. The sad thing is that such behaviour becomes so 'normal' to the spouse that he or she forgets the reality of the person's behaviour before the depression set in.

Improving and going home

As time goes by, your relative will get better. This may take weeks or even months. Before the time of discharge, it makes sense to plan a short holiday for the two of you, if possible. A simple holiday, not too far from home and with plenty of activity is best. Lazing around on a beach somewhere is probably the last thing a depressive should be doing.

Right from the day of the patients' discharge, be positive about their improvement, remind them to take their drugs regularly and ensure that they go to their follow up appointments at the hospital. Some people on modern drug therapy get better so dramatically that they're loath to go back to the hospital for follow up. This is a shame, because the doctors are human beings and want to hear some of the good news as well as the bad.

Long-term follow up will be carried out by the patient's general practitioner, and if you're at all worried about your relative's progress you should discuss it with the doctor. Having the person in hospital should have given you, the relative, a break and a chance to think things through without the daily pressures of being with a depressed person. This time can be valuably used to plan ways of overcoming some of the problems that led to the depression in the first place. Personality and interrelationship problems are often at the heart of the matter and the time you have free from day-to-day (or even hour-to-hour) problems can be just the opportunity you need to work things out. Talk to your doctor, priest, closest friend or even friends or relatives of the patient to try to get to the bottom of the underlying troubles. There are very few situations in life that can't be remedied with caring, professional help; but most of us are too stubborn to avail ourselves of the help that is available. Social services departments can often assist with practical problems; going to a marriage guidance counsellor, getting help with troublesome children and scores of other things are available for those who really want to get out of the rut that originally made them depressed.

So, if you really want to see your relative well again, use the time he or she spends in hospital to do your thinking and getting help, so that when they come home you can really start building your life together again.

CHAPTER 9

Suicide

It may seem to be strange to devote a whole chapter of a book on depression to suicide, but depression is a potentially lethal condition, and it's suicide that so often kills depressed people. Studies of people with depressive illness show that about fifteen per cent eventually kill themselves. This makes suicide a very serious hazard of depression.

Depression is by far the commonest cause of suicide. Several surveys have found that between sixty and ninety per cent of all suicidal people were suffering from (or just recovering from) depression. It is because of this startling and undeniable fact that the prompt and serious treatment of depression is so essential. Depression isn't a condition to be taken lightly – it kills people.

If you've never really thought about suicide seriously before, it might come as a deep shock to think that anything could be so bad as to make you actively want to kill yourself. After all, life is so precious and we spend most of our existence preserving, nurturing and creating new life. Suicide strikes at the very heart of man's social ethics and still carries a very considerable social stigma. Even in these 'permissive' times, suicide remains a taboo subject.

Suicide was certainly occurring 4,000 years ago and there is every reason to believe that man has been killing himself since his existence on earth began. A small minority of societies throughout history have condoned suicide, but the great majority condemn it. In Ancient Rome and Greece it was considered a crime against the state, and in England in the Middle Ages the bodies of suicides were dragged through the streets before they were hung upside down or impaled on stakes at public crossroads. In the eleventh century, the suicide's family was punished by being refused permission to bury the body in a church or city cemetery and the survivors often had their property confiscated.

It wasn't until 1961 that the Suicide Act was passed in the UK – an Act which finally declared that a person who committed suicide hadn't broken the law. (Helping someone to commit suicide is still illegal, however.)

In the US, where the law is to a great extent drawn from English law, suicide is still a crime in several states although legal action is no longer taken against the families.

Even in the UK, where suicide has been 'legal' for twenty years, there is still a tremendous sense of shame and guilt attached to the death. A suicide in the family can be a real social stigma and one which can last for years. Even apart from the religious and cultural taboos, people assume that the family is in some way to blame, and that had they been any good they would have prevented it happening somehow. This is usually unfair, because in most cases there is little that could have been done. After all, most suicides are late middle aged and elderly men, who are determined to kill themselves whatever their family might do.

The trouble with a suicide in the family is that there is a double dose of bad feelings. It's bad enough when anyone in a family dies, but when society censures or even threatens to condemn a family, there's always the dreadful, unspoken question – 'Did we *really* kill Dad?' These emotional traumas take their toll of the surviving relatives, who are statistically more likely to become victims of depression and suicide as a result. Fortunately though, the negative results on the rest of the family are not as bad as one would expect. For more details of this, see page 230.

It's important here to draw a distinction between suicide and attempted suicide, because research shows that they are different conditions. People who commit suicide are by and large male, suffering from depression and are over the age of fifty-five. Those who make attempts at suicide are young, female and often have no real wish to die. We shall look at attempted suicide (parasuicide) later, but first let's look at suicide itself.

How common is it?

Suicide is not a common cause of death, but it is an important and often preventable one. Only about one per cent of all deaths in the UK are caused by suicide, but it is the second commonest cause of death under the age of twenty (accidents alone cause more deaths). Statistics for suicide rates around the world are notoriously inaccurate, and certainly cannot be compared from country to country because of the different criteria used for defining and recording suicide. Some countries are loath to label a death as being due to suicide unless the evidence is extremely clear. There is no doubt that vastly more people commit suicide than official statistics suggest and that many of them do it in ways that are impossible to prove. For example, it is well known that some people who are depressed throw themselves into their work in an over-zealous way, only to die prematurely from stress-related diseases such as heart attacks. Other depressed people drink too much, in the knowledge that it will damage their livers and so shorten their lives. Others drive recklessly and undertake flagrantly dangerous pursuits in which they dice with death.

No figure can, or ever will, be available for the number of those who kill themselves unnecessarily in these ways, so they are lost to the suicide statistics.

Recorded suicide deaths have been falling since the mid-1960s in the UK. This has probably come about because of the introduction of safe domestic gas. Coal gas, with its lethal carbon monoxide, was a readily available way out for would-be suicides, but now that it has been removed and replaced by natural gas, they take tablets, which they have usually recently received from the doctor.

It's tempting to believe that increased services and care for the mentally ill and the efforts of the Samaritans have brought about this fall in the suicide rate, but there is no evidence for either. Improved medical services have certainly resulted in some attempted suicides being saved, but this cannot account for the whole drop in numbers.

Having said that the figures are dropping, there is still no room for complacency. Suicide is twice as common as homicide in America – a country known for its considerable murder rate. In the US, suicide in all its forms has been ranked as the fifth most common cause of death and it is probably the same in the UK.

The currently falling suicide rate is almost entirely accounted for by a fairly big drop in suicide among the elderly. Suicide rates for men under thirty-five and women under twenty-five are however still rising. In 1980 in England and Wales 2,436 men and 1,586 women committed suicide, according to official figures; but as we have seen, these grossly underestimate the real size of the problem.

Who commits suicide?

In simple terms, it's people who are depressed who commit suicide. Alcoholism and drug abuse are certainly not far behind as causes, but as we have seen (page 74) these two conditions are so closely related to depression that many leading psychiatrists see them as depressive equivalents.

Men tend to commit suicide more often than women, but evidence from several countries shows that women are fast catching up.

The vast majority of people who commit suicide are *not* mentally ill by any reasonable definition of the term. They are usually temporarily unbalanced as part of a more longstanding depressive illness, and will have had a recent emotional upheaval that triggered the suicide. More 'normal' people commit suicide than do psychiatric patients. Some schizophrenics kill themselves, it is true, but in terms of death rates they make little impact on the suicide statistics.

People at particular risk of committing suicide are those with any features in the following list. If a person has two or more features from the list, then he or she must be considered to be a serious risk and needs professional help at once.

Depression
Severe insomnia
Severe hypochondriacal preoccupations
Previous attempts at suicide
A male over fifty-five years
A history of alcohol or drug abuse
Schizophrenia

212

A disabling painful disease or serious physical illness
Social isolation
Repeated suicidal thoughts
A history of suicide in the family
A history of recent bereavement
Unemployment or financial problems
Recovery from depression

Suicide is no respecter of persons. People of all races, colours, educational levels, social classes and ages kill themselves, so don't think of the above list as comprehensive. The only group in which suicide is rare is in children under twelve. (For more details of childhood suicide see page 215.)

As we have seen, depression is the single commonest cause of suicide and some studies have shown that being depressed raises one's chances of dying by suicide 500 per cent above the rest of the population.

But whatever background, disease, mental disturbance or personality type suicidal people may have, they'll have one or all of the following experiences: loneliness, helplessness, hopelessness, the loss of something they valued, severe disappointment, a marital infidelity, a sense of personal failure (often not real but nevertheless seen as real by the person). These and a host of other trigger factors can all tip the balance from simply feeling depressed to actually doing something to end it all.

Suicide is three times commoner among divorced people than among the married, and occurs more among the single than the married. Perhaps the partner of a potential suicide can so tip the balance as to avert suicide when the going gets tough. (Divorced doctors in the US, for example, are thirteen times more likely to kill themselves than are their married colleagues.)

It has recently become apparent that black people (who had been thought to have lower suicide rates) are committing suicide more frequently. Minority racial groups are now recognized to be at increased risk of suicide in almost every country. Classical studies in the US show that American Indians are five times more likely to commit suicide than other citizens (both directly and by lethal overdrinking), and in

213

many US cities deaths among young blacks far outnumber those among comparable whites. Studies among white families have found that a significant factor in suicide is the lack of an effective father figure in the home and this has been found to be a problem in black families too. Early separation, death, divorce, poor relations with the mother and inadequate father-son relationships have been found in both racial groups.

Although approximately twice as many women are thought to suffer from depression as men (for a further discussion of this see page 22), many more men kill themselves than do women. The ratio varies according to the age group studied. The highest differential in one survey was found to be in the eighty to eighty-four year age group, in which seven times as many men killed themselves as women.

Suicide rates among the elderly are falling from this high peak, but they still have the highest rate for any age group. Men, and especially men over the age of fifty, continue to be the most at risk of actually killing themselves.

For a quarter of a century suicide levels have been highest among professionals and executives, and several studies have shown that the rates are exceptionally high among health professionals. One survey found that suicide among health personnel outnumbered suicides among other technical/professional people of the same sex by 2.3:1. Twice as many doctors kill themselves as do other professionals, with doctors over sixty-five showing the highest rate. Unfortunately, it looks as though there is some kind of a spin off to their spouses, who also have a far higher suicide rate than would be expected. Half of all suicide deaths among doctors occur in their most productive years professionally (thirty-five to fifty-four years of age) and retired doctors have about four times the suicide level of other retired men. A major factor in the high suicide rate among doctors clearly is their ability to obtain, and their knowledge of, the drugs needed to complete the act successfully.

In general, western people commit suicide when they are mentally disturbed through depression, alcoholism or an acute emotional crisis. Suicide, carried out coldly and rationally, whilst it does occur, is very rare.

Suicide in children and young people

We saw on page 126 that children suffer from depression far more commonly than most people realize and a great deal of research shows that adolescents too are commonly depressed. The myth that children and young people don't get depressed has been squashed by many surveys, but because the depression is often presented in ways that adults don't expect (boredom, being fed-up, nothing worthwhile to do, aches and pains, excitement-seeking and delinquency), it can easily be overlooked.

Suicide in children is, however, very rare under the age of twelve. In the UK, on average only fourteen children under twelve kill themselves each year. It appears that what tips the balance (as judged by suicide notes) is a home discipline crisis or a high parental opinion about to be shattered by school reports of anti-social behaviour. Quite a few have parents or school friends who have killed themselves.

It is thought that children don't commit suicide much before the age of twelve years because until then they have no real concept of death, are free from pubertal changes and are closely supervised for much of the time. Even some of those who do try to kill themselves have no real concept of death and are doing something which they think will buy them time until unpleasant or intolerable situations pass. They do not see death as permanent. 'My mother will be sorry when I'm dead' is a common thought in children contemplating suicide, and the tragedy is that they don't realize that they won't be around to witness the sorrow. Children's suicidal threats are, however, often very real and should be taken seriously, especially over the age of twelve. Just *how* seriously these threats should be taken is difficult to assess, because only forty per cent of child suicides makes threats beforehand. Such threats should be taken as cries for help, but they are not predictive of suicide itself in children or young people. This is not the case in adults, as we shall see.

One survey of child suicides found that they fell into two broad groups. One was composed of the loners, often very intelligent children, who felt distant from their parents because the parents were less well educated. They were taller than most of their age group and closer to puberty. Their mothers were often mentally ill. Children in the other group were aggressive, impetuous, resented criticism and were suspicious of everyone.

More boys than girls kill themselves – the girls doing it with drugs and the boys using more ingenious ways such as drowning, hanging and even some rather extraordinary methods. Most suicides occur after an absence from school, and disturbed or broken homes are commonly part of the picture.

Childhood suicide is therefore rare and is likely to remain so. It is, however, a real hazard of childhood depression and severely depressed children are at risk, albeit to a small degree.

Once we move into the teens, suicide (or, more often, attempted suicide) becomes an important side-effect of depression. Suicide rates among the adolescent age group are rising, yet to keep the matter in perspective, suicide is still far commoner in older age groups.

Suicide among older children is more often triggered by the loss of a significant person in the child's life than by failure at school and other factors. Many of the youngsters who commit suicide have never had one person they could admire or trust and so tend to become loners. Such youngsters, when away at college or university for the first time, find making relationships difficult and their depression can lead to suicide. This is all the more likely to be triggered by the loss of a girlfriend or boyfriend, as this loss is more poignant for such young people.

One US study found that young men at college who committed suicide were likely to have lost a father (either through death or divorce) before the age of sixteen. If the father *was* alive he was highly successful, deeply involved in his work and hadn't taken time to relate to his son. Girls who committed suicide were more likely to have come from homes where the mother was domineering and the father weak and ineffectual. When such a girl is disappointed in her boyfriend she feels desperately let down, may put the boy under sexual pressure or even become pregnant.

Particularly in the US, drugs are increasingly playing a role in teenage suicides. The underlying problem in the first place is probably depression, but many drugs can themselves produce depression which can lead to suicide (see also page 70). Mind-altering drugs, such as LSD, can lead a person to suicide because they give him or her a sense of invulnerability to truly dangerous pursuits.

Why do people do it?

Studies show that almost everyone has thought of committing suicide at some time in their lives, so it is a feeling we can all identify with. However, it's a big step from fleeting thoughts of suicide to actually doing something about it. It is this step that is so easily bridged by depression. But it's not only depression that can make the difference between thinking about it and doing it, though depression is the commonest cause. Here are some reasons people frequently give.

'Why go on living?' is a common thought when depressed people contemplate suicide. Life has got to the point where it has no meaning for them, where they're no use to anyone, have nothing to offer the world and can see no future or end to their problems. These thoughts are especially indicative of trouble if they are out of character. They are often a sign that people are heading for self-destruction and must be taken seriously.

A sudden impulse, in the middle of an argument, after a disappointment, a loss or a let down can lead to suicide on the spur of the moment. This is relatively uncommon and far more frequently leads to an unsuccessful attempted suicide. Sometimes the trigger-factor so dazes the person that, for example, a husband learning of his wife's infidelity will walk under a car, oblivious of its presence. In moments of anger or frustration our minds can become temporarily blurred and we can, in a flurry of emotions, do something which, even if it doesn't kill us, can bring us too near the brink for our liking. I say this because this sort of impetuous action is often soon regretted. Such suicides are easily prevented if distraught people are protected from themselves during the 'at risk' period.

Physical or mental exhaustion can trigger suicidal thoughts, even in non-depressed individuals. Repeated sleepless nights coupled with other mental and emotional trauma can lead a young mother, for example, to feel suicidal even though she isn't clinically depressed. The world simply gets on top of her for a while. Such people rarely commit suicide if they are tided over this dangerous initial phase. If they are not depressed they have no real desire to die. A good rant, a holiday or the sorting out of an underlying personal problem is what these people need and respond to.

People with *a serious physical illness*, if they are in constant pain or believe the illness to be terminal, sometimes see suicide as an escape from their suffering. Some of these sufferers may be depressed as a result of the illness and, if this is so, the depression should be treated; but many more are in perfect mental health and simply want to end what they see as an intolerable burden on themselves and those around them. Euthanasia, 'mercy killing', is a highly emotive subject and feelings run high, especially among those who demand to be put out of their misery. This is no place to discuss euthanasia, but it is no coincidence that suicide rates soar as ageing proceeds. Many old people with life behind them (as they see it), failing faculties and increasing physical and emotional losses, believe there is little to live for and so take their own lives. This in many ways reflects our society's appalling treatment of the old in general, and those of us who are younger should have a real burden on our consciences.

Some people who try to commit suicide (and a few of those who actually succeed) are *trying to communicate* something to those around them or to one person in particular. A woman begging her husband to be faithful, a teenager trying to get some love and attention and a thousand other examples are all pointers to the desperation that many people can't express in any other way. Although these people rarely kill themselves, they are dicing with death. Sometimes their plans go wrong and they succeed all too well in their efforts. If the would-be rescuer couldn't be reached, the planned homecomer missed the train, or the drugs were taken with alcohol, the outcome can all too easily be more serious than expected and can even prove fatal.

How to tell if someone is thinking of suicide

As I have said, depression is a serious and potentially fatal disease. This means that if you or someone you know is

218

depressed you must be on the look-out for suicidal signs. Most people who succeed in committing suicide have been secretly planning it for some time, yet they often give subtle clues, if only you can recognize them.

Unfortunately, many people believe the old wives' tale that if people talk about killing themselves they won't do it. This is sadly not true, as many thousands of distraught families can testify. On the contrary, depressed people usually 'cry out' for protection against their self-destructive urge. Eighty per cent of successful suicides have talked about it before, sometimes even to their doctors. Talking about suicide or loneliness is a very dangerous sign and should never be ignored. Always take such talk seriously and get medical help.

Many old people, very young people and highly educated people don't talk about it and simply go ahead and make plans. A good clue here is if the person starts preparing for death. Some people clear out their drawers, gather personal things together, tidy their study, make a will, talk about life insurance policies or give away prized possessions. Any of these things combined with depression should arouse suspicion, as should any stockpiling of medicines.

'Suicide talk' is often taken simply as a gesture contrived to frighten people into giving the depressive more attention or to manipulate a situation to gain a desired goal. This may be true, but still cannot be ignored. Anyone who is this desperate to make their feelings of despair known deserves help and *needs* it. You can't dare people to act out their threats. You'll be alive if you 'win', but they won't and you'll never forgive yourself.

Individuals at particular risk are those who have already tried to kill themselves. Never think that because they didn't succeed first time they'll be put off trying again. If they're talking about it and they've done it before, statistics show that they'll do it again and are more likely to succeed.

Lastly, don't be fooled by religious or highly moral people who talk of suicide. Neither devoutness nor ethical or moral beliefs carry any weight at all when someone is depressed enough to consider suicide. Religious men of every creed have committed and do commit suicide, and I personally know one very spiritual man who has tried four times. Religion does seem to be something of a barrier though in global terms, because

Roman Catholics commit suicide less than those of other religions. On an individual basis, religious or spiritual beliefs give scant protection.

So, if you think a friend or a relative fits any of these descriptions, don't ignore them. It has been calculated that two million Americans living today have tried to kill themselves. This represents an enormous pool of potential suicides – given that those who have tried once are more likely to try again. Add to this known 'at risk' group all those who are contemplating suicide for the first time, and you'll see how likely it is that you'll come across someone who really means business. We who are not depressed owe it to those who are to help protect them from themselves during the very short-lived periods when life becomes intolerable for them. You never know, some day the tables may be turned and you'll wish someone had helped you.

What this means in practice is being aware of the danger signs and, if they are acute, not leaving the person alone, even to go to the lavatory. In the meantime, get someone else to seek medical advice or help from the social services department of the local authority. The Samaritans can also be helpful. (See below.)

How, when and where people do it

In the UK the vast majority of people kill themselves using drugs. In the US guns and explosives feature very prominently. Hanging, strangulation and suffocation with car exhaust fumes come next and jumping from high places and under trains are way down the list. Men, by and large, go for more bravado, favouring the dramatic methods, whilst women almost all take tablets.

Most suicides occur in the spring. It seems that the majority of depressions start around September and that the person attempts to deal with the illness for about six months before medical help is sought. During this time the depression may be undetected, 'masked' (see page 39) or inadequately treated. This leads to a peak in hospital admissions for depression in March/April and a peak in suicides in May. This is, of course, a very over-simplified conceptual model of suicide and lots more research needs to be done, but it could lead to a better understanding of suicide and its prevention.

People working in this field are always surprised that there are so few suicides over the Christmas holiday period. A lot of people certainly become depressed at a time when everyone else is enjoying themselves, but this doesn't seem to be reflected in an increase in suicide. No one knows why this should be.

Traditionally, Monday has been a particularly prominent day for suicides, which gives some support to the existence of the 'Monday Blues'. One might expect that Saturday night would be a vulnerable night, what with an increased alcohol intake and the end of a disappointing or frustrating week, but this isn't so. In fact Sunday is more popular for suicides than Saturday.

It's a sad irony that treatment for depression can not only save a lot of lives, but can also contribute to the suicide level. The four months after release from hospital are a dangerous time for potentially suicidal people. They feel more active and sufficiently better as a result of drug treatment to kill themselves. Prior to treatment, their inertia and low feelings probably prevented them from 'getting round' to suicide.

Most people commit suicide at home – usually in the morning.

Suicides that don't succeed (parasuicide)

For every person who succeeds in committing suicide, between five and ten others try and fail, or never really mean to kill themselves in the first place. That they 'fail' is no reflection on their ability to carry out the task successfully, but rather demonstrates their different motivation from the 'true' or successful suicide. Researchers in this area view these two types of suicide as substantially different in several important ways, as we shall see.

Self-poisoning (the commonest form of attempted yet unsuccessful suicide) has escalated to become one of the foremost acute medical hazards in the western world. It is now the commonest reason for emergency non-surgical admission in people under fifty and at least 100,000 people poison themselves every year in the UK alone. If this trend continues self-poisoners will fill every available emergency medical bed in 1984.

Although ten per cent of parasuicides inflict injury on themselves, the other ninety per cent take drugs so 'overdosing', 'self-poisoning' and 'parasuicides' are terms that have all come to be used interchangeably. It's a sad fact that 'taking an overdose' has become a recognized (if not yet totally acceptable) way of drawing attention to oneself in a crisis situation. There is no evidence at all that there is more psychiatric illness than ever, so it must simply be that people are using self-poisoning as a means to an end.

Unfortunately, we in the medical profession are mostly to blame for this epidemic, because the rise in the level of self-poisoning has gone hand in hand with a gigantic increase in the prescribing of mind-altering drugs. Many surveys show that most overdose patients have consulted their doctor in the previous month and have been given more than enough tablets to kill themselves. In many UK practices, the doctors allow mind-altering drugs to be repeat-prescribed without seeing the patient at all, and under these circumstances long-term addiction (be it physical or psychological) can occur, in addition to the undoubted stockpiling that provides tools for the overdose. This excessive and often indiscriminate prescribing of such drugs is a blot on the medical profession and is directly responsible for most of the increase in self-poisoning that we are seeing today.

Most people who take an overdose have either had unpleasant childhood experiences, are currently going through an emotional upheaval or both. A broken home in childhood renders people more likely to be hurt by the loss of a loved one in later life and makes them less able to forge good relationships as adults. It's often against such a background that an acute problem is superimposed. Most people who take an overdose are not 'mad' in any sense but are going through a temporary, disabling emotional crisis, albeit superimposed on a psychological disturbance.

Alcohol plays an important part in overdoses. One study found that about half the men and a quarter of the women were either drunk or had taken alcohol at the time of their overdose, and alcoholism was diagnosed in forty per cent of the men and

222

seven per cent of the women. We have seen how alcohol goes hand in hand with depression in chapter one, so this will come as no surprise to the reader.

Of all the triggers that precipitate an overdose, a break or threatened break in a personal relationship is by far the commonest. It's a sad fact that, on questioning, most overdose patients tell of their poor relationships with all kinds of people for almost all their lives. This makes it even sadder that they get so badly treated in hospital and by health care professionals in general. Junior doctors and the nursing staff on whose backs the main burden of caring for overdose victims falls, often treat them with a singular lack of concern and compassion. Several studies have found that the medical profession looks upon these people as making annoying attempts at self-destruction. This evokes a hostility towards the patient which is often ill-disguised. Unfortunately, most doctors and nurses see themselves as being there to treat 'really ill' people, by which they mean really physically ill. It is sad to see the most pleasant and caring of medical and nursing staff become spiteful and even vindictive when faced with an overdose. By and large, the principle that's adopted is to treat them as perfunctorily as can reasonably be endured and to discharge them as quickly as possible.

Officially every overdose patient should receive a psy-chiatric assessment, but in practice this doesn't happen. Most doctors feel that overdose patients are unsatisfactory to treat and that they do not benefit from what a hospital has to offer. Doctors and nurses like treating patients who fit into their concept of the 'model patient'. Such a patient is physically ill, passive, appreciative and grateful. Our training in modern medicine fits us very poorly for the compassionate treatment of the countless thousands of people who don't fit into this cosy stereotype, yet who are seriously ill. It is a tragedy that the very 'overdose' personalities that most annoy doctors are the least likely to get further help and the most likely to end up killing themselves.

Even when overdose patients are offered out-patient follow up appointments to see a psychiatrist, only about half attend. There are several reasons for this high default rate. First, parasuicide is usually an interpersonal event which occurs at the height of a crisis and can be seen as a primitive kind of problem solving. Within a week the major components of the problem will have changed, albeit temporarily, and the patient no longer feels he or she needs the help or wants to be reminded of the event. Second, a week's interval may be too long for a really troubled person who'll write off psychiatrists as irrelevant. Third, to many overdose victims the thought that their problem is going to be classed as 'psychiatric' is simply too much for them.

Many studies have looked at why people take overdoses and the reasons are both numerous and complex. Some people do it in a fit of rage, often after a loved one has hurt them. This, they reason, will make the other party feel guilty and bring them back, physically or emotionally. Another group are seeking a way out of an emotional situation from which they can see no other exit. Others (about half) say they really want to die, but on more careful questioning they clearly don't. Probably the most common motive – even if the individual doesn't realize it at the time – is an appeal for help. It's a way of telling the world that the depressive can't cope any more – either with life in general or with a particular crisis situation. Often, more than one of these motives can be present in the same person.

Are those who succeed different from those who don't?

There has been a lot of research on this subject over the years and the answer is definitely 'yes'. Experts in this field have divided people into two distinct but overlapping groups.

Parasuicides are mostly female (2.5 women to every man); are under forty (eighty per cent); come from the lower social classes; are living with others in relatively overcrowded accommodation; have a lifelong history of major, recurring conflicts in personal relationships; and have a diagnosable personality disorder. Typically, their self-poisoning acts are impulsive and they usually make sure they'll be found. They not infrequently actually take the overdose in front of someone.

Suicides, on the other hand, are more usually male; are over forty (about eighty per cent); from the higher social classes; live in social isolation; and suffer from depression and possibly also a serious physical disease. Their acts of suicide are generally

224

well planned, guaranteed to succeed and are carried out in private.

There is, of course, some overlap between the two groups. About a third of suicides have made previous attempts. Alcohol and drug dependence are found in both groups, as are previous contacts with psychiatrists and evidence of recent personal stress.

Following up self-poisoners (which clearly cannot be done with successful suicides) shows that within one year of the overdose, a fifth will have done it again and between one and two per cent will have killed themselves. Over a ten year period, a tenth will have killed themselves.

The severity of the self-poisoning act doesn't predict whether individuals will eventually succeed in killing themselves. Even trivial overdoses must be taken seriously, because these people are just as likely to succeed the next time as the apparently 'more serious' person.

It would be comforting to think that this epidemic of self-poisoning could be reduced by some social or medical means but, unfortunately, this looks unlikely. With the quality of today's parenting falling generally, the number of single parent families rising and the urban social environment unlikely to improve substantially, the scene is set for the production of even more potential overdose patients. It's a sad fact that many parasuicidal girls (and they are mostly girls, as we have seen) have mothers who are on psychiatric drugs and who have made suicidal attempts themselves. This type of suicidal gesture is seen by many experts as a learned response to certain trying situations in life. In general, these girls are not highly educated and are not used to verbalizing their problems. As one doctor in the field put it, 'As a form of dramatic, non-verbal communication, a call to the Samaritans isn't in the same league as an overdose'. There is no sign that doctors in general are reacting to pressure from the most aware of their peers and curtailing their use of psychological active drugs, and the relentless pressure from patients to use such chemicals as an emotional crutch in times of need makes their lives doubly difficult. Too many people today, particularly young people, turn to drugs at every little upset in life. It seems that many of us have lost the ability to cope with life's stresses and are far too prone to look outside ourselves for support.

Society as a whole can slowly change the situation by educating children at home and in schools to see drugs as poor substitutes for real relationships with people – relationships that stand up in the face of crises. The medical and paramedical professions will have to provide a lot more psychological support for those with emotional problems who have no one to turn to, and we'll all have to be a lot more aware of the problems likely to lead to self-poisoning in order to stop people getting that far.

In day-to-day terms, though, preventing suicide starts with recognizing depression and ensuring that the affected person gets effective treatment. Far too many people become suicidal as a result of an unrecognized depression, simply because doctors and lay people alike aren't aware of the real nature of the problem. The recognition of atypical and masked depression is discussed in chapter one.

Preventing suicide and parasuicide

Although some of the measures outlined above could undoubtedly help prevent some suicides and parasuicides, nothing done so far has had any meaningful impact. One preventive organization which has already been set up that might be useful is the Samaritans. I say 'might be', because it's very difficult to prove the effect they are having.

The Samaritans were founded in 1953 in London by an Anglican priest, the Rev Chad Varah, and since 1960 there has been a rapid expansion of Samaritan services throughout the UK. There are now more than 170 branches throughout the country, but the organization needs more people in order to keep up with the demands placed upon them.

Since 1973 the number of callers to the Samaritans has increased by sixty per cent, while the number of volunteers has increased by only seventeen per cent.

When the Samaritans came into being the suicide rate was 12 per 100,000 of the population, and today it is 8 per 100,000. Some of this drop has been accounted for by the replacement of coal gas with natural gas, as we have seen, but the Samaritans are claiming much of the rest to be the result of their efforts.

The way the Samaritans work is as follows. They publicise a local telephone number which people are encouraged to ring at any time of day and night if they need help. The people operating the scheme are lay men and women who have no training in psychotherapy, but who have undergone a short course which prepares them for their work. The main aim of the training is to enable the volunteer to recognize a serious problem on hearing it and to be able to suggest a suitable course of action. It has been estimated that about a quarter of those phoning the Samaritans are at serious suicidal risk and that a further quarter are in need of psychiatric help.

By and large, the Samaritans offer simple 'talk therapy' over the phone, although they may be able to offer social support in some cases. Their main aim is to prevent those who are thinking of committing suicide from doing so.

Studies in several towns both before and after the arrival of the Samaritans show that they might have a small effect on the suicide rate – though this is not certain. However, they probably do not affect the parasuicide rate. In one South London study nearly three-quarters of the overdose patients knew what the Samaritans were and how to contact them (this is high compared with other studies), but teenagers – a group at particular risk from overdose – were least well informed. Having said this only 1.4 per cent of the attempted suicide patients in this survey did in fact contact the Samaritans immediately before the suicidal attempt. Of 235 patients who knew how to contact them, only five did so. The reasons they gave for not contacting the Samaritans were: 'Didn't think of it' (twenty per cent); 'Wanted temporary oblivion' (twenty per cent); 'Samaritans are no help' (sixteen per cent); and 'Wanted to die' (eleven per cent). It's interesting to note here that of those who said they 'wanted to die' when asked for a reason for trying to kill themselves, eighty per cent later said that they were glad they didn't succeed. Other work has shown that even if people do contact the Samaritans they still have a thirty times greater chance of committing suicide than the general public – but to be fair to the organization, this is a self-selected, probably determined population. Nearly half of the Samaritans' clients who wanted to kill themselves had a 'disrupted marital relationship' according to one study (for the population at large, the figure is seven per cent).

Unfortunately, it appears that the elderly (who, we have seen, are at especially high risk of suicide) are not well informed about the Samaritans. One survey found that even if they knew about the Samaritans, many could not get to a phone, often because they lived alone or could not use one. The Samaritans clearly need to get to this 'at risk' population, but to do so they'll need many more trained volunteers and publicity aimed particularly at elderly people living alone. By definition, such people are not easy to get at.

So all in all, the work of the Samaritans, whilst difficult to assess, is probably valuable in preventing some suicides. Those who are determined to kill themselves are difficult to reach by any means. Samaritans also do valuable counselling work in other areas of human misery and undoubtedly help thousands of people every year. Their work will always be a labour of love because at the crucial moment when someone is thinking of committing suicide he or she may not (as the South London study found) think of phoning or want to phone the Samaritans. For those that do though, there is always an understanding non-judgemental person at the end of the phone who has heard it all before and can usually say something to defuse the situation. Samaritans can't work miracles and even a highly trained psychiatrist on the spot might not be able to either, but they do save lives and one day that life could be yours or a friend's.

The trouble with assessing the worth of suicide prevention is that the statistics conceal individuals. This is both their strength and their weakness. Just because it can't be proved that the Samaritans prevent most people from killing themselves does nothing to detract from the success they do have, and to those families who have had a member 'saved' the statistics mean very little. If someone doesn't commit suicide after a talk with the Samaritans, one is left with 100 per cent of the person, not a faceless statistic.

On a more 'scientific' level of suicide prevention, some researchers have tried to develop blood tests that would predict a suicidal tendency in 'at risk' populations. Such efforts have not met with much success. Several studies have correlated the severity of a depression with the urine output of a natural body

228

steroid and others have looked at blood changes. Unfortunately, no blood or urine tests are as yet of any value in suicide prediction, but there is hope for the future.

What can doctors do?

It may seem ironic after all that has been said in this chapter, but until about twenty-five years ago doctors didn't take suicide very seriously. Suicide patients were either ignored or locked up in a mental hospital. Changes in society's ideas about long-term incarceration meant that fewer psychiatrists were prepared to resort to this dramatic answer to the problem. This did, however, leave a very real problem which still had to be answered.

Today, medical therapy for suicidal people takes the form of emergency hospitalization, ECT or drug therapy (if the danger to life is immediate and great), or some kind of psychotherapy. Most prospective suicides are seen by their general practitioners who, using a combination of talk and sedative drugs, can often take the sting out of the acute situation so that the person either comes to terms with the precipitating factor that brought about the suicide attempt or benefits from drugs that can cure the underlying depression. (For a full discussion of the treatment of severe depression, see page 55.)

If the family doctor is at all concerned, a psychiatrist can be asked to come to the house to give an opinion. If the specialists are worried that the person really might commit suicide, they can arrange for admission (against the patient's will if need be) to a mental hospital or to the psychiatric wing of a district general hospital. Very severely depressed and suicidal people often benefit from ECT, but this will by no means be given as a routine in such cases.

Even quite severely suicidal people are surprisingly well within a few days in the secure, caring environment of a hospital ward, and if the underlying depression responds to treatment the person will be allowed home within a few weeks. It's important to remember that whilst severely depressed people may well try to kill themselves, there are other categories of illness that provoke a person to commit suicide and these may need longer and different hospital treatment. Other neuroses, some people with paranoia, certain personality disorders and a few schizophrenics fall into this category; so don't assume that depression is the only cause of suicidal thoughts – even though it is by far the most common.

Once the immediate danger to life is over, with or without a hospital stay, drug therapy can enable people to live relatively normal lives and give them enough peace of mind to be able to start thinking about their problems. The life crisis that precipitated the suicidal event or thought won't have gone away but, under the umbrella of the right drugs, people can begin to face the world again. The drugs themselves answer nothing, of course, but in such dire situations they're an invaluable crutch, as time and psychotherapy combine to heal the emotions and the underlying social problems. Today's good doctor will work not only on the 'medical' side of the problems that caused the suicidal crisis, but will enlist the help of social workers and other professional and voluntary agencies if necessary. Doctors can't necessarily provide answers to the many social and environmental ills that people suffer from, but they can often organize help from those who can.

Medical and social help is available in abundance compared with even twenty years ago, yet ironically this is not what people who try to succeed in committing suicide need most. What they *do* need is a commodity that can't be bought with taxpayers' money – a personal relationship. When suicidal people cry out for help they don't want a cold, clinical ward and a well-run institution – they want people who care for them. And close interpersonal relationships seem to be in increasingly short supply.

The aftermath of suicide

Although people who have suicides or parasuicides in their close families are more likely than the general population to try the same, this is a relatively minor risk of having a suicide in the family. Far more numerous are the potential problems associated with the legal inquiry, the moral disapproval, the social censure and the almost universal long-term feelings of loss and guilt.

An inquest is required by law on those who die from suicide, homicide or accident and this can be painful for the surviving spouse. The most distressing part is usually identifying the

230

body. It's reasonable for someone other than the spouse to do this, if at all possible. Many people find giving evidence at the inquest upsetting and most complain of the legal setting of the whole thing, which they associate with breaking the law and being 'on trial'. This seems further to reinforce their guilt feelings and is not at all helpful soon after a suicide. Newspaper accounts of the death are also very distressing to many people, but these are difficult to influence in a society which allows open access to reporters.

Now that twenty years have passed since suicide was 'legalized', it is not too surprising to learn that most spouses don't encounter too many negative attitudes to the event. One survey found that most people's comments were neither positive nor negative, and that people were not, for example, more likely to move house to get away from social censure after a suicide. It seems that suicide is increasingly likely to provoke sympathy and compassion and not hostility.

Of course a suicide in the family doesn't always produce bad results in the survivor. Surveys have shown that spouses of suicidal alcoholics; of suicides with abnormal personalities; of those with illnesses that had lasted for two years or more; of those with hypochondriacal symptoms; and of those who had made previous suicidal attempts were better off after the suicide. Those who had at some time been separated also fared better. One study found that of those spouses that had remarried within five years of the event, the vast majority were better off than before.

It is well known that widows and widowers run an increased risk of death and that widowers' excess mortality is confined to the first year after the bereavement. The mortality of the widows and widowers of the suicides is no different from that associated with widowhood from other causes.

So in summary, even though many people immediately fear that the loss of a spouse through suicide will of necessity alter their lives for the worse, this is not usually so. Often, the underlying problems that led to the suicide have made life difficult and even intolerable for a long time and the outcome can be very positive. Needless to say, this is a gross generalization and occasionally a much-loved spouse will leave an emotionally devastated partner – but this is not the norm.

The people who seem to come out best after the suicide of a spouse are the young with a history of an unstable marriage or those whose spouse had a problem with alcoholism, abnormal personality, chronic mental illness, hypochondria and previous attempts at suicide. Most people bereaved through suicide are certainly shocked and distressed, but the much feared increase in mental ill health, social criticism and social dislocation seems to be relatively uncommon.

How about the effects on the children? Very little is known on this topic but recent research shows that any changes that are observed could just as easily have come from being with a disturbed parent; the effects of bereavement at a formative time; the circumstances of the death; and the social and financial problems of living in a one-parent family. A major study found no damage to the children's health in the short-term, although it is known that in the long-term such children are more likely than their peer group to suffer from depression.

The absence of any adverse consequences suggests that the children studied had enough resilience to weather the crisis, helped by the fact that the ill parent died and the healthy one lived.

Theories of assortative mating suggest that like attracts like in marriage, and this would infer that in such families the remaining spouse was simply the less ill of the pair and that a repeat marriage might bring similar problems. Insufficient research has been done on this, but short-term (five years) follow up studies have not shown this to be the case.

Suicide in a family is rarely an isolated event; it is usually a major event in an unhappy series of events. Certainly grief and mourning follow – but so too does relief in many cases.

Where to go for help and what you can do yourself

In an acute crisis the Samaritans are always there, as we have seen, but more often you'll be worried about recurrent suicidal thoughts in yourself or in others and will want to do something about it.

We've already noted how people often give unspoken clues to their suicidal intent and it's up to all of us to pick these up and act on them.

Anyone contemplating suicide needs help from professionals at once. Don't gamble with life – it's too precious and too many fine human beings have been lost because help was delayed for all kinds of seemingly justifiable reasons. The family doctor should be the first person to be told, but all kinds of other people find themselves being involved in these situations. They include social workers, teachers, clergymen, close friends, bar staff, hairdressers, employers and even police officers. The person closest to the potential suicide is often the last one he or she wants to confide in.

Doctors will use their skills to defuse the situation when possible or, if the risk of suicide is great, will arrange for the person to be admitted to a hospital (not necessarily a psychiatric hospital) for their own safety.

Here are some basic rules for dealing with people who are talking about or threatening suicide.

Do take every suicidal threat or action seriously. Don't be afraid to ask if the depressive is really serious about committing suicide. You won't give them ideas – don't worry about that. On the contrary, it shows them that you're taking them and their problem seriously and proves that they are better understood than they expected.

Don't be flippant or dismissive. Never say 'You wouldn't kill yourself', 'You're not the type', 'You don't really mean it', or similar remarks. These only act as a challenge to severely depressed, suicidal people. They might just do it, not to spite you, but to show you that their depression was deadly serious. Any desperate individuals, no matter what their beliefs, morals, aspirations or personality, *can* and *just might* commit suicide, especially if challenged in this way.

Never try to bluff your way through with comments like, 'OK, go ahead then!: they might just take you up on it and you'll have it on your conscience for ever.

Don't go in for any do-it-yourself psychoanalysis – this should be done later by a professional.

Don't get drawn into arguments about whether they should live or die: you can't win that one. They are so low that nothing you say will convince them and it could in fact annoy them so much that they'll be precipitated sooner into suicide.

Do be prepared to listen – let them talk themselves out of it, if possible while you await professional help.

Even if you get over the acute crisis, *don't* assume that things will necessarily improve – they won't. Any life crisis that has driven a previously normal person to threaten suicide needs to be examined carefully and the root cause attended to. Never accept a suicidal threat as an idle show of emotion – it always mirrors an underlying problem that demands attention. Unfortunately, it comes very hard to most relatives (and especially spouses) to learn that they can't be of any great help in sorting out the root causes, but this is all too often the case. Outside help is usually needed if the suicidal threats are not to be repeated or acted upon.

Age Concern (England)
Bernard Sunley House,
60 Pitcairn Road,
Mitcham,
Surrey CR4 3LL
01 640 5431

Al-Anon Family Groups
(UK and Eire)
61 Great Dover Street,
London SE1 4YK
01 403 0888

Alcoholics Anonymous
P.O. Box 514,
11 Redcliffe Gardens,
London SW10 9BG
01 834 8202
See local phone book
for details of local groups.

British Association of
Psychotherapists
121 Hendon Lane,
London N3
01 346 1747

British Pregnancy Advisory Service
Austy Manor,
Wooton Wawen, Solihull,
West Midlands B95 6DA
05642 3225

Cancer Information Association
Marygold House, Carfax,
Oxford OX1 1EF
0865 46654/43621

The Compassionate Friends
25 Kingsdown Parade,
Bristol BS6 5UE
0272 47316

Cruse
Cruse House,
126 Sheen Road,
Richmond,
Surrey TW9 1UR
01 940 4818

Depressives Anonymous
83 Derby Road,
Nottingham,
NG1 5BB

Disabled Living Foundation
346 Kensington High Street,
London W14 8NS
01 602 2491/2/3

Family Planning Association
27-35 Mortimer Street,
London W1N 7RJ
01 636 7866

The Health Service Commissioner
Church House,
Great Smith Street,
London SW1
01 212 7676

Marriage Guidance Council
Herbert Gray College,
Little Church Street,
Rugby,
Warwickshire
0788 73241

Mastectomy Association
Secretary: Mrs Westgate,
1 Colworth Road,
Croydon CR0 7AD
01 654 8643

MIND (see National Association for Mental Health, below)

National Association for the Divorced and Separated
13 High Street,
Little Shelford,
Cambridge

National Association for Mental Health (MIND)
22 Harley Street,
London W1N 2ED
01 637 0741

National Council on Alcoholism
3 Grosvenor Crescent,
London SW1
01 235 4182

National Council for One-Parent Families
255 Kentish Town Road,
London NW5 2LX
01 267 1361

National Council for Voluntary Organizations
26 Bedford Square,
London WC1
01 636 4066

National Federation of Solo Clubs
Room 8,
Ruskin Chambers,
191 Corporation Street,
Birmingham 4
021 236 2879

National Institute of Adult Education
19b De montfort Street,
Leicester LE1 7GE
0533 551451

National Schizophrenia Fellowship
78/79 Victoria Road,
Surbiton,
Surrey KT6 4NS
01 390 3651/2

Parents Anonymous
See local phone book or press,
or phone 01 668 4805 (24-hour service) for details of local groups.

Patients' Association
11 Dartmouth Street,
London SW1 8BN
01 222 4992

Pregnancy Advisory Service
27 Fitzroy Square,
London W1P 5HH
01 387 3057

Relatives of the Mentally Ill
7 Selwyn Road,
Cambridge CB3 9EA

The Samaritans
17 Uxbridge Road,
Slough SL1 1SN
75 32713

Schizophrenia Association of Great Britain
Hon Secretary:
Mrs Hemmings, BSc,
Tyr Twr,
Llanfair Hall,
Caernarvon LL55 1TT
0248 670 379

Community Health Councils and Social Services Departments are under these headings in local telephone directories.

INDEX

238